AF394800

# 101
# SURREALISTS

# DESMOND MORRIS

# 101

# SURREALISTS

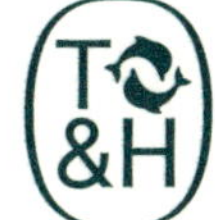

# CONTENTS

# INTRODUCTION

Surrealism is the most important art movement of recent times, and 2024 is officially its centenary year. The usual way of marking such a milestone might be to offer biographies of 100 surrealists, but in keeping with the perverse spirit of the movement, this book offers 101.

The official date of the birth of the surrealist movement is 15 October 1924. This is the date that saw the publication of André Breton's first manifesto, in which, for the first time, he presents a formal definition of surrealism. He comments boldly that 'there can be no doubt that this word had no currency before we came along'. This is not strictly true, but it is true that Breton's genius gave the word new meaning and tied it to an entirely new theory of irrational creativity – free, as he put it, 'from any aesthetic or moral concern'.

To be historically correct, this was not the first use of the term 'surrealism'. The word was coined in 1917 by Pablo Picasso, who mentioned it to Guillaume Apollinaire, who was the first to use it in print. Because of this, most art historians credit Apollinaire with its coinage.

In fact, Picasso had been searching for a term to describe what he was doing in his revolutionary new work. He wanted a word that captured his attempt to make his paintings more real than reality itself. 'I value a more profound resemblance, realer than real, attaining the surreal,' he said – further explaining, in 1945, 'That's how I viewed surrealism, but the term was used differently.' Still later, he commented: 'If surrealism hadn't been used to designate another movement, I think it would describe my painting.'

Although art historians have largely ignored this, Breton made no secret of Picasso's important role when he said, 'We loudly claim him to be one of us.... Surrealism...need merely follow where Picasso has gone before and will go again.'

Picasso himself was less complimentary. Recognizing that he had lost the term to Breton – who was now using it in connection with what was initially a literary and philosophical movement, rather than one concerned with the visual arts – he said: 'That's why surrealism has done so much damage. They've completely forgotten the main thing – painting – in favour of lousy poetry.... They didn't understand what I meant by surrealism when I coined the term – something more real than reality.'

As time passed, Breton gradually came to understand the importance of the visual arts in surrealism. Four years after his manifesto, he published an important essay called 'Surrealism and Painting' in which he admits the power of the visual image: 'A few lines, a few blobs of colour, hold me in their thrall as nothing else can do.'

He attacks traditional art that merely copies the appearance of the external world, and is at pains to praise Picasso for rejecting this approach: 'For fifteen years now, Picasso has been exploring...advancing deep into unknown territory, bearing rays of light in each hand.... What miracle has endowed this man...with the facility to give materiality to what had hitherto remained in the domain of pure fantasy? What a revolution must have taken place within him.... We cannot fail to acknowledge the immense responsibility that Picasso assumed in so heightening his awareness of the treacherous nature of tangible entities that he dared break openly with them.... If surrealism ever comes to adopt a particular line of conduct, it has only to accept the discipline that Picasso has accepted and will continue to accept.'

With praise like this, it is easy to see why Picasso was willing to show his paintings at early surrealist exhibitions and include illustrations of his work in early surrealist publications; however, his lack of interest in their literature and philosophizing meant he never attended the surrealists' meetings or joined their group. He went on to become a solitary giant, while Breton flourished as the leader of the surrealist group. After the Second World War they broke off all contact, but this had nothing to do with art – it was purely a political difference.

Today most people see surrealism as an art movement, and the early surrealist writings are largely forgotten. The literature still arouses scholarly interest, but the wider public knows nothing of it – meanwhile, visual surrealism has spread its wings to influence photography, cinema, television, advertising and popular culture in general. Nowadays, when something unusual occurs, instead of saying, 'That was so strange,' it is common practice to say, 'That was so surreal.'

The turbulent 20th century generated countless art movements. Surrealism has outlived them all. While fauvism, expressionism, cubism, futurism, suprematism, synchronism, orphism, rayonism, vorticism, dadaism, purism, letterism and all the rest have faded into history, surrealism has continued to go from strength to strength.

The film director Luis Buñuel summed it up better than anyone when, speaking of the early surrealists, he said: 'We were nothing, just a small group of insolent intellectuals who argued interminably in cafés and published a journal; a handful of idealists easily divided where action was concerned. And yet my three years' sojourn in the exalted – and yes, chaotic – ranks of the movement changed my life.'

Indeed, it changed the lives of everyone it touched. We all like to dream, not only when we are asleep, but also when we are awake, and surrealism, to quote Hans Richter, gave us 'dreams that money can buy'. It celebrated the irrational and legitimized the outlandish. It fostered a disrespect for authority and a joy in eccentricity.

The 101 brief biographies that follow introduce to you to its most interesting proponents.

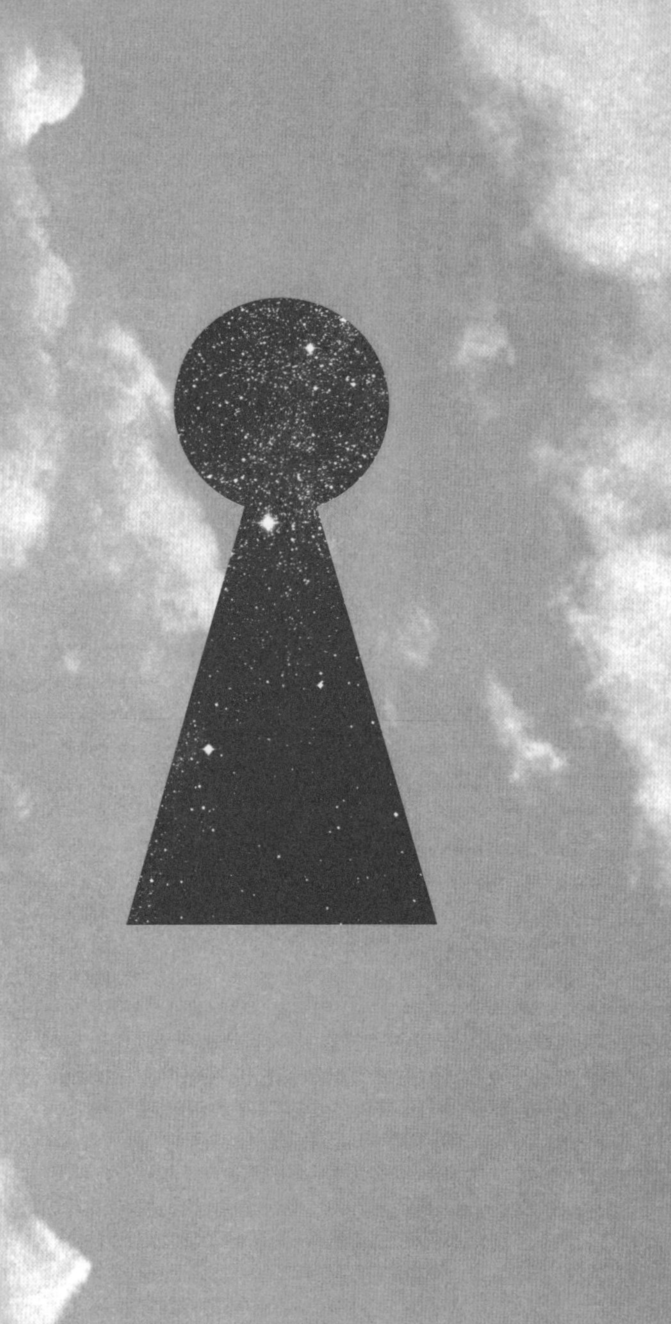

# MARION ADNAMS



## The quiet, provincial art teacher with a powerful surrealist vision

**BORN**: 3 December 1898, Derby

**PARENTS**: Father a woodwork teacher at Derby School

**LIVED**: Derby, 1898–1995; France, 1960s

**DIED**: 24 October 1995, Derby

Although Marion Adnams produced highly accomplished surrealist paintings, she was never involved in the surrealist movement. Instead she lived a quiet academic life in the city of Derby, where she taught art. She died in the same house where she had been born, and her funeral was held in Derby Cathedral.

The nearest Adnams came to direct contact with the surrealist movement was when, from time to time, she exhibited her paintings in London galleries alongside those of Max Ernst, Henry Moore and Eileen Agar. Her choice to lead a quiet life in a provincial city meant that she became one of the 'forgotten surrealists', rarely mentioned in books or articles. There was nothing remotely surrealist about her lifestyle or her philosophy of life. She only became a surrealist when she was sitting in front of her easel.

Adnams was first and foremost a teacher. From an early age she expressed the desire to study art but was diverted from this by her family, who persuaded her to attend college in nearby Nottingham to study modern languages. Dutifully, she obtained her degree in 1919. After graduating, she set off on art tours to Belgium, France and Italy. The work she created during these 1920s trips was exhibited at the Derby Art Gallery. In the 1930s she attended evening art classes in Derby, where her teacher, an artist called Alfred Bladen, aroused her interest in surrealist painting.

The two masters of surrealism who had the strongest influence on her work were Magritte and Dalí. She began to make meticulous landscapes in which familiar objects appeared in irrational relationships with one another. She would go out to explore the local countryside, often collecting natural objects, as Paul Nash was doing, and bringing them back to her studio. There she would start painting and enter what she called 'the enchanted country' – her personal dream world. Asked about her themes, she replied that she had a special interest in 'death and resurrection – life coming out of death in varied and curious ways'.

Towards the end of the 1930s Adnams began her teaching career, not as a language teacher but as art mistress at a girls' school in Derby. She also started to devote more and more time to her surrealist paintings. She soon moved on to teach at a grammar school and eventually ended up as head of art at Derby Training College – a lifelong career as a dedicated art teacher in middle England, well away from the surrealist activities in the capital.

Adnams retired from teaching in 1960, at the age of sixty-one, and was then able to devote more of her time to painting. She acquired a second home in Provence, and when painting there she was strongly influenced by the French countryside.

Tragically, in 1970, her sight failed. Her blindness was so severe that for the last twenty-five years of her life, from the ages of seventy-one to ninety-six, she could not see well enough to paint.

There have been two retrospective exhibitions of her work: in Nottingham in 1971, and at the Derby Museum and Art Gallery in 2017.

# EILEEN AGAR



## The rebellious beauty who found in surrealism a welcome escape from the tedium of high society

**BORN**: 1 December 1899, Buenos Aires **PARENTS**: Father a Scottish businessman; mother American English **LIVED**: Buenos Aires, 1899; London, 1911; Paris, 1927; London, 1930 **PARTNERS**: Robin Bartlett, m. 1925–9; Joseph Bard, 1926; Paul Nash, 1935–44; Paul Éluard, 1937; Joseph Bard, m. 1940–75 **DIED**: 17 November 1991, London

Although there was nothing especially erotic about her paintings, in life Eileen Agar was more sexually adventurous than many women of her generation. According to her husband, she was always 'trying to do something in a way that cannot be done, such as making love standing up in a hammock'. And she was not averse, it seems, to being involved with three separate lovers at one time.

Agar was born in Argentina to an American mother and a Scottish father who was there to sell windmills to the locals. Her parents were wealthy and sociable and the children often saw them just once a day, at bedtime. When Eileen was ten, her father retired to England; on the journey from Argentina the family were accompanied by a cow and an orchestra, ensuring they had plenty of fresh milk and music while travelling. In England they lived in a large mansion in Belgrave Square, complete with ballroom. After overcoming her parents' objections, Agar was allowed to attend the Slade School of Art, although she had to be delivered there and collected each day in the family Rolls.

At the age of twenty-one, tired of family restrictions, she packed her bags and left home for good. She found a small studio in Chelsea and began painting seriously. She married Robin Bartlett in 1925, but soon left him for the man who would become the love of her life: a handsome Hungarian writer called Joseph Bard. The couple travelled to Paris, where, in the late 1920s, Agar encountered André Breton at the very peak of the surrealist revolution. She spent time with many of the major figures of the day, including Evelyn Waugh, Ezra Pound, Cecil Beaton, Aldous Huxley, W. B. Yeats, Osbert Sitwell, Ernest Hemingway and Scott Fitzgerald.

Back in London, she received encouragement as an artist from Henry Moore, and they became close friends. He never forgot that she beat him at tennis. In 1935, while passing the summer on the south coast of England, Agar met the artist Paul Nash and his wife. Agar and Nash fell in love and, after a while, became lovers, causing much heartache for their still actively involved partners.

Early in 1936, Roland Penrose arranged a major exhibition in London to introduce surrealism to the British public. Three of Agar's oils and five of her surrealist objects were selected for the show. She was fascinated by her new surrealist friends. She found Max Ernst bird-like, André Breton leonine, Yves Tanguy bizarre, nervous and excitable, Salvador Dalí conspicuous with an explosive temper, and Joan Miró childlike and poetic.

The following year, Agar's love life became even more complicated when she succumbed to the charms of the French surrealist poet Paul Éluard. She described him as a living Eros and was soon in his arms and in his bed, despite the presence of his delightful second wife, Nusch, an ex-circus performer.

Such were the complexities and intricacies of relationships within the surrealist group Eileen Agar had joined. And she took to this new life with a joyous sense of release from the formal restrictions of her younger years, saying, 'I have spent my life in revolt against convention, trying to bring colour and light and a sense of the mysterious to daily existence.'

# JOHN ARMSTRONG

## The British loner who stood outside the surrealist movement, but created imaginative dreamlike landscapes

BORN: 14 November 1893, Hastings, Sussex  PARENTS: Father a parson
LIVED: Hastings, 1893; West Dean, Sussex, 1895; London, 1913–39; Dunmow, Essex, 1940; Lamorna, Cornwall, 1945–55; London, 1955–73
PARTNERS: Benita Jaeger, m. 1936–8; Elsa Lanchester; Elizabeth Smart; Veronica Sibthorp  DIED: 1973, London

As an artist, John Armstrong was a loner – an independent spirit who had no links to the surrealist group, but whose paintings were often undeniably surrealist in character. The reason for this is simple. He described his mode of working as follows: 'These things come to me as complete images, often when I am half asleep.... Afterwards I may have ideas about what they mean, but I suppose only a conference of psychologists could really analyze them.' In other words, he was painting from the unconscious mind, in keeping with the central surrealist tradition.

Armstrong was the delicate son of a strict Victorian parson in the south of England. He grew up in a country vicarage, where he and his siblings were tutored at home by their parents. He soon rebelled against his rigorously imposed religious upbringing, and saw art as his way of escape.

During the First World War he was fortunate to be posted to the Middle East, where he could study the art of ancient civilizations at first hand. Back in London, he devoted himself to painting but was so poor that he often went hungry. On one occasion he was so starved that he lapsed into a coma and had to be rushed to hospital to save his life.

He escaped from this period of poverty by painting set designs and murals, but did not give up his easel work, and in 1928 was rewarded with his first solo show in London. It was a success, with half the works sold – but the Great Depression of the 1930s was soon to throw a dark shadow over the art world.

A compensation was his friendship with the actor Charles Laughton and Laughton's wife, Elsa Lanchester. Armstrong had been a witness at their wedding in 1929 and in the 1930s he moved into the world of the cinema with them, working on various design projects. While Laughton was away filming *Mutiny on the Bounty*, Lanchester made three short films starring Armstrong and his new girlfriend Benita Jaeger, who later became his wife. Their marriage lasted only two years. When Benita told him she was having an affair, Armstrong kissed her hand and it was all over.

His work in the late 1930s became more richly surrealist and bizarre. A review from this period in the *Telegraph* refers to him as 'our foremost surrealist painter'. The critic is at pains to point out that Armstrong is not slavishly copying a foreign fashion, but deriving his strange, dreamlike landscapes from a much earlier, purely English visual tradition. Another important critic, Wyndham Lewis, controversially declared that there were only two British surrealists: Armstrong, and Paul Nash.

Interviewed many years later, Armstrong made the important distinction that he himself had not been a true surrealist, although some of his paintings were surrealist works. This was not as contradictory as it might sound; there were a number of painters who created surrealist pictures but knew nothing at all about the surrealist movement itself or its manifestos and theories. They arrived at surrealist images via a strange, private, personal, individual obsession. Like Armstrong, they were natural surrealist artists, but strictly on their own terms.

# JEAN (HANS) ARP

## The dadaist who became a pioneer of the surrealist movement and one of its greatest sculptors

**BORN**: 16 September 1886, Strasbourg  **PARENTS**: Father German; mother French  **LIVED**: Strasbourg, 1886; Paris, 1904; Weimar, 1905; Paris, 1908; Berlin, 1913; Switzerland, 1915; Cologne, 1919; Paris, 1920; Grasse, 1940; Zurich, 1942; Paris, 1946  **PARTNERS**: Sophie Taeuber-Arp, m. 1922–43; Marguerite Hagenbach, m. 1959–66  **DIED**: 7 June 1966, Basel

Arp was a key figure in the early days of the surrealist movement. His nationality was complicated. He was born in Strasbourg, Alsace, on the border between Germany and France, a city whose complex history saw it switching back and forth between German, French and Alsatian. As a child he had two names and spoke three languages. His German name was Hans Peter Wilhelm Arp and his French name was Jean-Pierre-Guillaume Arp. He spoke French with his mother, German with his father and Alsatian in daily life.

When he was six, the young Arp fell ill, and during his convalescence he passed the time making drawings. As a teenager he spent most of his time in the studios of local artists and at the age of eighteen made his first trip to Paris and fell in love with the city.

In 1907, when Arp was twenty-one, his family moved to Switzerland. At his new home he started experimenting and, in 1911, organized an exhibition in Lucerne that included works by himself, Picasso, Klee, Matisse and Gauguin, among others.

In Zurich in 1915 Arp met his future wife, the abstract artist Sophie Taeuber. The following year he provided decorations for the Cabaret Voltaire, where the dada movement was born. The first dada exhibition took place in Zurich in 1917 and Arp was actively involved. In his work he was now creating what he called 'fluid ovals' – biomorphic shapes often presented as reliefs. Always ahead of his time, he had become a full-blown surrealist artist seven years before the surrealist movement officially began.

When the war ended, the dadaists were beginning to disperse and the movement was starting to lose its impetus. In Paris Arp joined up with the surviving dada group there, which included André Breton – but by 1922, the end of the movement was in sight, and in September Tristan Tzara formally delivered its funeral oration. The following month, Arp and Sophie Taeuber were married. A new phase was about to begin.

In Paris in 1924, Breton and his circle replaced the negativity of the dada movement with a new concept, based on the exploration of irrationality and the unconscious: surrealism. Although they welcomed Arp's work, he himself still felt he was a dadaist at heart.

Arp became a French citizen in 1926 and settled outside Paris. He continued to exhibit with the surrealists, but kept his distance from their political posturing and their theorizing. When war broke out again in 1939, as a protest, Arp stopped signing his work 'Hans Arp' and switched to 'Jean Arp'. He and Sophie moved to the South of France, in the unoccupied zone, where they could continue to work in their studio. In 1942 they travelled to Switzerland in the hope of gaining visas to the United States, but tragedy struck the following year when Arp found his wife dead one morning, asphyxiated by the fumes from a gas stove. His bereavement brought his sculptural work to a halt for four years, and his moods became darker.

In 1949 he visited New York for the first time and met up with many old friends. In 1959 he married Marguerite Hagenbach, who had by then been his constant companion for some years. Arp's work was now in great demand and his final years were full, busy and rewarding. He died of a heart attack in Basel in 1966. Max Ernst said of him that he taught us to understand the language of the universe.

# FRANCIS BACON

**The greatest British surrealist, foolishly rejected by the movement**

**BORN**: 28 October 1909, Dublin  **PARENTS**: Father an English racehorse trainer; mother a wealthy socialite  **LIVED**: Dublin, 1909; England, childhood; Ireland, 1918; Gloucester, 1924; Ireland, 1926; London, 1926; Berlin and Paris, 1927; London, 1928; Monte Carlo, 1946; London, 1948  **PARTNERS**: Eric Hall, 1929–50; George Dyer, 1964–71; John Edwards, 1974–92  **DIED**: 28 April 1992, Madrid

It may seem strange to include Francis Bacon in this volume, but the fact is that he considered himself to be a surrealist; he wanted to be a member of the British surrealist group and to be included in their great 1936 exhibition. Herbert Read and Roland Penrose visited Bacon's studio in London to decide whether to include him or not, but when they saw his work, they were dismayed by what they thought were religious elements in it. On this basis they rejected him, to his great disappointment. This was a tragedy for British surrealism because, had they accepted him, Bacon would have gone on to become a major figure in the movement. Instead he found international fame as an independent artist.

The rejection was based on a misunderstanding. There was nothing even faintly religious about Bacon's art. His interest in crucifixions was based not on Christian iconography but on his own private sexual fantasies – Bacon was deeply involved in sadomasochistic practices, and the crucified figures were self-portraits. His early life provides some context for this interpretation.

Bacon's father was a racehorse trainer in Ireland, and young Francis was a great disappointment to him. Living in an intensely masculine world, Bacon senior was horrified to learn that his son was less than 'manly'. His reaction to this discovery rebounded on him in spectacular fashion.

His first mistake was to have Francis whipped by the stable grooms for being effeminate – as it turned out, Francis thoroughly enjoyed this. A later mistake was to send him off to Berlin, the sexual capital of pre-war Europe, where anything went. Francis was in his element. His father had lost their family feud and the young man was now, at last, free to do as he wished.

Without going into the precise details of Bacon's sexual preferences later in life, it is generally acknowledged that he enjoyed being beaten. He once told the American poet Allen Ginsberg that he had obtained gambling money by allowing himself to be whipped, with a bonus for every stroke that drew blood. This type of background knowledge does shed some light on the tortured images in his paintings – but it does not explain their greatness. It is easy to imagine an artist so preoccupied with masochistic sexuality producing embarrassingly lurid images with no merit whatsoever. In Bacon's case, however, it is the restraint and the ambiguity of his images that make them so powerful and so haunting.

Critics have spoken grandly of Bacon's depiction of the 'spiritual isolation' of modern man, but the truth is that his paintings are almost totally personal and sexual in meaning. The boxes in which he depicts many of his human figures are not symbols of spiritual isolation – they represent the confinement of sexual slavery and bondage.

Francis Bacon was a creative genius who also, at times, was a thief, a compulsive gambler, a drunkard and a liar. Even his published statements, by his own admission, are unreliable: 'I often say anything, you know, to pass the time.' Although there were many flaws in his character, Bacon was also, it must be said, a great conversationalist, with a caustic wit and a wanton generosity towards those he liked. He radiated charisma when he entered a room and was endowed with great charm whenever he wished to exercise it.

# ENRICO BAJ

## The Italian anarchist whose grotesque images appealed to the surrealists

**BORN**: 31 October 1924, Milan
**PARENTS**: From a wealthy background
**LIVED**: Milan, 1924; Geneva, 1944; Milan, 1945
**PARTNERS**: Married twice
**DIED**: 16 June 2003, Vergiate, Varese, Northern Italy

The Italian anarchist Enrico Baj created grotesque paintings which are often full of scurrilous political humour. He was strongly associated with the surrealists without actually belonging to the group. One of his exhibitions was raided by the police and the gallery showing his work was closed down, an event that would certainly have appealed to the surrealist elite.

Baj came from a wealthy Milanese family. As a boy, he was provocatively rebellious. He spent his childhood in Milan but was strongly opposed to the fascist regime of Mussolini, and fled Italy in 1944 to escape being called up for army service. He settled in Switzerland and lived in Geneva until the end of the war.

Returning to Milan in 1945, he obtained a degree in law from Milan University and practised law there. He later said that this experience only taught him about the folly of bureaucracy, and his greatest desire was to escape from that world into the realm of the imagination. In his studio, he focused his attacks on warfare, pomposity and arrogance, but always did so with ironic humour and a satirical amusement.

During trips to Paris he encountered André Breton, Marcel Duchamp and Max Ernst. Breton said of him: 'Baj's playful and ironic side masks a constant and coherent engagement against all the forms of destructiveness and oppression that man inflicts on man.' His favourite humanoid figures often have heads that are torsos, or torsos that are heads, so that the mouth lies in the genital region. The effect is of a heavy mask with arms and legs. These monsters straddle the landscapes like marauding giants; Breton called them 'a ridiculization of a triumphal arch transformed into an unwieldy figure'.

Baj held his first solo exhibition in 1951. In 1963 he collaborated with Man Ray in founding an Institute of 'Pataphysics in honour of Alfred Jarry, the French symbolist writer best known for the play *Ubu Roi*. He also worked with Duchamp on a parody of the *Mona Lisa* in 1965, superimposing Duchamp's face onto her body.

As an attack on war, in the 1960s Baj created a series of ludicrous, demented generals covered in medals. He repeated this anti-military motif more than forty times and its impact led André Breton to declare that Baj was a true surrealist.

Disillusioned by the direction modern art was taking, Baj's bizarre response was to paint large copies of works by the great masters, from Seurat to Picasso. He even produced his own version of *Guernica*, with his personal monsters added to the composition. This huge work is 3.6 × 7.8 metres in size – the same dimensions as the original Picasso painting.

Baj was married twice and had five children. His second wife, Roberta Cerini Baj, was twenty years his junior; thirty-seven years after his death, she donated his archive and part of his extensive library to the Museum of Modern and Contemporary Art of Trento and Rovereto in northern Italy.

# BALTHUS

## The master of his art, who was obsessed with the threshold of sexuality



**BORN**: 29 February 1908, Paris, as Balthasar Klossowski **PARENTS**: Erich Klossowski, an art historian; Elisabeth Dorothea Spiro, an artist **LIVED**: Paris, 1908; Morocco, 1930; Paris, 1933; Champrovent, near Aix-les-Bains, Savoy, 1940; Bern, 1942; Geneva, 1945; Paris, 1946; Rossinière, Switzerland, 1977 **PARTNERS**: Antoinette de Watteville, m. 1937; Setsuko Ideta, m. 1967 **DIED**: 18 February 2001, Rossinière

Balthus is one of the most controversial modern artists. His technique may be traditional but his subject matter has often caused outrage, with his depictions of pre-pubescent girls troubling many gallery-goers. In the present century, as people have become increasingly ready to question material that hints at paedophilia or exploitation, objections to his work have gained more traction. In 2014, a German museum cancelled a planned exhibition on the grounds that it 'could lead to unwanted legal consequences'.

It is impossible to avoid the conclusion that Balthus was sexually obsessed with young girls between the ages of about twelve and sixteen. He was fascinated by the visual appeal of the female body on the threshold of sexuality, and his work asks the viewer to admire the casual innocence and unselfconscious physical beauty of its subjects. When interviewed, however, he claimed his admiration went no further – that in his opinion paedophiles were sick and that to him, the young girls he portrayed were 'untouchable, sacred'.

Balthus was a strange, very private individual. He was born in Paris, where his childhood was disrupted by the First World War. His family were Polish emigrants who had become German citizens; when war broke out they were forced to flee the city, lost all their possessions, and settled in Berlin. After the war Balthus moved restlessly between Switzerland, France and Germany and started painting in earnest, strongly influenced by the old masters and largely self taught.

In 1933 he encountered the surrealists and was visited by André Breton, Paul Éluard and Alberto Giacometti. It was the start of a close friendship with Giacometti that would last for thirty years. Towards the end of his life, Balthus still kept a bronze bust given to him by Giacometti on his mantelpiece.

He was visited by Picasso in 1934 and subsequently had a controversial exhibition at the Galerie Pierre in Paris, a stronghold of surrealism. His painting *The Guitar Lesson* caused a scandal, and not a single work was sold – Balthus was in despair, and a few months later he attempted suicide. However, he survived and busied himself with a variety of commissions, including portraits, set designs and illustrations. A few years later he married Antoinette de Watteville, a girl he had first met in 1924 when she was twelve years old, but after nine years of marriage they separated. One of their two sons remembers Balthus as a passionate individual with a quick temper, who threw tax inspectors downstairs and got into fist-fights in cafés.

In 1962 he visited Japan, where a young Japanese girl called Satsuko Ideta was his interpreter. She followed him back to Europe, and five years later she and Balthus were married. In 1977 they moved with their daughter to a grand manor house in the Swiss Alpine village of Rossinière. This would be their home until 2001, when Balthus died at the age of ninety-two.

In his later years Balthus received honours and accolades and held many exhibitions. Because of its masterly qualities, his work was revered by the art world despite its problematic content. His obsession with privacy, however, meant that he was not widely known to the public. He would rarely talk about his art and always kept his studio locked, even from his wife.

# JOHN BANTING

## The joker in the surrealist pack, whose life was a surrealist event

**BORN**: 12 May 1902, Chelsea, London
**PARENTS**: Father a bookbinder; mother a teacher
**LIVED**: London, 1902; Ireland, 1947; East Sussex, 1950s; Hastings, 1965
**PARTNERS**: Close friendship with Nancy Cunard
**DIED**: 30 January 1972

John Banting was one of the jokers who frequented surrealist circles. Painting surrealist pictures was not enough for him – life itself had to become a surrealist event. He was once seen dancing at a club in a smart business suit, wearing shoes on which he had made a realistic painting of his toes complete with nail varnish: his personal tribute to Magritte's iconic work *The Red Model*. On another occasion, he went round a London art exhibition signing all the works on show 'Marcel Duchamp'. After all, if Duchamp could sign a print of the *Mona Lisa*, why not other works of art as well?

John Banting was born in Chelsea and grew up in Edwardian London. The first artistic movement to attract him was vorticism, but since he had to earn a living by working as a bank clerk, he could only attend art classes in his spare time. At the age of twenty-three he was able to set up his first studio, working on book illustrations and making set designs for ballet companies.

Banting met some important members of the avant-garde on a visit to Paris in 1922, including Man Ray, Peggy Guggenheim and Constantin Brancusi. But it was during a later visit, in 1930, that he encountered André Breton, Alberto Giacometti and

Marcel Duchamp, all of whom made a significant impact on him. Under their influence he became a serious convert to the surrealist cause and remained devoted to the movement for the rest of his life.

In 1936 he took part in the International Surrealist Exhibition in London, showing five works: two oils, two watercolours and one surrealist object. He strongly supported the communist leanings of the early surrealists, and throughout his life was intensely left-wing. Impressed by his work, Duchamp invited him to show in the next major surrealist exhibition, in Paris in 1938.

At the start of the Second World War Banting failed his medical exams for the military. He spent the war years as an air raid warden and worked for the Ministry of Information, making propaganda films along with Dylan Thomas. In London after the war he created a remarkable surrealist publication, the *Blue Book of Conversation*, for which he provided both text and illustrations. It amounts to a vitriolic attack on English high society, whose representatives appear as formally dressed carcasses with hideous names such as 'Lady Crevice Raikes-Bagge' or 'Mrs Fuschia Stingwing'.

In 1956 Banting moved to Rye in Sussex to live near his friend, the eccentric artist Edward Burra. He produced little work in his later years, but kept busy writing as well as showing his early works in surrealist exhibitions. At this stage in his life Banting was plagued by alcoholism, ill health and poverty, and seems to have survived on an annual allowance from a rich boyfriend of his youth.

In his sixties, Banting was always complaining to Burra about his ailments. There is a poignant letter, written by Burra ten days before Banting's death, in which he describes a visit to see his old friend in hospital in Hastings, awaiting an operation to 'rehabilitate' his pelvic region. Banting describes his forthcoming surgical procedure as 'distinctly Picasso cum Heath Robinson'. His body ruined by years of alcohol abuse, he never recovered from the operation.

# WILLIAM BAZIOTES



**BORN**: 11 June 1912, Pittsburgh, PA
**PARENTS**: Of Greek heritage
**LIVED**: Pittsburgh, 1912; New York, 1933
**PARTNER**: Ethel Copstein, m. 1941
**DIED**: 6 June 1963

The American surrealist William Baziotes is largely forgotten today, swept away by the tidal wave of abstract expressionism that came to dominate the world of modern art in 1950s New York.

Baziotes was born in Pittsburgh in 1912, of Greek immigrant parents. He lacked a higher education, leaving school at the age of sixteen. In 1931 he visited the recently opened Museum of Modern Art in New York, where he saw a Matisse exhibition. It had such an impact on him that he decided to move to that city and become a painter.

In the 1940s, he found himself surrounded by refugee surrealists from Europe who had fled the horrors of the Second World War. Baziotes had already begun producing surrealist works in the 1930s, but when he met Matta in 1940 and was then introduced to the other exiles, their influence on him was considerable. Automatism became more important to him and he allowed his unconscious mind to influence his biomorphic shapes more than before. He expressed it well himself: 'What happens on the canvas is unpredictable and surprising.... Each painting has its own way of evolving.... Each beginning suggests something. Once I sense the suggestion, I begin to paint intuitively. The suggestion then becomes a phantom that must be caught and made real.'

Baziotes met and married Ethel Copstein in 1941. Unlike so many surrealist marriages, theirs would last a lifetime. The couple shared a love of the art of ancient Greece, and it has been claimed that this influenced Baziotes' imagery, although it is hard to see how.

Of all the young American artists who were attracted to the exiled surrealists, it was Baziotes who received the warmest welcome. The Europeans sensed his genuine affinity for their approach. He became a regular at the weekly evening meetings run by Matta. He and his wife were also invited to Peggy Guggenheim's extravagant parties at her new Manhattan home.

Guggenheim expressed an interest in seeing his paintings and arranged to visit his studio. This was something of a predicament, because Baziotes and his wife were so poor that they had no furniture – Ethel later recalled, 'My husband went out and bought a chair in which she sat for an hour and it broke.' Nevertheless, the visit was a success and Guggenheim soon offered Baziotes an exhibition at her New York gallery, Art of this Century.

After the war, when most of the surrealists had returned to Europe, Baziotes continued to paint in a surrealist manner but earned his living teaching art in a variety of posts in New York. This was necessary in part because his method of painting was so very slow – he typically completed only one or two pictures a year. He would not be rushed, explaining that each work 'has its own way of evolving'. He was always reluctant to talk about his artistic practice. All he would say was, 'It is the mysterious that I love in painting. It is the stillness and the silence. I want my pictures to take effect very slowly, to obsess and haunt.' He quoted Baudelaire, saying: 'I have a horror of being easily understood.'

Baziotes died young, in 1963 at the age of fifty, from lung cancer. His significance as an artist was recognized by a memorial exhibition of his work at the Guggenheim Museum in New York.

# HANS BELLMER

## The surrealist who was obsessed with female anatomy



**BORN**: 13 March 1902, (German) Kattowitz; now (Polish) Katowice **PARENTS**: Father a severe, humourless bourgeois Nazi **LIVED**: Kattowitz, 1902; Berlin, 1923; Paris, 1938; prison camp, 1939–40; southern France, 1941; Paris, 1949 **PARTNERS**: Margarete Schnell, m. 1928–38; Elise Cadreano, 1938; Joyce Reeves, 1939; Marcelle Celine Sutter, m. 1942–7; Nora Mitrani, 1945–9; Unica Zürn, 1954–70 **DIED**: 23 February 1975

The controversial artist Hans Bellmer created some of the most disturbing images in the history of the surrealist movement. His work suggests an obsession with violating the female body in as many ways as possible. Technically speaking, however, he was a master of design, and many of his worst sexual excesses are immaculately depicted.

Bellmer was born in what was then the east German town of Kattowitz, now Katowice in Poland. At the age of twenty he held his first exhibition, for which he was arrested by the police, accused of undermining morality. He escaped by bribing an official, and the following year his father took him off to Berlin to study for a degree in engineering. When Bellmer abandoned his studies his father cut off all financial support, and he was forced to earn his living as a commercial artist. In 1926 he opened his own design agency and two years later married a fragile young girl called Margarete Schnell.

In 1933, supposedly in an act of rebellion against the state, Bellmer closed his agency and started making surrealist dolls, combining parts of real dolls to create strangely erotic monsters. In 1935 he visited Paris, met Breton for the first time and became a regular surrealist exhibitor. Early in 1938, Margarete died of tuberculosis and Bellmer left Berlin to live in Paris, where he met Marcel Duchamp, Max Ernst, Yves Tanguy and Man Ray.

When war broke out in 1939, Bellmer was detained as a German national in France. In 1939, he and Ernst found themselves together in an internment camp in the South of France. Later, when Ernst managed to make passage to the United States, Bellmer decided to remain in Vichy France and in 1942 he married a French citizen, Marcelle Celine Sutter. As the war rumbled on, he worked in secret as a forger, preparing false identity papers for refugees. When peace was declared, he and his wife separated, and in 1947 they were divorced.

On a visit to Berlin to see his mother in 1953, Bellmer met the German writer Unica Zürn, and the following year he moved back to Paris with her. In Zürn, Bellmer had found a partner with whom he could act out his strange sexual fantasies – there are some extraordinary photographs he took of her, naked and tied up tightly with string. The string cuts into her flesh, creating startling distortions of her body shape. It was as though Bellmer was transforming her into one of his erotic doll figures.

By 1970 Bellmer had ceased to be productive, and his life with Zürn had become unbearable. She was eventually taken away to a psychiatric clinic, after which Bellmer became so miserable that he expressed a wish to die. In her clinic, Zürn's condition started to improve and she was allowed out for five days to visit him. They spent a pleasant evening chatting about their problems, but the following morning Zürn took a chair out onto the terrace of the top-floor apartment, climbed up onto it, and leapt to her death.

Bellmer was distraught and his condition deteriorated rapidly. A moment of relief came in 1971, when he was taken to a retrospective of his work in Paris. He was so moved to find himself honoured in this way that he broke down and wept in the gallery. He eventually died in 1975, from cancer of the bladder.

# JOHN BIGGE



## The surrealist with an inherited title, who escaped his aristocratic background through dream landscapes

**BORN**: 20 June 1892, Oxford **PARENTS**: Father Sir Amherst Selby-Bigge, permanent secretary to the Board of Education **LIVED**: Oxford, 1892; King's Sutton, 1900; London, 1913; war service in Greece, 1915; London, 1923; Austria, France, Portugal, Spain, 1936; London, 1941; Austria, 1945; London, 1946; Le Bugue, Dordogne, 1950s to 1973 **PARTNERS**: Rachel Humphries, m. 1914; Marija Bacik, m. 1946 **DIED**: 1973, Le Bugue, Dordogne

John Bigge was not a typical surrealist – for one thing, he held the hereditary rank of baronet, and his full title was Sir John Amherst Selby-Bigge, Bart. He can best be described as a 'gentleman surrealist', something of a contradiction in terms. There was certainly a period when he painted surrealist pictures, but he would never have considered joining a formal group or signing any manifestos or declarations. Nor did he lead a surrealist lifestyle.

The fact was that Bigge painted for pleasure, and his surrealist landscapes reflected this. They were expertly painted but lacked any sense of surrealist passion or rebellion. He took natural forms, modified them slightly and then presented them in unnatural settings, making them seem novel and intriguing. The result was an appealing, dreamlike landscape that lacked any sort of threat or sinister undercurrent.

John Bigge was born in Oxford towards the end of the 19th century and educated at Winchester and at Christ Church, Oxford. In 1912, at the age of twenty, he abandoned formal education and adopted a nomadic lifestyle, announcing his rejection of 'the banalities of the sophisticated world'.

The following year, however, he changed his mind and was admitted to the Slade School of Art in London. There he met a fellow art student, Rachel

Ruth Humphries, whose family ran the publishing company Lund Humphries. He and Rachel were married in 1914 and would have four daughters, but no son and heir to carry on the title.

At this crucial point in his career, Bigge's studies were cut short by the start of the First World War. He was called up for military duty and served with the Macedonian Mule Corps in Greece, with the unusual title of Inspector of Muleteers.

At home, his wife had made many connections in the world of art and literature and enjoyed giving dinner parties. The writer and founder of the Bloomsbury Group, Lytton Strachey, after dining with the Bigges, wrote of John: 'He had evidently been crushed flat by the war – not its worst horrors but the stupidity of everyone he was with, and the appalling dullness of existence.... I thought he was really one of the most truly good people I had ever met.'

Like several other surrealists, Bigge had a dramatic moment of 'conversion' when he saw the early work of the Italian Giorgio de Chirico. This encounter took place at Tooth's Gallery in London, where de Chirico was having an exhibition in 1928. It was at this point that Bigge decided he must become part of the surrealist movement.

He became friendly with the artist Edward Wadsworth, and this connection had a considerable influence on his work. As time passed, Bigge became more and more serious about his painting, and in 1931 he was afforded his first solo exhibition at the Wertheim Gallery, London. The following year he had a solo show in Paris, and in 1936 he was included in the major International Surrealist Exhibition in London. He was quoted as saying that he admired the surrealist movement because 'Its sur-realities... are more real than the conventional realities of the modern world.'

When Bigge's father died in 1951, he inherited the title of baronet – a shock for André Breton, had he heard of it. After the war, he moved to France and lived in the Dordogne until his death in 1973.

# PAUL-ÉMILE BORDUAS



## The Canadian surrealist who formed a group called the 'Automatistes'

**BORN**: 1 November 1905, Mont-Saint-Hilaire, Quebec **PARENTS**: Father a carpenter and blacksmith **LIVED**: Saint-Hilaire, 1905; Montreal, 1923; Paris, 1928; Saint-Hilaire, 1930; Montreal, 1933; New York, 1953; Paris, 1955 **PARTNER**: Gabrielle Goyette, m. 1935–51 **DIED**: 22 February 1960, Paris

In 1924, André Breton defined surrealism as 'Psychic automatism in its pure state, by which one proposes to express the actual functioning of thought, in the absence of any control exercised by reason...' It was this definition that inspired the Canadian artist Paul-Émile Borduas to form a group called Les Automatistes in Montreal in the 1940s. His form of automatism was abstract surrealism at its most direct.

Borduas was born in Canada, in the village of Saint-Hilaire near Montreal. He showed an early interest in creating art objects and won a scholarship to the Montreal school of fine arts. In 1928 he left Canada to study at an art college in Paris, but soon had to return home when his money ran out.

Back in Canada in 1930, he encountered Breton's writings. They made a powerful impact on him and he began painting 'automatically'. He explained: 'Faced with the white sheet, my mind free of any literary ideas, I respond to my first impulse.... Once the first line is drawn, the page has been divided and that division starts a whole series of thoughts which proceed automatically.'

His first exhibition as an abstract surrealist took place in 1942, and he quickly attracted a group of young artists around him who became known as 'the automatists'. As the leader of this new movement in Canada he organized group exhibitions in 1946, in both New York and Montreal. This was the first time Canada had encountered such work, and it had a mixed reception.

Borduas's group of sixteen artists became increasingly rebellious until, in 1948, they issued a manifesto that caused outrage. Called *Refus global* (Total Refusal), it demanded the separation of the church from the state, and especially from the arts. The diatribe against religion could have been written by Breton himself and its impact was inevitable. Twenty-six days after its publication, Borduas was dismissed from his position as an art teacher; he would never again hold an official teaching post of any kind in Canada.

The following year he issued a pamphlet in which he cried out, 'At last free to paint!' In reality, what this meant was that he had no money. In 1951, to his great distress, he returned home from a trip to Toronto to find that his home was empty; his wife and children had left him.

He decided to sell his house in Saint-Hilaire and move to the United States. There he continued painting, and some observers likened his work to that of the newly emerging school of abstract expressionists. There was, however, a crucial difference. In Borduas's compositions there was a background on which strange foreground shapes floated and hovered. It was as though he was painting figures in a landscape, but without any recognizable representational details. This is why he can be called an abstract surrealist rather than a purely abstract artist.

In 1955 Borduas finally left North America for good, settling in Paris for the last five years of his short life. But back in Canada, his rebellion was having a greater impact than he could have imagined: there was a so-called 'quiet revolution' under way, in which creative artists were being liberated and released from their traditional chains. In retrospect, Borduas can be seen as a pivotal figure who helped to bring about the widespread modernization of social life in his home country.

# CONSTANTIN BRANCUSI

## The Romanian artist who was a great surrealist sculptor before there was a surrealist movement

**BORN**: 19 February 1876, Hobitza, Romania
**PARENTS**: Poor peasants; father a bully
**LIVED**: Hobitza, 1876; Craiova, 1892; Bucharest, 1898; Paris, 1904
**PARTNER**: Vera Moore, 1930
**DIED**: 16 March 1957, Paris

Brancusi was a surrealist sculptor before there was a surrealist movement. Even before the First World War, he was producing sculptural forms of which any later surrealist would have been proud. Like de Chirico's early paintings, they heralded things to come. Brancusi's reputation, however, goes beyond surrealism: he has been described as the pioneer of all modern sculpture.

Brancusi – *pronounced* Brancoosh, not Brancoozy – was born in the forested foothills of the Transylvanian mountains in Romania. His parents were poor peasants and his childhood was harsh. To escape his bullying father, he ran away from home three times. On the third occasion, when he was still only eleven, he did not return. He survived by working at menial jobs until he was able to enter the School of Arts and Crafts in Craiova. There he worked so hard that he received grants enabling him to move on to Bucharest and enrol at the School of Fine Arts. In Bucharest, his juvenile work was so good that he was soon winning prizes and even gaining commissions.

At the age of twenty-seven, in 1903, he left Romania and set off across Europe on foot. After more than a year of travel he arrived in Paris and enrolled in an art school there. He earned his living by washing dishes and singing in the local Romanian church. The following year he exhibited some of his sculpture and it was seen by Auguste Rodin, who praised it highly. From this point on, commissions and exhibitions became regular events for Brancusi. In the heady atmosphere of artistic rebellion in Paris, he became part of a wide circle of avant-garde friends that included Picasso, Matisse, Modigliani, Cocteau and others.

When the First World War broke out he was not accepted for military service, so avoided the battlefield slaughter of that terrible period. After the war he began exhibiting again, but there was trouble ahead. In 1920 one of the sculptures he exhibited in Paris was considered to be obscene. The authorities pronounced it too phallic, and it had to be withdrawn. In 1926 he was involved in another scandal, this time with American customs officials: when they saw his bronze *Bird in Space*, they decided that it was not a work of art, but should be classed as 'an object of manufacture'. This meant that it would have attracted a high import tax, which Brancusi had to fight hard to avoid.

Two of his works were included in the 1936 International Surrealist Exhibition in London. The surrealists had always admired him and his work, but he himself remained stubbornly outside any group or movement. In 1955 he was awarded a large museum retrospective in New York, but was too ill to attend. The end was close, and in March 1957 he died. As he had never married and recognized no children, he left his studio and its contents to the Museum of Modern Art in Paris. He was buried in Montparnasse.

Little is known about Brancusi's love life except that he had a passionate affair with an Australian pianist called Vera Moore, starting in 1930. They had a son, John Moore, in 1934, but Brancusi never acknowledged him.

# VICTOR BRAUNER

## The brilliant Romanian surrealist, whose bizarre images are greater than his reputation


**BORN**: 15 June 1903, Piatra Neamț, Romania  **PARENTS**: Father a timber manufacturer, involved in spiritualism  **LIVED**: Piatra Neamț, 1903; Vienna; Brăila, Romania, 1914; Bucharest, 1916; Paris, 1925; Romania, 1927; Paris, 1930; Bucharest, 1935; Paris, 1938; South of France, 1940; Paris, 1945  **PARTNERS**: Margit Kosch, m. 1930; Jacqueline Abraham, m. 1946  **DIED**: 12 March 1966, Paris


Victor Brauner was born into a Jewish family in the Carpathian mountains of northeastern Romania in 1903. At school he developed a passion for zoology, heralding the presence of zoomorphic figures in his later paintings. When he was sixteen he enrolled at the Bucharest School of Fine Arts, but was later expelled for 'non-conformist behaviour' when some of his pictures were described as 'scandalous'.

By 1924, when he was twenty-one, he was aware of the dadaist movement; illustrations of his were appearing in a magazine to which the Romanian-born dadaist Tristan Tzara was also contributing. Soon after this, Brauner left Bucharest for the avant-garde art world of Paris, where he managed to survive for two years until his money ran out and he had to return penniless to Romania.

In 1930 he married Margit Kosch, a jewelry artist. Together they moved to Paris, where Brauner made contact with his compatriot, the sculptor Constantin Brancusi. His close neighbour was Yves Tanguy, who introduced him to André Breton. In 1933 he formally joined the surrealist group and began attending their café meetings. The following year he was given a solo exhibition, with Breton writing the preface to his catalogue.

At this point Brauner was fully established as a member of the surrealist circle, but sadly, despite earning some money by working as a movie extra, he once again ran out of funds and he and his wife had to return to Bucharest. He kept in touch with the Parisian surrealists, however, and was able to continue exhibiting with them. In 1936 he was represented at the International Surrealist Exhibitions in London and in New York.

The year 1938 was traumatic for Brauner, as he suffered a truly surrealist injury. When an argument developed into a fight and Óscar Domínguez threw a missile at Esteban Francés, it missed Francés but struck Brauner in the face with such force that it destroyed his left eye. What made the injury so strange was that seven years earlier, in 1931, Brauner had painted a portrait of himself in which he depicted his face with one eye severely wounded.

Despite the injury, Brauner was soon painting again, and several exhibitions of his work were held in Paris in 1939. That same year, he and Margit divorced. When the Nazis occupied Paris in June 1940, Brauner fled to the South of France, where he spent the rest of the war destitute and in hiding. He returned to Paris after it was liberated in 1944, occupying a studio that had once belonged to Henri Rousseau. It would be his home for the next fourteen years, shared with his second wife, Jacqueline Abraham, whom he married in 1946.

Brauner was reunited with the returning surrealists after their exile in the United States, but in the following year he clashed with Breton over the expulsion of Matta from the group. Brauner not only refused to sign a letter expelling the Chilean artist, but publicly accused Breton of hypocrisy. Breton expelled him from the group, but later, in 1959, he was formally reinstated.

The 1960s saw many more exhibitions of Brauner's work, but in 1965 he was admitted to hospital with stomach ulcers. He died the following summer, after a long illness. The inscription on his tomb in Montmartre reads, 'Peindre, c'est la vie, la vraie vie, ma vie' (Painting is life, true life, my life).

# ANDRÉ BRETON

## The godfather of the surrealist movement, whose autocratic leadership gave it its lasting strength

**BORN**: 19 February 1896, Tinchebray (Orne), Normandy **PARENTS**: Father a policeman; mother a seamstress **LIVED**: Normandy, 1896; Nantes, 1914; Paris, 1922; New York, 1941; Paris, 1946 **PARTNERS**: Georgina Dubreuil, 1919–20; Simone Kahn, m. 1921–31; Leona Delacourt (Nadja), 1926–7; Suzanne Muzard, 1927–30; Claire, 1930; Valentine Hugo, 1931; Marcelle Ferry, 1933; Jacqueline Lamba, m. 1934–45; Elisa (Bindorff) Claro, m. 1945–66 **DIED**: 28 September 1966, Paris

André Breton was the most central, most important figure in the history of surrealism. It was he who defined it, described it and defended it against all comers. Nobody played a more significant role in organizing and promoting the surrealist movement, and for that Breton must always be respected. He was a notable surrealist poet and an occasional surrealist artist. Having established all of this, it must also be said that he was widely disliked, even among his followers.

Breton was born in Normandy at the end of the 19th century, to a father who was an atheist policeman and a mother who was a pious seamstress. Surrealism owes his mother a great debt, because it was her cold, harsh treatment of young André that set him off on a lifelong search for the wonders of his lost childhood. In the fantastic daydreams and dark imaginings of a child's mind, Breton saw a possibility of a new kind of adult creativity. And as a young man in his late twenties, it was this form of creativity that he was able to foster with the founding of the surrealist movement in Paris.

Gathering around him a small group of rebellious poets and writers, he laid out his master plan in the form of a manifesto. Together the surrealists were to start working directly from the unconscious mind, without any rational, moral or aesthetic censorship.

At first the movement was essentially literary

and philosophical, but several brilliant visual artists were immediately attracted to it and wanted to join. They, of course, had a great advantage, because visual artists face no language problems. Eventually Breton found himself internationally regarded as the founder of an art movement rather than a rebellious philosophical collective.

In his private life, he experienced some difficulty forming long-lasting relationships. Throughout the 1920s and 1930s, while he was controlling and developing the movement in Paris, he enjoyed a series of love affairs, none of which lasted very long – until, in 1934, he met an ambitious young artist by the name of Jacqueline Lamba, who was spirited, intelligent and well read. Unable to survive on her income frompainting, she was earning a living as a nude dancer in a Montmartre cabaret. Breton fell in love with her immediately, and three months later they were married.

In 1939, with the outbreak of the Second World War, Breton's world collapsed. He and the other surrealists fled to New York, where they sat out the war. It was a depressing time for him, but in 1946 he was at last able to return to his beloved Paris, where his old apartment awaited him. As a way of relaunching surrealism in the city, he began planning another major International Surrealist Exhibition. It took place in 1947 and made a considerable impact, but that impact was not sustained. There was a general feeling that as an organized movement, surrealism was over. Breton did his best to keep it going until his death in 1966, but the major surrealists were now all scattered and group activity in post-war Paris was hard to maintain.

Breton was arrogant and sometimes pompous, but he was the central driving force of the surrealist movement, and it would have been much the poorer without him. His charismatic presence gave surrealism its gravitas, elevating it from the level of an intellectual prank into one of the major art movements of the 20th century.

# EMMY BRIDGWATER



## The British artist whose surrealist ideas were more impressive than her technical ability

**BORN**: 10 November 1906, Edgbaston, Birmingham
**PARENTS**: Father a chartered accountant
**LIVED**: Birmingham, 1906; Oxford, 1926; Birmingham, 1937; London, 1948; Birmingham, 1986
**PARTNER**: Toni del Renzio, 1942
**DIED**: 13 March 1999, Birmingham

Emmy Bridgwater was born into a middle-class family in Birmingham towards the end of the Edwardian period. At the age of sixteen she attended Birmingham Art School, and four years later she moved to Oxford to continue her studies there. Being short of funds, she worked as a secretary to pay her way.

In 1936 she visited the International Surrealist Exhibition in London, and the experience changed her life. From this point onwards she knew that she had to devote herself to working in the surrealist tradition. For a further year of study she enrolled at the Grosvenor School of Modern Art in London, again supporting herself through secretarial work.

Bridgwater returned in 1937 to Birmingham, where she joined the local surrealist group led by Conroy Maddox. A few years later she also joined the London surrealist group that had gathered around the Belgian Édouard Mesens. In 1942 she had a brief but passionate affair with the Russian surrealist Toni del Renzio, who unsuccessfully challenged Mesens for leadership of the British surrealist group. She also had her first solo exhibition, at the Bilbo Gallery in London.

After the war, in 1947, she was one of the signatories of the formal declaration of the British surrealist group, still led by Mesens. In the same year, André Breton was sufficiently impressed by her work to invite her to participate in the International Surrealist Exhibition in Paris.

Bridgwater's paintings are difficult to describe, but they had a powerful impact on those who encountered them. Toni del Renzio said of them, 'We do not see these pictures. We hear their cries and are moved by them. Our own entrails are drawn painfully from us and twisted into the pictures whose significance we did not want to realize.' Robert Melville commented that 'although they are dreamlike in their ambiguity they are realistic documents from a region of phantasmal hopes and murky desires'. Michel Remy described Bridgwater as an 'explorer of the sulfurous lavas and springtimes of the unconscious'.

In the late 1940s, her career as a surrealist came to a sudden, unexpected halt owing to family emergencies. Her elderly mother, who had been looking after Bridgwater's disabled sister, now needed care herself, and Bridgwater had to take on the family duty of caring for both of them. This consumed so much of her energy that she was unable to continue full time with her painting. She kept exhibiting and painted whenever she could find a spare moment, but eventually, in 1950, admitted defeat and gave up painting altogether. In 1953 she moved to Stratford-upon-Avon to take up her role as a full-time carer.

This state of affairs would continue for nearly twenty years until, around 1970, she became active once more and started to make collages. After this she took part in a variety of surrealist group shows, and in 1990 had a solo exhibition in London. Sadly, after 1986, she was incapable of painting or drawing. She suffered this enforced inactivity for many years, until her death in a nursing home in 1999 at the age of ninety-two.

# EDWARD BURRA

## The wealthy, arthritic loner of British surrealism, whose dark imagery was laced with an 'impotent venom'

BORN: 29 March 1905, South Kensington, London
PARENTS: Father a barrister; inherited wealth
LIVED: Rye, East Sussex
DIED: 22 October 1976, Hastings

Edward Burra was one of the rich surrealists. Thanks to his inherited wealth, he never had to experience the indignities of poverty suffered by many others in the group. He did, however, have his own cross to bear in the shape of crippling, lifelong rheumatoid arthritis that began at the tender age of five and stayed with him until he died many years later, at seventy-one.

The son of a wealthy lawyer, Burra was raised in Rye on the south coast of England. As a child, he loved drawing and was encouraged in this by his family. When he was twenty, he wrote to a friend saying, 'I should like to draw all day without stopping.'

Apart from his art, Burra's other great passion was travelling – a passion at odds with the weakness of his body. He once told a friend, 'I must sit down most of the time.' It is true that his travels did involve a great deal of sitting down, drinking and observing in bars, cafés and music halls. He was particularly taken with the then notorious district of Harlem in New York.

His first surrealist work did not appear until 1930. From this point onwards he would repeatedly abandon his satirical works and plunge into the darker world of surrealist imagery, but it cannot be said that he had a marked surrealist phase. His surrealism was spasmodic, interspersed with his more typical satirical observations and his landscapes. His total output was small. In the half-century when he was active he produced only 413 paintings, and of these no more than sixty were surrealist works. They were, however, works of great intensity and complexity, and three of them were included in the International Surrealist Exhibition of 1936.

Burra's biographers have suggested that the greatest factor limiting his surrealist output was his dislike of certain aspects of the movement. André Breton had always emphasized that the movement was essentially a collective; Burra, a devoted individualist and non-joiner, found Breton's passion for trying to control his followers irksome. He told one surrealist: 'I didn't like being told what to think, dearie.'

What he did like about the surrealist movement was the way it released him to explore the recesses of his unconscious, and the fact that it was essentially a rebel group, opposed to the establishment. For these reasons, he kept returning to surrealist imagery and was happy to exhibit with the group when invited to do so.

In personality, Burra was often difficult and acid-tongued. He hated being interviewed and on the rare occasions when he permitted this intrusion into his private life, his responses were typically brief. When asked what really mattered to him, his reply consisted of a single word: 'Nothing.'

Needless to say, during his travels he disliked being quizzed by customs officials. On one occasion during the Prohibition era, an American customs man spotted the bulge caused by a bottle of whisky hidden in his hip pocket. When the official demanded to know what it was, Burra escaped by exploiting his misshapen body, snarling, 'It's a growth.'

# ALEXANDER CALDER

## The brilliant surrealist blacksmith who brought mobility to sculpture

**BORN**: 22 July 1898, Lawnton, Pennsylvania **PARENTS**: Father a sculptor; mother a portrait artist **LIVED**: Pennsylvania, 1898; California, 1906; Philadelphia, 1909; New Jersey, 1915; New York, 1923; Paris, 1926; Connecticut, 1933; Indre-et-Loire, 1953 **PARTNERS**: Louisa James, m. 1931 **DIED**: 11 November 1976

Barrel-chested Sandy Calder was one of the most original artists of modern times. Only Calder created 'mobiles' – sculptural works that made their impact by moving in the wind. They were his unique contribution to modern art.

Born in Pennsylvania at the end of the 19th century, Calder was fortunate in having a mother who was a painter and a father who was a sculptor. As a result, he started young, producing his first sculpture at the age of eleven. As a young adult, Calder continued to develop his childhood fascination with metalworking, and when he was twenty-one he obtained a degree in mechanical engineering.

In 1926, at the age of twenty-eight, he made his first wire sculpture. In the summer of that year he worked his passage to Europe on a freighter, making his way to Paris. Once there, he took a studio and started work on what would become known as the *Cirque Calder*, an early example of performance art. It consisted of a miniaturized circus in the form of mechanical sculptures operated by Calder himself in front of an audience.

In 1928 he arranged a meeting with Joan Miró in his Montmartre studio. Although their personalities were very different, Calder and Miró soon became friends and would remain close for the rest of their lives.

Travelling back to New York on a liner, Calder met an attractive girl by the name of Louisa James. They became acquainted and she invited him to stay at her house in Cape Cod, declaring afterwards that he was the perfect guest who 'mended everything in sight'. They were married in January 1931 – the beginning of a lifelong bond that would last until Calder's death in 1976.

Returning to Paris, the young couple set up home. At this point Calder was spending more time with surrealist artists such as Jean Arp and Marcel Duchamp, and he became fascinated by the abstraction of natural shapes. As a result, he started to create abstract organic shapes that floated in the air or were moved by small motors. These completely novel kinetic sculptures could not have been created without Calder's special double life, first as an engineer and second as a sculptor. It quickly became clear that he had invented an entirely original art form and it was Duchamp who christened the new works 'mobiles'. Calder's later, non-moving works were then given the name 'stabiles' by Jean Arp.

In the summer of 1933, the Calders sold their house in Paris and moved back to the United States – Calder said they had not liked the rumours that Europe seemed to be heading for another war. In this respect, they were years ahead of the other surrealists, who did not leave Europe until it was almost too late.

Back in America, the Calders found a broken-down 18th-century farmhouse on eighteen acres near the small town of Roxbury, Connecticut. It would remain their home for the rest of their lives. From this point onwards, Calder's story was one of increasing success.

After Calder's death in 1976, his old friend Miró wrote a touching poem for him. It ended with the words: 'Your ashes will fly to the sky,/to make love to the stars./Sandy,/Sandy,/Your ashes caress/The rainbow flowers/That tickle the blue of the sky.'

# LEONORA CARRINGTON

## The rebellious daughter of a British tycoon, who joined the Paris surrealists and created an arcane dream world

**BORN**: 6 April 1917, Clayton Green, Chorley, Lancashire **PARENTS**: Father a textile magnate; mother Irish **LIVED**: Lancashire, 1917; London, 1935; Saint-Martin-d'Ardèche, 1938; Spain, 1940; Portugal, 1941; New York, 1941; Mexico, 1943 **PARTNERS**: Max Ernst, 1937–9; Renato Leduc, m. 1941–4; Emérico (Chiki) Weisz, m. 1946–2007 **DIED**: 25 May 2011, Mexico City

Leonora Carrington was one of those attractive, rebellious young women who were drawn to the surrealist circle in Paris. She found the surrealist gatherings in Parisian cafés and bars exhilarating. After her stifled childhood, this was not surprising.

Carrington was born in northern England, the daughter of a Lancashire textile tycoon, and grew up in a large household. Despite its grandeur, she saw her family home as little more than a huge prison. At school she was soon in trouble because she could write with both hands, even backwards. The nuns who taught her told her that she was abnormal and punished her. This was the moment when her distrust of religion began. She was expelled twice, but despite this, her family had her presented at court and gave her a debutante's ball at the Ritz in London.

In 1935, at the age of eighteen, she left home permanently for the life of an art student in London. In 1937 Max Ernst had a show in London; Carrington, then aged twenty, met him at a dinner party and was soon his lover and his protégée. When he left for Paris she followed, telling her outraged family that she was going abroad to live in sin with a forty-six-year-old, married German artist. Her father declared that she must never return to the family home.

In 1937, Carrington became an active member of André Breton's circle. In 1938, however, both she and Ernst started to find Breton's interminable squabbling tiresome, and they left Paris to live in an old farmhouse in a French village. With the outbreak of the Second World War, their idyll came to a juddering halt. Ernst, being German, was immediately interned in a French prison camp, and Carrington found herself suddenly isolated in a foreign country. She sold up and moved to Madrid, where she was discovered one day screaming that she wanted to kill Hitler.

From a distance, her father had her committed to a Spanish lunatic asylum and made arrangements for her to be transferred to a mental institution in South Africa. He sent her old nanny over by submarine to escort her there. As soon as they reached Lisbon, Carrington escaped and found her way to the Mexican embassy, where an acquaintance of hers, Renato Leduc, was working. She pleaded with him to get her out of the country, but this was not easy. The only way was to marry – which they did, and moved to America.

In 1943, Leduc decided to move back to his homeland and took Carrington with him. Not long afterwards, they were amicably divorced. In Mexico City she fell in love with Emérico 'Chiki' Weisz, a photojournalist, and they were married in 1946. Carrington continued to paint well into her nineties.

Carrington's paintings take the viewer into a fantastic private world full of monsters and arcane rituals. Some are like demented fairy tales, others like elegant nightmares. They make an impact even though their precise meaning is obscure.

When she was ninety years old, Carrington was asked whether certain strange animals in one particular scene were acting as guardians. She replied, 'I don't really think in terms of explanations.' Her view was that if images came from the unconscious, they should also be received by it. When another interviewer asked about the meaning of one of her works, she retorted sharply, 'This is not an intellectual game. It is a visual world. Use your feelings.'

# MARC CHAGALL

## The Russian romantic whose irrational dream world preceded the surrealist movement



**BORN**: 6 July 1887, Liozna, near Vitebsk, Belarus (then Russia), as Moishe Shagal **PARENTS**: Father a herring merchant; mother sold groceries **LIVED**: Liozna, 1887; St Petersburg, 1907; Paris, 1910; Vitebsk, 1914; Moscow, 1917; Berlin, 1922; Paris, 1923; New York, 1941; France, 1948; Vence, Côte d'Azur, 1950 **PARTNERS**: Bella Rosenfeld, m. 1915–44; Virginia Haggard, 1945–52; Valentina (Vava) Brodsky, m. 1952 **DIED**: 28 March 1985, Saint-Paul-de-Vence

Chagall, like de Chirico, was a natural surrealist who preceded the movement. He was ignored by the surrealists once their movement got under way in the 1920s, but in 1928, in his essay 'Surrealism and Painting', Breton apologizes for this: 'It is a deplorable omission that Chagall's contribution to the beginning of the movements of Dada and Surrealism has not been fully recognized…. Nothing shows a more positive magic than this work…. His positive explosion of lyricism dates from 1911, the moment when, under his sole impulse, metaphor made its triumphal entry into modern painting.'

Chagall was born in 1887 in a Jewish suburb of Vitebsk. His father was a fishmonger's assistant and his mother ran a small shop. The cramped wooden house that was home to his parents and their nine children was always humming with social activity and there was dancing, laughter, shouting and music. All these elements would become lodged in the mind of the young Chagall, to be regurgitated later in his paintings, mixed up together in distant echoes of childhood dreaming.

In 1907 Chagall went to the Russian capital, then St Petersburg, where he spent four years as an art student. After this he moved on to Paris, where, with artistic rebellion in the air, he began placing his dreams on canvas in an irrational jumble. There were lovers floating in the air, heads detached from bodies, a fish playing the violin, a donkey holding a parasol, and animals turning into humans. His friend Guillaume Apollinaire called his work *surnaturel*.

During the next few years, Chagall produced some of his greatest pre-surrealist work – but then, while he was on a visit to his hometown of Vitebsk in 1914, war broke out and he was stranded there. The following year he married Bella Rosenfeld, whom he had met in 1909 while he was studying art in St Petersburg. After the First World War ended, he made the decision to return to the freer atmosphere of Paris. There he was able to continue with his painting, and in 1937 he took French citizenship.

When the Second World War broke out in 1939, Chagall and his wife fled to New York, arriving in June 1941 on the very day that the Nazis invaded Russia. In 1944, Bella died from a viral infection. A year later Chagall met Virginia Haggard, daughter of a British diplomat, and they began an affair that would last for seven years and give them a son.

When the war ended, Chagall found himself centre stage as a major artist in New York, with a retrospective of his work at the Museum of Modern Art in 1946. In 1948 he returned to France but abandoned Paris for the south, settling near Nice. He would remain there until his death in 1985.

In 1952, his seven-year relationship with Virginia Haggard came to a sudden end. Now in his late sixties, Chagall needed a housekeeper and was lucky enough to find one in the shape of Kyiv-born Valentina Brodsky, known to everyone as Vava. Three months later, they were married, and Vava soon took over his whole life – caring for him, travelling everywhere with him and organizing his business affairs. For the ageing artist, nothing could have been more perfect. Without her constant support, he would certainly not have lived to the advanced age of ninety-seven; nor would he have been able to take on major art projects in his later years, including the painted ceiling of the Paris Opéra.

# GIORGIO DE CHIRICO

**BORN**: 10 July 1888, Volos, Greece **PARENTS**: Father Sicilian; mother Genovese **LIVED**: Volos, 1888; Athens; Munich, 1905; Milan, 1909; Florence, 1910; Paris, 1911; Italy, 1915; Rome, 1918; Paris, 1925; Italy, 1932; Rome, 1944 **PARTNERS**: Raissa Gurievich, m. 1925; Isabella Pakszwer Far, m. 1930 **DIED**: 20 November 1978, Rome

## The Italian master whose early work heralded and deeply influenced the surrealist movement

Giorgio de Chirico's life story as an artist is split into two. In the early part, which runs from 1911 to 1918, he produced a group of 'metaphysical' paintings of sinister figures and street scenes that are among the greatest surrealist works ever made. What is more, they preceded the surrealist art movement, serving as a herald for its approach. And yet, in the later part of his life – from the age of thirty until his death at ninety – de Chirico's work became boringly traditional.

De Chirico was born into an Italian family living in Greece in 1888. His father was an engineer in charge of building a new railway line. The small boy showed a talent for drawing and was sent to study in Athens, where he spent six years learning to paint.

In 1904, when he was sixteen, his father died and his mother took him to Italy, where they lived in Milan. In 1911 they moved to Paris, but following the outbreak of the First World War, de Chirico joined the Italian army. He managed to secure a clerk's post at a military base, where he had plenty of free time in which to paint. It was during these war years that he was able to produce his most important metaphysical works.

In 1923 he held an exhibition of his metaphysical paintings in Paris. One of his strangest early works, *The Child's Brain*, was exhibited in the window of the gallery and seen by Breton, who said that he could not rest until he had acquired it. Before he had done so, however, the work was also spotted by a young Yves Tanguy, who leapt from a moving bus in order to examine it more closely. What he saw changed his life, converting him from being a merchant seaman to devoting the rest of his life to painting.

During the 1920s, de Chirico's art underwent a change that saw it diverge from its surrealist beginnings, but in 1925 he returned to Paris and attended some of André Breton's surrealist gatherings. His welcome was to be short-lived, however, for he was about to hold an exhibition of his new, more conventional work. The surrealists were horrified by what they saw. In their eyes, he was now producing complete rubbish. The man they had admired so much had, for them, become an embarrassment. They launched an attack on him and all bonds of attachment were completely broken.

De Chirico did not take this lying down. He went into counter-attack mode, accusing the surrealists of 'behaving like hooligans and petty delinquents'. This battle would rumble on and on – in 1928, Breton summed up the situation in his book *Le Surrealisme et la peinture*, where he stressed his admiration for de Chirico's pre-1919 work and his condemnation of the later work.

From the 1920s until his death in 1978, de Chirico produced a long stream of highly traditional, representational work, with just an occasional reversion to his early metaphysical themes. He married twice, exhibited widely and lived at various times in Florence, Milan, Rome, Paris and the United States. During the Second World War he remained in Italy, painting in Florence and Rome. After the war he settled permanently in Rome, where he continued to paint for the remainder of his days.

# CECIL COLLINS



**BORN**: 23 March 1908, Plymouth
**PARENTS**: Father an engineer
**LIVED**: Plymouth, 1908; London, 1927; Devon, 1936; London, 1944; Cambridge, 1948; Chelsea, London, 1970
**PARTNER**: Elizabeth Ramsden, m. 1931
**DIED**: 4 June 1989

## The British artist whose strange landscapes would be rejected by the surrealists

Cecil Collins has to be included in a list of surrealist artists because his work was shown as part of the landmark event in London in 1936 – the International Surrealist Exhibition at the New Burlington Galleries. Superficially, his paintings do appear to be in the surrealist mould, but a closer examination reveals that they have religious themes and therefore break one of the basic rules of the surrealist movement. A possible explanation of Collins' acceptance as a member of the surrealist group is that his depiction of mystical, religious themes was viewed as a satirical attack on the subject.

Cecil Collins is one of those idiosyncratic, isolated, individualistic British artists whose work is immediately recognizable and has no close parallels in modern art. He was born in middle-class Edwardian Plymouth, the son of an engineer. A sickly, delicate boy, he was often away from school and spent many hours on his own, convalescing from various illnesses. The solitude he experienced helped him to develop his visionary imaginings. In his mind, he occupied a magical, spiritual world inhabited by figures from dark Cornish legends.

When Collins was nineteen, his father died. His mother, who had always been sympathetic to his interest in drawing and painting, was delighted when he won a scholarship to the Royal College of Art in London. There he became the golden boy of his year and, strangely, went through an anti-religious phase during which he painted a picture entitled *There Is No God*. By the early 1930s his brief atheist period was over and he was in love with a fellow student, the lively, intelligent and beautiful Elizabeth Ramsden. She seemed happy to share his eccentricities, and they were married in 1931.

In his art, Collins became obsessed with a figure he called simply 'the Fool' – a sad but slightly comical figure, a universal clown, an innocent abroad. He is usually depicted wearing a dunce's cap, as if being punished for stupidity.

Collins had a passionate dislike for the school of modern art known as hard-edge abstraction and complained bitterly about 'sterile geometric art with its tyrannical cultural snobbery'. This view, expressed in 1935, may explain why he was attracted to the surrealists and they to him. But when André Breton realized that surrealism had been invaded by despised spiritual imagery, the end came rapidly. Breton issued a statement condemning work such as Collins', ensuring that any paintings submitted by him to future surrealist exhibitions would be instantly rejected.

After his split from the surrealists, Collins continued to paint his visionary scenes. When the war came, with his frail health making him exempt from military duty, he took up teaching at Dartington Hall in Devon.

In 1959 a major retrospective of over 200 of his works was held at the Whitechapel Gallery, London. In the catalogue he struck back at his detractors, saying: 'Pure art is the prettier side of the utterly empty mechanical desert we call modern civilization.' Critics were once again divided, but there was enough praise for Collins to take some comfort from the event. Until the end of his life, his work was both coldly rejected and deeply admired.

# ITHELL COLQUHOUN



## The occultist of British surrealism, whose obsession with witchcraft saw her expelled from the group

**BORN**: 9 October 1906, Shillong, in what was then Eastern Bengal and Assam, British India **PARENTS**: Father a civil servant **LIVED**: Shillong, 1906; Cheltenham, 1925; London, 1927; Paris, 1931; London, 1933; Paris, 1937; London, 1939; Cornwall, late 1940s **PARTNER**: Toni del Renzio, m. 1943–7 **DIED**: 11 April 1988, Lamorna, Cornwall

Ithell Colquhoun was one of those artists who had an intense surrealist phase, but whose main focus lay elsewhere. She was first and foremost an occultist. Her interest in witchcraft meant that she was opposed to official religion, and this was something she shared with the surrealists. She was also obsessed with the mysterious – again, this was something that appealed to the surrealist mind.

Colquhoun was born in Shillong, British India, in the middle of the Edwardian period. Her father was a Scottish civil servant and she enjoyed an exotic and uninhibited childhood, full of rich and colourful imagery. Her family sent her to the Slade School of Art in London, where, in 1929, one of her paintings was so good that it won a prize and was exhibited at the Royal Academy. It was while she was a student at the Slade that she visited Paris and became fascinated by the dark surrealist fantasies of Salvador Dalí. In 1931, after graduating from the Slade, she set up a studio in Paris and became more deeply involved with the surrealist circle there.

She attended the International Surrealist Exhibition in London in 1936, but was not included among the exhibitors. It was not until 1939 that she formally joined the British surrealist group, then led by the London-based Belgian surrealist Édouard Mesens. However, in 1940 Mesens expelled her. She wanted to remain in the group but refused to give up her obsession with the occult, and Mesens could not accept this. This expulsion did nothing to dampen Colquhoun's interest in surrealism, nor to slow her output of surrealist works. It simply meant that she had to work outside the now small clique that gathered around their Belgian leader.

In 1942, at the height of the war, Colquhoun met a Russian surrealist by the name of Toni del Renzio. He moved into her studio, they became lovers, and in March 1943 they were married. When Mesens heard that del Renzio was making a bid to usurp his role as leader, he promptly expelled del Renzio from the surrealist group. In defiance of Mesens, del Renzio and Colquhoun organized a surrealist poetry reading in London. This threw down the gauntlet to Mesens, who reacted violently. He gathered together a gang of loyal friends and they attended the poetry reading armed with rotten eggs, which they hurled at the platform, where Colquhoun and her husband took refuge behind a grand piano. After about half an hour, the meeting had to be abandoned.

After the disastrous poetry evening, del Renzio was defeated and Mesens had regained his crown. But none of this put Colquhoun off producing surrealist paintings, which she continued to do for many years. Her marriage to del Renzio, however, did not last so long. Because of his infidelities, they separated in 1946 and were finally divorced the following year, with much rancour.

Devastated by the collapse of her marriage, Colquhoun moved down to Cornwall, where she would spend the rest of her life. There she became increasingly involved in the arcane world of magic, witchcraft and the occult.

A final word about Ithell Colquhoun's name: according to Toni del Renzio, it was pronounced 'Eye-thel' rather than 'Ith-el'. Most people have always mispronounced her.

# JOSEPH CORNELL

## The creator of irrational surrealist objects in the form of magical boxes

**BORN**: 24 December 1903, Nyack, New York

**PARENTS**: Father a designer and merchant of textiles; mother an ex-kindergarten teacher

**LIVED**: Nyack, 1903; New York City, 1917

**PARTNER**: Yayoi Kusama, 1960s–72

**DIED**: 29 December 1972, New York

Joseph Cornell belongs to that special category of artists whose work was relentlessly surrealist, but whose lifestyle was alien to the surrealist philosophy. His creations were almost entirely in the form of collages. The early ones, influenced by his discovery of Max Ernst, were two-dimensional, but his main body of work consisted of three-dimensional collages or assemblages – little wooden boxes filled with carefully arranged but irrationally juxtaposed objects. In 1941, André Breton said that he only approved of two American artists: David Hare and Joseph Cornell. He commended Cornell for having 'evolved an experiment that completely reverses the conventional usage to which objects are put'.

Joseph Cornell was born in Nyack, a village about thirty miles north of New York City. He was a lonely boy who relished the family trips to Manhattan, where they visited vaudeville shows and he saw Harry Houdini. It was Houdini escaping from locked boxes that he remembered most vividly. The box as a magic place would haunt him for the rest of his life, playing a major role in his art.

His father, a textile salesman and designer, died when Joseph was thirteen. By the time he was seventeen he was supporting his family financially.

During the Depression of the 1930s, as an escape from the drudgery of his daily life, he started making artworks from his extensive collection of old books, oddments and bric-a-brac. In 1931 he came across Max Ernst's classic book of collages, *La Femme 100 têtes*, in which old Victorian engravings were cut up and rearranged to create startling new compositions. Cornell immediately set about cutting up old books and making his own versions of Ernst's collages. From this beginning, he soon moved on to making three-dimensional collages inside small boxes.

Although eccentric and reclusive, Cornell had the initiative to show some of this early work to the Julien Levy Gallery in New York. This was the start of a long career as an exhibiting artist and, in the 1940s, when he was discovered by the refugee surrealists who were sitting out the Second World War in New York, he was welcomed into their ranks, exhibiting with them repeatedly and mixing with them socially.

During the 1950s Cornell's work became more widely recognized and he kept on making more and more of his surrealist boxes. His success culminated with a major retrospective at the Guggenheim Museum in New York in 1967. It was also in the 1960s that met the only woman with whom he nearly had an affair. He had fancied many girls in the past, but had never done anything physical about his crushes. This one was different. She was a Japanese artist called Yayoi Kusama, who liked his work and agreed to pose for him as a model. He became obsessed with Kusama, but looked upon the sex act as an ordeal and something that, if he indulged in it, would rob him of his ability to make works of art.

Despite his financial success as an artist, Cornell did not change his lifestyle, continuing to live frugally until his death in 1972. It was typical of the man that his will left everything he possessed, including all works of art, to provide aid for children with disabilities. At his funeral, his ashes were buried in a small coffin with the dimensions of one his famous boxes.

# ARTUR DO CRUZEIRO SEIXAS

## The leading figure of Portuguese surrealism, whose lively imagination was active for almost a century

**BORN**: 3 December 1920, Amadora, Lisbon, as Artur Manuel Rodrigues do Cruzeiro Seixas **PARENTS**: Father a railway clerk; mother made embroidery and lace **LIVED**: Lisbon, 1920; India and East Asia, 1950; Angola, 1952; Estorial, Portugal, 1964; Algarve, 1982; Estorial, 1988; Famalicão, Portugal, 2013 **DIED**: 8 November 2020

Cruzeiro Seixas, a key figure in Portuguese surrealism, modestly preferred to call himself 'a man who paints' rather than an artist. He grew up in Lisbon as an only child. Later in life, he recalled, 'We come from bourgeois roots. I miss the love of my parents, some exceptional parents.... They loved me so much that the world for them was the three of us.'

Surrealism came relatively late to Portugal. There had been isolated surrealist artists there from earlier years, but it was not until 1947 that André Breton encouraged the formation of a Lisbon surrealist group, and Cruzeiro Seixas was one of its members. The group's first major exhibition took place in 1949 and caused a scandal, with police involvement.

As so often in surrealist groups, there were arguments and expulsions and a splinter group was formed, called simply 'the surrealists' (Os Surrealistas). This group, which included Cruzeiro Seixas, held two exhibitions of its own, one in the summer of 1949 and another the following year.

After exhibiting in the second group show, he became restless and joined the merchant navy, visiting Africa, India and East Asia. He explored Goa, Hong

Kong, Macau and Timor. In 1952 he settled in Africa, at the Angolan capital of Luanda. There he explored the interior, collected tribal artefacts, and began creating art again, holding exhibitions of his paintings, collages and objects in Luanda in 1953 and 1954. Once again, his work caused heated debate and many of the Portuguese colonials living there were hostile.

In 1964 he decided to return to Europe, visiting France, England, Holland, Spain and Italy. He then settled at Estorial, Portugal, a few miles west of Lisbon. His exhibitions were more frequent now, including major retrospectives, and his reputation continued to grow. From 1968 to 1974 he was the director of the São Mamede Gallery, and from 1976 to 1983 he served on its board. He continued to produce surrealist works throughout his life even though, as an organized group, the surrealist movement in Portugal had come to an end back in 1950. In 1999 he donated his entire collection to help form the Museum of Surrealism in the Cupertino de Miranda Foundation, northern Portugal.

'The soul and the reason only interest me if they are really surreal,' he told an interviewer. 'I do not believe in religions, they do not touch me. I recognize religion as an extraordinary human characteristic, but I cannot grasp it…. Freud without doubt taught us a great deal about humanity, and then surrealism opened a huge door…but people are foolish and do not know what to do with it.'

Asked about his sexuality, he responded: 'Homosexuality for me was always a form of freedom against organized society…. For me, there was never any doubt that…homosexuality would be my great door to freedom, one of my doors at least.'

During his long life, Cruzeiro Seixas often had to take on mundane employment in order to survive, but admitted that 'I was always a bad employee because I spent so much of my time doing drawings.' For him, creating visual works of art that presented viewers with a strange world of irrationally juxtaposed elements was an obsession that never waned.

# SALVADOR DALÍ

## The Spanish genius who, in public, chose to play the surrealist clown

**BORN**: 11 May 1904, Figueres, Spain
**PARENTS**: Father a lawyer and notary
**LIVED**: Figueres, 1904; Madrid, 1922; Paris, 1929; Port Lligat, 1930; New York, 1940; Port Lligat, 1948
**PARTNER**: Gala Éluard, m. 1934
**DIED**: 23 January 1989, Figueres

Dalí was, without question, the most skilful and most accomplished of all the surrealists. In his early work he was also the most darkly imaginative and inventive. He enjoyed acting the fool in public, a device that made him well known to a wide audience. As a result, he became the most famous of all the surrealists and boldly proclaimed, 'I AM surrealism.'

Dalí was born in northern Spain in 1904, making him slightly younger that most of the other key surrealists. His father was a successful notary in Figueres and the family lived well. Dalí persuaded his parents to let him have a small studio where, at the age of ten, he produced his first oil painting. When he was seventeen he left Figueres to attend art school in Madrid. There he spent many hours in the Prado, studying the paintings of Hieronymus Bosch.

In 1925, at the age of twenty-one, Dalí made his first trip to Paris, armed with an introduction to Pablo Picasso. For the young artist, he said, it was like an audience with the Pope. The impact of Paris was such that Dalí decided then and there to somehow enter its avant-garde world, away from the restrictions of Figueres. He finally managed this in 1929, when he moved there to make a film with his old friend Luis Buñuel. The film was *Un Chien Andalou* and it contained images so shocking that it created a sensation. Breton declared it the first surrealist film.

When the film was completed, Dalí returned to Spain. It was then that he met Paul Éluard's wife, Gala, and began an intense relationship with her. Realizing that his abilities as an artist could make them both rich, Gala dumped Éluard and set her sights on Dalí.

Dalí's first exhibition in Paris was a huge success – every single painting sold. He became increasingly active in the surrealist circle and was soon an official member of Breton's select group. Back in Spain, he and Gala bought a fisherman's cottage in Port Lligat and converted it into a snug home for themselves, with a quiet studio where Dalí could paint in peace.

In 1931, exhibitions of his new work in Paris and New York were a resounding success. His painting *The Persistence of Memory* appeared at this time, with its soft watches that would live on to become one of the icons of 20th-century art.

A few years later, he and Gala married – a decision motivated less by romantic love than by her determination to inherit his estate if he should die or go mad. They decided to visit New York, where Dalí's eccentric behaviour set the stage for a lifelong love affair with the American art world. When war broke out in 1939, the couple returned to New York and remained there for the following eight years.

In 1948, they came back to Port Lligat, where Dalí resumed painting in his studio – but his late output, from the 1950s until his death, was generally disappointing. In the 1960s he acquired a theatre in the centre of his hometown of Figueres, which he began converting into a personal museum. It finally opened in 1974, displaying a treasure trove of Dalínian conceits. Years later, when he died, Dalí's body was entombed there, beneath the centre of the old theatre stage.

# JULIO DE DIEGO



## The Spanish artist who ended up in Hollywood, his flamboyant lifestyle overshadowing his surrealist work

**BORN**: 9 May 1900, Madrid **PARENTS**: Father a jeweler **LIVED**: Madrid, 1900; Morocco (army service), 1920; Paris, 1922; New York, 1924; Chicago, 1926–42; Mexico, 1939; New York, 1942; Los Angeles, 1956; Woodstock, 1961; Sarasota, Florida, 1967–79 **PARTNERS**: Rosalind Mallery, m. until 1932; Gypsy Rose Lee, m. 1948; Denny Joyce, 1955 **DIED**: 22 August 1979

As a child, Julio de Diego became obsessed with drawing and made it his ambition to become a visual artist. His domineering father was violently opposed to this career choice, and matters came to a head when he raged through the house destroying every work of art that his young son had lovingly created. The boy was only fifteen at the time, but his father's demolition of his dreams was too much for him and he bravely left home, never to return.

This youthful act of defiance meant that de Diego now had to find work in order to survive. He managed to get a job as apprentice to a set designer who was painting the scenery for an operatic company. He held his first exhibition of paintings at a gambling casino when he was seventeen, and was thrilled when he managed to sell one of them.

An extraordinary moment occurred when Serge Diaghilev of the Ballets Russes enlisted him to dance on stage with the great Nijinksy. Impressed by the teenager's flowing body movements and natural agility, Diaghilev asked him to join the company, but de Diego refused. Instead, still aged only nineteen, he moved into the world of the cinema and became an art director. He then served in the army, enlisting in the Spanish Cavalry. On returning to civilian life, he travelled in 1922 to Paris, where he worked for a while as an apprentice in Picasso's studio.

At the age of twenty-four he decided to investigate the Americas and travelled to New York. He was soon designing scenery again, this time for a Broadway musical. Eventually he settled in Chicago, where he would stay from 1926 until 1942. It was here that he settled down to lengthy bouts of painting, exhibiting regularly each year. He said of his pictures: 'All of my paintings are autobiographical, full of mystery, incongruous monsters, visions, sensous personages, sybaritic dreamers, sentimentalists, romantics and comic sadists.'

During the Second World War, when the major surrealists had all fled from Europe to live in exile in New York, Max Ernst, Marcel Duchamp and Man Ray became interested in de Diego's work and gave him encouragement. After the war, he exhibited with them at the major Exposition Internationale de Surrealisme in Paris in 1947.

In 1948 he gained some notoriety when he married for the second time, to the famous burlesque dancer and striptease artist Gypsy Rose Lee. The walls of her home were adorned with paintings by Miró, Picasso, Chagall and Ernst. Sadly, despite their similar interests, the marriage did not last, and they were divorced in 1955.

De Diego eventually arrived in Hollywood, where he took the role of a pirate called Miguel alongside his friend Yul Brynner in *The Buccaneer*, a 1958 film produced by Cecil B. DeMille. In 1967 he made his final move, going south to the warmth of Sarasota in Florida, where he remained until his death from cancer in 1979.

Julio de Diego was a serious surrealist artist, who always returned to painting between his other, more conspicuous activities. These did, however, overshadow his work as an artist, and as a result he has never figured historically as a major exponent of the surrealist movement. He scattered his talents too widely, but it has to be said that he did enjoy a wonderfully varied and colourful life.

# TONI DEL RENZIO

## The White Russian aristocrat who fled his country to end up as an active London surrealist

**BORN**: 15 April 1915, Tsarskoye Selo, now Pushkin, near St Petersburg, Russia **PARENTS**: Father an Italian aristocrat attached to the Russian court; mother a Romanov and great-granddaughter of Nicholas I **LIVED**: Russia, 1915; Yalta, then Formia, Italy, 1917 (refugee); Switzerland and Britain (schools); USA and Italy (universities); Abyssinia, 1935 (Italian cavalry); Morocco, 1936 (deserter); Spain, 1936 (anti-Franco fighter); Paris, 1937; England, 1939 (refugee); Italy, 1948; London, 1951; Paris, 1962; California, 1967; UK, 1969; Canterbury, 1975; London, 1980; Margate **PARTNERS**: Ithell Colquhoun, m. 1943–8; Doris Miller, m. 1971 **DIED**: 7 January 2007, Margate, Kent

Toni del Renzio was a White Russian nobleman with the splendid birth name of Antonino Romanov del Renzio dei Rossi di Castellone e Venosa. His father was an Italian aristocrat attached to the Russian court. His mother was a Romanov, making Toni the great-great-grandson of Tsar Nicholas I.

His life story reads like the plot of a Hollywood movie. He was two years old when the Russian revolution of 1917 occurred and his aristocratic family had to flee from their splendid palace. They headed south, ending up at his father's estate in Italy, where he enjoyed an idyllic childhood. He was educated in Switzerland and in Britain, then went on to gain university degrees in the United States and Italy, graduating in philosophy and mathematics.

After graduating, he decided to explore Eastern Europe, and it was when he visited Prague as a teenager that he made his first contact with surrealism. The Prague group of surrealists that he met included Toyen and Jindřich Štyrský. The impact they made on del Renzio would last a lifetime.

Having excelled at horse-riding when he was at school, in 1935 he was conscripted into Mussolini's Tripolitan cavalry, but soon deserted and took flight through North Africa, heading west across the great desert disguised as a Bedouin Arab. Joining a camel caravan, he eventually reached Morocco, and from there made his way to Spain. As luck would have it, he arrived in Spain just as the Civil War was about to break out, and was co-opted into the Trotskyite forces. War-weary, he eventually moved on again, reaching Paris in 1937.

There he managed to mingle with the avant-garde artists, including Picasso, Masson and other surrealists. Under their influence he started to paint seriously, but then the Second World War started and he moved on yet again, this time ending up in London, where he worked for General de Gaulle's Free French Fighters.

In London, he was beginning to make contact with the surrealist group there when the Blitz arrived and surrealist activity was disrupted. The London group became dispersed but del Renzio decided that, war or no war, he would single-handedly revive the surrealist movement in London. Personal relationships became complicated at this point. Del Renzio had had a brief affair with the British surrealist Emmy Bridgwater but, at the same time, had accepted financial support from another of the group – Ithell Colquhoun. He then fell in love with Colquhoun, and they were married the following year.

Around this time, del Renzio decided to make himself the head of the London surrealist group. Édouard Mesens, who had always seen himself as the group's leader, viewed this as the action of an impudent upstart. A nasty squabble ensued and rumbled on until 1944, when Mesens finally regained control.

In 1947, del Renzio and Colquhoun divorced, and in the years that followed he earned a living as a journalist, a lecturer, an actor (using his cavalry skills to ride a horse in a spaghetti Western) and a film director – but in private, he never gave up his obsession with surrealist collage and painting.

In 1971, del Renzio married for a second time. When he was seventy years old, his wife Doris presented him with quadruplets, ensuring him a place in the record books as the oldest known father of test-tube quads. The family were now living in the seaside town of Margate, southeast England, where del Renzio eventually died at the age of ninety-one.

# PAUL DELVAUX



## The creator of a mesmeric dream world dominated by a naked muse

**BORN**: 23 September 1897, Antheit, Liège, Belgium **PARENTS**: Father a lawyer at the Brussels Court of Appeals **LIVED**: Antheit, 1897; Brussels, 1916; France, 1949; Brussels, 1949 **PARTNERS**: Suzanne Purnal, m. 1937–47; Anne-Marie de Maertelaere, m. 1952 **DIED**: 20 July 1994, Veurne, Belgium

Paul Delvaux is without doubt one of the great atmospheric surrealists. André Breton summed him up perfectly when he wrote: 'Delvaux has turned the whole universe into a single realm in which one woman, always the same woman, reigns over the great suburbs of the heart.'

Delvaux was born in Belgium at the end of the 19th century and died at the end of the 20th, at the remarkable age of ninety-six. He was the son of a lawyer and appears to have been a rather scholarly schoolboy, studying Latin and Greek and reading Homer. To the alarm of his family, he decided to become an artist and was enrolled at the Academy of Fine Arts in Brussels in 1916. When his studies were completed and he had done a period of military service, he started painting in earnest.

The year 1926 was a turning point for him because it was then, at the age of twenty-nine, that he paid a visit to Paris and encountered for the first time the early paintings of Giorgio de Chirico. He wrote: 'He is the poet of emptiness. He was an extraordinary discovery for me, a point of departure.'

Another moment of revelation occurred at the Brussels Fair in 1930, when he saw a strange tableau, the centrepiece of which was a naked girl lying on a velvet couch. She was asleep and, as he watched, her chest rose and fell gently with each breath she took. She was accompanied by two skeletons. Closer examination revealed that she was, in fact, a cleverly operated mechanical mannequin. Delvaux was fascinated by this figure and described her as 'an amazing revelation...a very important turning point'. She became the model for all his later nudes.

In 1936 he began to depict a strange, eerily silent city where human figures, often completely naked, are engaged in some sort of ritual. These works transport the viewer to a precisely delineated dream world, academically painted and carefully composed.

To an unbiased observer, the art of Paul Delvaux is clearly surrealist, but historically his link with the movement is tenuous. He himself said of surrealism: 'What attracts me is the poetic meaning. What repels me is the theory.' He felt that the rules and restrictions introduced by Breton were fundamentally opposed to surrealism's most valuable idea – allowing the unconscious mind to express itself during the creative act. It would be reasonable to suppose that this point of view would mean Breton would be against him, but strangely the opposite was the case – Breton was keen to invite Delvaux into the surrealist fold and happy to include him in important group exhibitions.

Delvaux's most important period of painting began in 1936 and ended in the mid-1940s, at the conclusion of the Second World War. His very best work was done during the darkest days of that war. His most successful painting, the *Sleeping Venus* of 1944, was painted in Brussels while the city was being bombed – it is easy to imagine him standing in front of his huge canvas and losing himself in his dream world, shutting out everything else.

In Belgium Delvaux was viewed as a national treasure. In 1982 he was honoured in a way that few modern artists have enjoyed: a museum devoted entirely to his work was opened, in the Belgian seaside resort of Saint-Idesbald.

# LEO DOHMEN



## The charismatic Antwerp artist, whose scandalous lifestyle was a surrealist master-class

Leo Dohmen was a founder member of the Antwerp surrealist group, who considered themselves to be distinct from the Brussels group that gathered around Magritte.

Dohmen was born in Antwerp in 1929. His father was a tram driver by day and a black marketeer by night. Living as a street urchin, Leo managed to catch the eye of a benevolent lady who took pity on him and arranged a scholarship for him to go to school, where he was a model pupil. He specialized in chemistry and when he left school, worked for a photographic firm. He then began a series of profit-making schemes, some of which were legal.

In the 1950s, by which time he was married, he developed an interest in surrealism and met Marcel Mariën. Mariën was deeply involved in producing surrealist publications, and Dohmen took suitcases full of these to Paris to hawk them around bookstores. During these visits he met André Breton, Man Ray and Hans Bellmer, intensifying his involvement with the movement.

Dohmen's underground activities in the 1960s gave him little sleep. During the day he was at work and then, at night, he was swallowed up by the dark world of pornographic photography, gambling,

**BORN**: 3 July 1929, Borgerhout, Antwerp
**PARENTS**: Father a tram driver
**LIVED**: Antwerp and New Mexico
**PARTNER**: Mireille Sprengers, m. (n.d.)
**DIED**: 13 March 1999, Antwerp

drinking, art dealing and call girls. In 1965 the law caught up with him and he was arrested for selling obscene photographs. The police searched his home and confiscated what they considered to be offensive works by Max Ernst and Marcel Duchamp. He was held in a cell for three days, with the result that he was given the sack by his employers.

Being Dohmen, however, he soon bounced back, working at an art gallery whose owner was eventually jailed for fraud for not paying artists when he sold their work. Dohmen was saved by being offered a job with a chemical company, where he became a marketing manager and was once again able to resume his shady nocturnal activities. This time, they involved art dealing. It was said that he had a stock of works to satisfy every lack of taste. He used all kinds of underhand tricks, buying 150 surrealist paintings for a knock-down price from an American black marketeer and labelling them as 'bought in a Paris flea market'.

Dohmen made so much profit that in the 1970s he was able to buy a house and open his own art gallery there. All the art hanging on the walls was for sale, and the house was fitted with listening devices so that Dohmen could retire to his office and eavesdrop on his clients' discussions about possible purchases.

Dohmen's lifestyle was outrageous and, in a way, was a surrealist act in itself, ignoring all the rules of established society. He took endless risks but managed to survive all of his exploits. He also found time to make surrealist photographs, collages, assemblages and sculptures. Some of his collages – a performing sealion balancing a crucifix on its nose, a portrait of a woman with her mouth upside down, a nude female body with a leopard-skin pubic triangle, or a girl with a tap on the back of her head from which pours not water but hair – are hard to forget.

On his funeral notification in 1999, Dohmen was quoted as saying: 'If I can make people reconsider their way of thinking for ten minutes, my life will be a success.'

# ÓSCAR DOMÍNGUEZ

## The Tenerife surrealist, whose violent conduct overshadowed his wonderfully inventive works

**BORN**: 3 January 1906, San Cristóbal de La Laguna, Tenerife  **PARENTS**: Father a banana exporter who also worked in Les Halles market, Paris  **LIVED**: Tenerife, 1906; Paris, 1927; Marseille, 1940; Paris, 1941  **PARTNERS**: Roma Damska; Maud Bonneaud, m. 1948; Nadine Effront, 1950; Marie-Laure de Noailles, 1952–7  **DIED**: 31 December 1957

The Spanish surrealist Óscar Domínguez was born on Tenerife in the Canary Islands, in 1906. His father was an exporter of bananas. His mother died when he was only one year old, and Óscar was raised by his grandmother. While he was still very young, a serious illness affected his growth; his bone structure, especially his face and limbs, was badly affected. To occupy his time after the onset of the disease, he began painting in a traditional manner.

In 1927, at the age of twenty-one, Domínguez was sent to Paris to work for his father in the great central market of Les Halles. Like many young men from the provinces, he plunged into the city's nightlife, spending most of his evenings drinking in cabarets, bars and cafés. When his father died, Domínguez left the family business and took employment as an art designer.

He took a lover, a Polish pianist called Roma Damska, and she introduced him to the avant-garde art scene, where the surrealist movement was just beginning to gain strength. Domínguez met André Breton in 1933 and, through him, joined the surrealist circle in 1934. He exhibited regularly with them and contributed five works to the 1936 International Surrealist Exhibition in London.

That same year, Domínguez introduced the technique of decalcomania: by pressing painted paper against glass and pulling it free, he created complex accidental patterns. These appealed especially to Breton because they were automatic, and they became popular among other surrealists.

In 1938, during an evening gathering of surrealists, Domínguez was involved in a furious fight with Esteban Francés. He hurled a glass at Francés but it instead struck Victor Brauner in the face, destroying his left eye. As a result of this violent act, Domínguez was ostracized and fell into a deep depression. It was at this time that he made his first suicide attempt, after which he moved to a new studio in Montparnasse.

On the outbreak of the Second World War he joined the other surrealists in the South of France, where they were attempting to make passage to the United States. For reasons that are not clear today, Domínguez did not go with them, returning instead to Paris in the late summer of 1941. It is possible that he truly preferred to stay in France, but perhaps equally likely that the others were unhappy about travelling in the company of a man notorious for his fits of rage.

For the rest of the war Domínguez remained in Paris, where he became friendly with Picasso. As he became overwhelmed by the power of Picasso's art, his own work started to show signs of slavish imitation, to the detriment of his own artistic reputation. In his personal life the war years were particularly dark – his partner, Roma, who was Jewish, was taken away and executed by the Gestapo.

After the war, he began to drift away from the surrealist circle. He married Maud Bonneaud in 1948, but their marriage collapsed when he had an affair with the Belgian artist Nadine Effront in 1950. Later, in 1952, he began another affair, this time with Marie-Laure, Vicomtesse de Noailles, a great-great-great-granddaughter of the Marquis de Sade. It was she who would arrange Domínguez's burial in Paris when, on New Year's Eve 1957, he ended his own life by slitting his wrists in the bath.

# ENRICO DONATI

## The only surrealist to become a self-made multi-millionaire businessman

**BORN**: 19 February 1909, Milan  **PARENTS**: Father a scholar; mother a copyist of old master paintings  **LIVED**: Milan, 1909; Paris, 1930; USA, 1934; Paris, 1936; New York, 1939  **PARTNERS**: Claire Javal, m. 1934–65; Adele Schmidt, m. 1965  **DIED**: 25 April 2008, New York

Enrico Donati is unique among the surrealists, being the only one to have built a business empire that made him a multi-millionaire. It would be wrong, however, to assume because of this that he was a dilettante for whom painting was merely a sideline. On the contrary, there is a fierce intensity about Donati's work, and nothing about it suggests that it represented only one part of the artist's life.

Throughout his long career, Donati's art passed through at least five distinct phases. In the 1940s he was essentially a biomorphic surrealist. In the 1950s he moved on to organic abstraction. Then, in the sixties and seventies, he simplified his forms to become an exponent of abstract expressionism. In the 1980s he changed again, this time favouring abstract surrealism, and in the 1990s he returned to his first love of out-and-out surrealism.

Donati was born in Italy in 1909, into a scholarly family where the arts were encouraged. He attended Pavia University, where he took a degree in economics and a doctorate in sociology in 1929. After leaving university, he moved to Paris, where he spent a period composing avant-garde music. During breaks from composing he wandered around the Parisian art galleries and was excited to discover a new art form that was on display there – surrealism.

In 1934 he married Claire Javal, and together they travelled to the far west of the United States and Canada to study Native art and make a collection of tribal artefacts. After visiting the Apache, Hopi and Zuni cultures, Donati had gathered together an important collection of kachina dolls and masks that he would keep around him for the rest of his life.

At this point Donati realized that what he really wanted was to become a serious artist, so he and his wife returned to Europe in 1936 and set up home in Paris. There he met the surrealists and became part of their circle. When war broke out, he, Claire and their two daughters fled with the rest of the group to America.

In New York he became close to several key surrealists and in 1942 he met André Breton, who, on seeing his work, formally declared, 'He is one of us!' Breton took Donati under his wing and even provided him with titles for some of his surrealist paintings. He wrote about Donati poetically, saying that his work 'compels recognition from even the most stubborn adversary by the quality of its light'. Encouraged by Breton, Donati began exibiting his paintings in New York. At the end of the war, when most of the other surrealists returned to Europe, he stayed behind and became a naturalized American citizen.

In the early 1960s he gained a seat on the board of a large perfume company, and in 1965 he bought the company and became its chief executive. The same year, he separated from his wife and married Adele Schmidt, with whom he had another daughter. By now he was worth about $50 million and was able to take time off whenever he felt like it, disappearing into his studio to paint.

At the age of ninety-eight, Donati was injured in a New York taxi crash. He never fully recovered and died nine months later, when he was ninety-nine.

# MARCEL DUCHAMP

## The iconic trickster at the heart of the surrealist movement

**BORN**: 28 July 1887, Blainville-Crevon, Seine-Maritime, Normandy **PARENTS**: Father a notary; mother the daughter of a painter **LIVED**: Blainville, 1887; Rouen, 1895; Paris, 1904; New York, 1915; France, 1919; New York, 1920; Paris, 1923; Europe, 1928; Paris, 1933; New York, 1942 **PARTNERS**: Jeanne Serre, 1910; Yvonne Chastel, 1918–22; Mary Reynolds, 1923; Lydie Sarazin-Levassor, m. 1927; Maria Martins, 1946–51; Alexina Sattler, m. 1954–68 **DIED**: 2 October 1968, Paris

Marcel Duchamp is a paradox. He was the artist who was an anti-artist, the artist who destroyed art. When he exhibited everyday objects in art galleries, he made them into art by virtue of their context, not their form.

He was born in 1887 in Normandy, the son of a notary. The year 1912 was a key one for him, when he produced a series of brilliantly original works. His most famous painting – *Nude Descending a Staircase* – had a strongly surrealist flavour and was at least a decade ahead of its time.

When the First World War began, he left Europe for the United States. There, with Man Ray and Picabia, he established the New York dadaists. Like similar groups in Europe, it was their aim to undermine the establishment, and one of their most significant contributions was the 'readymade'.

According to Duchamp, it was in 1915 that the concept of the readymade came to him. Unfortunately for him, it has since come to light that he may have borrowed the idea from the New York dadaist Baroness Elsa von Freytag-Loringhoven. It was she and not Duchamp who was the first person to present a readymade as a work of art. In 1913 she found a large metal ring in the street and gave it the title *Enduring Ornament*, saying that if she commanded something to be art then it *was* art. Her most famous readymade was a piece of plumbing exhibited under the deliberately inflammatory title *God*.

The matter came to a head with the arrival of the most celebrated of all the readymades, a white ceramic urinal called *Fountain* and signed R MUTT 1917. It appears that the Baroness gave the urinal to Duchamp to place in the exhibition because he was a member of the committee running the show. If he wanted to claim it as his own, Duchamp's mistake was to write a letter to his sister in which he made the telling admission: 'One of my women friends, using a masculine pseudonym, Richard Mutt, submitted a porcelain urinal as a sculpture.' He probably thought that this letter would not survive, but unfortunately for him, it did.

Duchamp returned to Paris in July 1919, where he made a further assault on traditional art by disfiguring a reproduction of the *Mona Lisa*. He added a moustache and a beard and gave this 'modified readymade' the title of LHOOQ.

It was in Paris in 1921 that Duchamp met André Breton. Breton had such respect for Duchamp's intelligence that later on, after surrealism had taken over from the dadaist movement, he was always willing to treat Duchamp as an important presence, even though Duchamp never became a member of his inner circle.

In 1923, Duchamp made the momentous decision to cease being a creative artist and devote himself to playing chess. When he found himself penniless in Paris in 1927, he married Lydie Sarazin-Levassor, the daughter of a wealthy industrialist. Lydie adored Duchamp but he spent so many endless hours playing chess that, late one night, she glued all his chess pieces to the chess-board. After that, the marriage collapsed and she divorced him for desertion.

At the age of sixty-seven, in 1954, he married the American Alexina Sattler, ex-wife of the art dealer Pierre Matisse. The following year, he became a naturalized American citizen. Duchamp was at last able to enjoy a pleasant lifestyle free of money worries, and the marriage lasted for fourteen years until his death in 1968.

# MAX ERNST



## The most technically inventive of all the surrealists and also the most sexually active

**BORN**: 2 April 1891, Brühl, near Cologne  **PARENTS**: Middle-class Catholics; father a teacher of the deaf and a disciplinarian  **LIVED**: Brühl, 1891; Bonn, 1909; German army, 1914; Cologne, 1918; Paris, 1922; Southeast Asia, 1924; Paris, 1925; South of France, 1939; New York, 1941; Sedona, Arizona, 1946; South of France, 1953  **PARTNERS**: Luise Straus, m. 1918–22; Gala Éluard, 1924–7 (ménage à trois with Paul Éluard); Marie-Berthe Aurenche, m. 1927–37; Leonor Fini, 1933; Meret Oppenheim, 1934–5; Leonora Carrington, 1937–9; Peggy Guggenheim, m. 1941–6; Dorothea Tanning, m. 1946–76  **DIED**: 1 April 1976, Paris

Max Ernst was the ultimate surrealist. André Breton said that he had 'the most magnificently haunted brain'. Technically, he was also the most exploratory of all the surrealists, restlessly inventive and forever trying out new techniques. Very early on, he developed collage into a new art form. He experimented with frottage, with decalcomania and with the addition of solid objects to embellish his paintings. He even showed Jackson Pollock how to drip paint onto a canvas.

Ernst was born in Germany, a few miles from Cologne, in 1891. His parents were devout Catholics; his bourgeois father was good-natured but strict, while his mother was loving and humorous. At university he studied philosophy, art history, literature, psychology and psychiatry.

In 1912, when he was twenty-one, he saw work by Picasso that made a big impact on him, and in the same year he started exhibiting his own paintings. When war broke out in 1914, he was called up to serve in the German army. After the war, in 1919, he met Paul Klee and also encountered the early paintings of de Chirico – both important influences. In 1920 he and Hans Arp organized a dada exhibition in Cologne, with dramatic results. Angry visitors to the show destroyed some of the exhibits and the police closed the show.

In 1921, André Breton, then a member of the Paris dada group, contacted Ernst and invited him to hold an exhibition in the French capital. The following year he moved to Paris, where Gala Éluard, Leonor Fini and Meret Oppenheim were among his many lovers.

Then, in 1937, he fell deeply in love with a young English art student, Leonora Carrington. They met at a dinner in his honour in London. Despite the difference in their ages, Carrington found his sexual charisma irresitisible and soon followed him to Paris, where they became inseparable.

The following year, 1938, saw Ernst and Breton clash. Ernst was expelled from the surrealist group, and he and his new love moved out of Paris and spent a year or so living blissfully together in rural France. Carrington later described this as her period of paradise – but it was ruined by the outbreak of the Second World War. Max, a German, was interned, and Carrington was stranded and alone. She had a complete nervous breakdown that eventually destroyed her feelings for her lost lover.

It was the rich American Peggy Guggenheim who rescued Ernst and got him safely to New York, where they were married. The relationship only lasted for a couple of years; in 1943, Ernst started an affair with the American surrealist Dorothea Tanning. When the war ended, he and Guggenheim were divorced and he married Tanning. The couple settled in Sedona, Arizona, where they bought some land and built a house. Two years later, Ernst became an American citizen. Throughout the 1950s he would divide his time between the house in Arizona and studios in France.

In June 1954, Ernst was delighted to win the financially rewarding Grand Prize at the Venice Biennale. The Paris surrealists were not happy about his acceptance of this award and, much to his annoyance, expelled him from the movement for a second time. Despite this rejection, in 1958 Ernst changed nationality once more, this time becoming a French citizen, and in 1964 he and Dorothea settled in the South of France, where they remained until his death in 1976.

# MERLYN EVANS



## The Welsh artist whose surrealist paintings protested against inhumanity

**BORN**: 13 March 1910, Llandaff, Cardiff  **PARENTS**: Father an analytical chemist; mother a nurse  **LIVED**: Cardiff, 1910; Rutherglen, near Glasgow, 1913; London, 1931; Camberwell, 1934; South Africa, 1938; Army, 1942; London, 1946  **DIED**: 1973, London  **PARTNERS**: Phyllis Sullivan, m. 1933; Marjorie Few, m. 1950

The Welsh artist Merlyn Evans was born in Cardiff in 1910, but his family moved to Glasgow when he was three and he grew up in Scotland. At the age of twenty-one he won a scholarship to the Royal College of Art in London, where he met fellow student Phyllis Sullivan. They were married in 1933, but the marriage was dissolved during the Second World War.

Cubism and vorticism were the first major influences on Evans, and even after he had moved on to surrealist scenes there was often a marked angularity to his figures that suggested he had never quite shaken off his first loves. This angularity gave many of his compositions an aggressive, even savage quality. The title of one of his surrealist works, *Tyrannopolis*, sums up the violence inherent in his work.

Evans' personality was described as 'many-sided and complex'. He was well read, with a particular interest in Freudian psychology. He loved a good argument and was forever analysing issues involved in psychology, philosophy, politics and the history of art. In his spare time he wrote a great deal of poetry. He also played the piano and the trumpet, and was a skilled carpenter. These wider concerns can sometimes enrich an artist's visual vocabulary but there is also a risk that they can clutter the head with complex thoughts, interfering with the rush of pure, intuitive creativity that is required to produce the best surrealist painting.

Evans made many visits to Paris in 1934 and 1935, during which he met Mondrian, Kandinsky, Giacometti, Ernst and Hayter and learned about the new developments that were taking place there. He was a member of the surrealist group in England from its inception in 1936, and six of his works were included in the International Surrealist Exhibition in London that year. He exhibited with the surrealists again in 1937, but he was becoming increasingly uneasy and pessimistic about the mood of futility that he sensed was developing in the cultural and political life of Europe. He left England the following year to take up a teaching post in Natal, South Africa, which was soon disrupted by the outbreak of the Second World War. In the Eighth Army he saw service in the North African campaign, and then in Italy. He ended up working in war records in Rome, where he met Giorgio de Chirico.

Disillusioned by the horrors of war, Evans was quoted in 1944 as saying: 'Now we have no trouble in agreeing that humanity is very wicked indeed.' After the war he returned to London and began exhibiting there on a regular basis. In 1950 he met the pianist Marjorie Few, who became his second wife, and in 1965 he was appointed to a teaching post at the Royal College of Art.

He remained in England for the rest of his life, apart from a brief spell as artist in residence at the Art Institute of Chicago in 1967. While there, he was able to visit New York and make contact with abstract expressionist painters including Mark Rothko, Barnett Newman and Robert Motherwell. He retained his teaching position at the Royal College until his death in 1973.

# LEONOR FINI

## The highly skilled sex goddess of the surrealist movement



**BORN**: 30 August 1907, Buenos Aires **PARENTS**: Father an Argentine businessman and religious zealot; mother Italian **LIVED**: Buenos Aires, 1907; Trieste, 1909; Milan, 1924; Paris, 1931; Monte Carlo, 1939; Rome, 1943; Paris, 1946 **PARTNERS**: Prince Lorenzo Ercole Lanza del Vasto di Trabia, 1931; André Pieyre de Mandiargues, 1932; Max Ernst, 1933; Julien Levy, 1936; Federico Veneziani, m. 1939–45; Stanislao Lepri, 1941–80; Sforzino Sforza, 1945–52; Constantin Jelenski, 1952–87 **DIED**: 18 January 1996, Paris

Leonor Fini was one of the exotics of the surrealist movement, as fascinating in her person as in her art. Her adult love life was colourful to say the least, but the drama in her life story began much earlier, while she was still a baby.

Fini was born in Argentina in 1907, the daughter of a rich Argentinian businessman and an Italian mother. Before she was one year old, her parents' relationship had ended badly. The following year her mother scooped up the infant Leonor and fled back home to Italy. This made Leonor's father furious, and he hatched a plan to kidnap his daughter. He hired some men to do the job and they tried to grab Leonor from a street in Trieste, but the attempt was foiled.

Leonor's terrified mother fled south and adopted the subterfuge of pretending that she had a son. She disguised Leonor as a boy and kept this up for six stressful years until, at last, the child's father admitted defeat.

As she grew up, Leonor turned against religion. At school she was a rebel and was expelled three times. The one thing she loved doing was drawing and sketching, and her mother encouraged her in this. Leonor Fini held her first solo exhibition in Milan at the age of twenty-two. At around the same time, she began dressing in an unconventional way as a form of protest against authority. She had become a natural surrealist, both in the images she created and in her personal behaviour. At the age of twenty-four she fell in love with a handsome young Italian prince. They set up an apartment in Paris, but the relationship soon collapsed and the prince returned alone to Milan. Fini lost no time in finding a new lover. In the summer of 1932 she met a writer called André Pieyre de Mandiargues in a hotel bar, and within a week had moved into his flat.

In the social whirl of the French capital Fini proved to be an overnight success. Her beauty became the talk of Paris. She always dressed outrageously – sometimes as a cardinal – and made a dramatic entrance an any event. Picasso became infatuated with her and Paul Éluard wrote poems to her. Jean Genet composed letters of praise about her and Jean Cocteau called her a 'divine heroine'. Max Ernst was fascinated by her 'scandalous elegance' and soon became her lover. When Julien Levy, an American art dealer, visited her in Paris in 1936, he described her as having the 'head of a lioness, mind of a man, bust of a woman, torso of a child, grace of an angel, and discourse of the devil'.

When the war came, Fini left France for Monte Carlo; at the height of the conflict, in 1943, she moved to Rome. After the Americans liberated Rome in 1945, she returned to her beloved Paris. It was at this point that she acquired a menagerie of twenty-three pet cats, the only 'children' she would ever care for. Her return to Paris heralded a long period of creative productivity and solo exhibitions.

Fini's work was always technically skilful and in her best pieces there is a sense of some strange ritual taking place, fuelled by unconscious thoughts. When she died, aged eighty-eight, in 1996, one obituary spoke of her creation of 'an erotic dream world where women were in control...a world of dream or nightmare'.

# ESTEBAN FRANCÉS

## The Spanish surrealist who was the victim of a drunken assault by Óscar Domínguez

**BORN**: 30 July 1913, Port Bou, Girona, Catalonia
**LIVED**: Port Bou; Figueras; Barcelona, 1925; Paris, 1937; Mexico, 1940; New York, 1945; Deia, Majorca, 1970s
**PARTNER**: Remedios Varo, 1931
**DIED**: 21 September 1976, Barcelona

The Spanish painter Esteban Francés was one of the second wave of surrealist artists who gathered around André Breton in Paris and formed part of his official circle. Francés did not arrive there until 1937, by which time most of the old guard had already left. Now Francés, along with Gordon Onslow Ford, Óscar Domínguez, Matta and Victor Brauner, provided a new entourage that kept Breton in power as the leader of an official inner group.

Francés was born in Port Bou, Girona, and spent his childhood in Figueras. Later his family moved to Barcelona, where he studied law and art. It was there, in the early 1930s, that he met Óscar Domínguez, the surrealist from Tenerife in the Canary Islands who was already part of Breton's circle in Paris. For a while Francés shared a studio with Remedios Varo and they soon became lovers, even though she was apparently happily married at the time. In the summer of 1935 Francés, Domínguez and Varo passed the time by making collective collages in the form of 'exquisite corpses', seven of which survive.

When the Spanish Civil War began in 1936, Francés fought against Francó before going into exile in France in 1937. In Paris he encountered the surrealist group and soon joined them. Breton was glad of his support and praised him in glowing terms, saying: 'Francés contributes a nature emotionally impregnated with everything that makes life worth living today.'

According to Marcel Jean, Francés spent a lot of his time in Paris gambling and walking around the streets. Relations within the surrealist group did not always run smoothly. There was a terrible incident in 1938, when he and Domínguez were both very drunk at a surrealist party; Francés had criticized Varo for having several lovers at the same time, and Domínguez had drunkenly started defending her honour. As their argument developed into a shouting match and then a fight, Victor Brauner rushed to protect Francés and was struck in the face by a glass thrown by Domínguez, losing his left eye.

In the summer of 1939, Francés and several members of the surrealist group invited Breton to spend the summer with them at a château near the Swiss border that Onslow Ford had rented for a few months. With war clouds gathering, it was a strange summer interlude. Although they did not know it, it was in effect a farewell party for the great days of the surrealist movement. Soon they would all be fleeing from the horrors of the Second World War, leaving Paris with its surrealist ghosts.

Francés left for Mexico in 1940, where he was welcomed by the artist Diego Rivera and earned a living organizing surrealist exhibitions. Varo arrived there too in 1941, and she and Francés are known to have worked together on various projects to generate some income, including making stage sets to illustrate Allied war victories.

Francés finally said goodbye to Varo in 1944 and moved from Mexico to the United States, arriving in New York in 1945. There he took part in surrealist exhibitions while earning a living as a scenery and costume designer for ballets. Later, he returned to Spain and lived for a while in Deià, a small village in the north of Majorca. He was on a visit to Barcelona, organizing an exhibition there, when he died in 1976.

**BORN**: 7 February 1909, Copenhagen, as Frederik Wilhelm (Christian) Carlsen **PARENTS**: Father a laboratory supervisor **LIVED**: Copenhagen, 1909; Prison, 1937; Copenhagen, 1937; Stockholm, 1944; Copenhagen, 1950 **PARTNERS**: Emmy Ella Hirsch, m. 1930; Ingrid Lilian Braemer, m. 1938; Ellen Madsen, m. 1969–95 **DIED**: 26 October 1995



# WILHELM FREDDIE

## The only surrealist to be jailed for his subversive artwork

The Danish painter Wilhelm Freddie had the distinction of being the only surrealist artist to be imprisoned because of the images in his works of art. He was a total surrealist who would accept no compromise and resisted any attempt to persuade him to modify his work.

Freddie was born in Copenhagen in 1909. His father was a laboratory supervisor in the Institute of Pathology at the university there, and Freddie spent many hours at the Institute while growing up. This early exposure to detached limbs and preserved bodies in glass jars had a darkly stimulating effect on his youthful imagination.

At the age of twenty, he discovered the surrealist movement that was flourishing in the late 1920s in Paris. It made a huge impact on him, and in 1930 he was the first person to exhibit a surrealist painting in Copenhagen. The reaction was negative in the extreme.

In 1936 Freddie visited Paris, where he met Giacometti, and Brussels, where he met Magritte. Through his contacts with the other surrealists, he was invited to send work to the International Surrealist Exhibition being organized in London. He sent five works, three of which were confiscated by British customs officials as pornographic.

Later that year, he exhibited in the Danish city of Odense, but before the show could open a local police commissioner visited and had certain works removed.

Even the King of Denmark got involved. Looking at one of Freddie's paintings, he asked, 'Has this man been locked up?' The following year, that is precisely what happened.

Freddie held a show of his work in a Copenhagen restaurant. Saboteurs tried to close it down; one of them even jumped on Freddie and attempted to strangle him. The police confiscated all the exhibits and, after a prolonged court case, Freddie was fined 100 crowns and sentenced to ten days in prison for producing pornography.

With the arrival of the Second World War two years later, his situation became hazardous. Denmark was occupied by the Nazis in 1940 and Freddie's life, as a 'degenerate' artist, was at risk. In 1943 he went into hiding and the following year, aware that the Gestapo were still searching for him, he had no choice but to flee the country. He travelled north to Sweden, where he was able to paint and exhibit, and at last his work began to attract more favourable reviews.

After the war Freddie received a long, friendly letter from André Breton urging him to participate in a major surrealist exhibition in Paris. He did so, and the work he contributed was strongly praised – something he must have thought would never happen. It was the beginning of a new chapter in his life. In 1950 he left Sweden and returned to his hometown of Copenhagen. His six-year exile was finally at an end.

The second half of Freddie's life was far more positive. In 1965 he was glowingly described by a Danish art critic as 'Our first real artist...One of the few Danes on the international scene.' By the end of the 1960s, his works were being acquired by museums. The long battle for recognition had been won.

Despite this, even today, Freddie is less well known than the other major surrealists. The reason for this is partly geographical: his lonely defence of surrealism in Scandinavia had isolated him. This is neatly summed up by the title of the catalogue for his first ever solo exhibition in London, in 1972. On the cover, it asks: 'Where has Freddie been?'

# ALBERTO GIACOMETTI

## The most original of the early surrealist sculptors, who later became obsessed with anorexic figures

**BORN**: 10 October 1901, Borgonovo, Graubünden, Switzerland **PARENTS**: Father a post-impressionist painter **LIVED**: Borgonovo, 1901; Paris, 1922; Geneva, 1941; Paris, 1945 **PARTNERS**: Flora Mayo, 1925–7; Isobel Delmer, 1945; Annette Arm, m. 1946; Caroline Tamagno, 1959 **DIED**: 11 January 1966, Chur, Graubünden

Alberto Giacometti's life as an artist was in two halves. During the first half he created some of the most exciting surrealist sculpture ever seen; during the second he abandoned surrealism and focused on making elongated, emaciated human figures in bronze.

Giacometti was born at the turn of the 20th century in a small village in the Italian-speaking region of the Swiss Alps. His father was a post-impressionist painter and, with his encouragement, Alberto started sketching from nature when he was nine years old. When he was twenty he arrived in Paris, which would become his home for the rest of his life. His Paris studio was so small that he had to sleep in a nearby hotel. Giacometti was never interested in creature comforts – even when he was rich towards the end of his life, he still lived a simple existence, obsessed with his work.

In 1929 he met André Masson and, through him, the other surrealists. He became an official member of the group and at the age of twenty-nine exhibited his new work alongside that of Miró and Arp. For four and a half years, between 1930 and 1935, he was a dedicated follower of André Breton and the surrealist circle.

Giacometti's 1932 works, such as *Woman with Her Throat Cut* and *The Palace at 4 a.m.*, would become surrealist icons. His pure surrealist phase was, however, short-lived, and in 1935 he started working from nature again. The surrealists were horrified. At a surrealist meeting, Breton was about to expel him, but Giacometti called out, 'Don't bother, I'm going,' and swept from the room. It was the final moment of his involvement with surrealism.

With the arrival of the 1940s came an entirely new phase in his sculpture. An obsession developed that frightened him – 'to my terror, the sculptures became smaller and smaller'. It was said that when he returned from Switzerland to France after the war, he carried several years' worth of work with him in five matchboxes.

Back in his Paris studio, he started work on what would become his famous skeletal figures. These tiny figures grew taller and taller but retained their emaciated body shape. 'All I do is subtract,' he explained, 'yet it keeps getting so big that I have the impression it's twice as thick again as it really is. So I have to go on taking more and more off.'

In 1947 Giacometti exhibited his tall, spindly figures for the first time at a show in New York. Throughout the 1950s, he had many more major exhibitions and became internationally famous. At last he had plenty of money, but despite this, his lifestyle did not change.

In 1959, the Hollywood star Marlene Dietrich arrived in Paris with forty-four pieces of luggage and a strong desire to meet Giacometti, whose work she had seen and loved in New York. She sat in his dusty little studio, watching him work. She drank with him in his local bar, where nobody recognized her. He was entranced and gave her one of his sculptures.

In the 1960s Giacometti's worldwide fame reached its peak, with major exhibitions in both Europe and America – but this period of his life would not last for long. His health was rapidly deteriorating, not helped by his habit of smoking four packs of cigarettes a day, and he died in 1966 at the age of sixty-four.

# HENRI GOETZ

## The surrealist who stayed in Paris to fight in the French Resistance

**BORN**: 29 September 1909, New York  **PARENTS**: Father ran an electrical plant; mother 'quasi-intellectual'  **LIVED**: New York, 1909; Cambridge, Massachusetts, 1927; New York, 1929; Paris, 1930; Cannes, 1940; Paris, 1944  **PARTNER**: Christine Boumeester, 1935–71  **DIED**: 12 August 1989, Nice

The surrealist work of the American artist Henri Goetz has been underestimated in the past, possibly because it was not a lifelong pursuit. For the majority of his working life he was essentially an abstract artist, although always with what he called a 'surrealist climate'.

His life's work can be neatly divided into three distinct phases. In the first he was conventionally realistic. Then he encountered the surrealists and developed a darkly imaginative biomorphic world. After the Second World War, his work became more abstract and he created a world of floating shapes and lines. It is this third phase that has overshadowed his much shorter, decade-long involvement with surrealism.

Goetz was born in New York in 1909; as his first name suggests, he had French ancestors. At eighteen he left home and took a course in art history at Harvard University. After this he enrolled at the Grand Central School of Art in New York, but soon realized that the place he truly wanted to be was Paris, the centre of the art world.

He was twenty-one when he arrived there, and quickly decided to make France his permanent home. He took a studio next to that of the Romanian surrealist Victor Brauner, and through him was introduced to the other Parisian surrealists.

In 1935 he married the Dutch painter Christine Boumeester – a union that would last until her death in 1971 – and began to exhibit with the surrealists. He had his first solo exhibition in Paris in 1937, and his career was developing well by the time it was brought to a halt by the outbreak of war. Because they were not French citizens, Goetz and his wife had to go underground and adopt assumed names. While most surrealists were fleeing south to escape to America, the couple remained in Paris and started working for the resistance. Risking their lives, they used a secret printing press to make anti-Nazi leaflets and posters and their artistic skills to forge passports. A Czech poet was their undoing: they had made some false documents for him, and when he was caught by the Gestapo he betrayed them. With their lives in danger, they had no choice but to abandon Paris and head south to the unoccupied zone.

They ended up in Cannes with little money, and Goetz took on any mundane jobs he could find. During this difficult period he continued to paint his surrealist canvases, but when he and his wife returned to Paris after the liberation of the city in 1944, his work started to become more abstract. This did not happen immediately, and some remarkable surrealist canvases have survived from the period immediately after the war.

The couple became French citizens in 1949, and in the years that followed Goetz held more than 100 solo exhibitions. In 1965 he founded his own art academy, the Atelier Goetz. He was still actively painting in 1989, the year he died. When he fell ill and found himself in hospital, he decided to avoid further pain by climbing to the top of the five-storey building and jumping to his death.

# JULIO GONZÁLEZ

## The quiet Catalan surrealist who taught Picasso how to make metal sculptures

The Catalan sculptor Julio González was born in Barcelona into a family of goldsmiths and metalworkers. His father was a sculptor who taught him how to work in metal when he was only six years old. Encouraged by his family, he entered the School of Art in Barcelona and studied painting there, but his heart was always in metalwork – and by the age of twenty, he had exhibited his first piece of forged and beaten iron. He began spending time at the café Els Quatre Gats, a favourite haunt of local artists, and it was there, in 1897, that he first became friendly with Picasso, who was five years his junior. In 1900 he moved to Paris, where he met up again with Picasso and became acquainted with other artists from his circle.

During the First World War, González worked in the Renault factory, where he learned the technique of oxy-acetelyne welding. Once the war was over he settled on sculpture as his mature art form. Towards the end of the 1920s, Picasso wanted to make some welded iron sculptures and went to González for technical assistance. González explained oxy-acetelyne welding and cutting to Picasso and for four years,

**BORN**: 21 September 1876, Barcelona
**PARENTS**: Father a sculptor
**LIVED**: Barcelona, 1876; Paris, 1900
**PARTNER**: Marie-Thérèse Roux, m. 1937
**DIED**: 27 March 1942, Arcueil, near Paris

until 1932, the two men worked together in close cooperation. During this time Picasso's visual ideas had a strong influence on González, whose sculptural style showed a marked change.

The quiet González found Picasso busy, restless and impatient, commenting that he was 'such an anxious man, always wanting to surpass himself'. Sometimes all Picasso would do was make some small sketches and hand them over to González, leaving his friend to actually make the sculptures. Picasso was pathologically protective of his hands – to the extent that he would not even drive a car – so when it came to wielding an oxy-acetelyne torch, he could not face it; González had to do the actual welding work under his direction. Such was their affection for one another, however, that there never seems to have been any tension between them. Picasso paid González well for his work and was in awe of the older man's technical skill, telling him, 'You work the metal like a clump of butter.'

Eventually González came to be regarded as a pioneer of sculpting in iron, and in later years he would exert an important influence on the work of many modern sculptors. He wrote movingly about the material he used: 'The age of iron began many centuries ago by producing arms. It is time this metal ceased to be a murderer.'

In the early 1930s, González began a series of more abstract sculptures. It was around this time that he became friendly with Breton, Tanguy, Dalí and the other surrealists and started to exhibit with them. When the Second World War broke out he began work on a plaster figure of a kneeling, screaming woman that he intended to be his indictment of warfare; sadly, he died of a heart attack before completing it. Picasso attended the funeral of his old friend, a modest, reserved man he had known and respected for forty-five years.

Today, the biggest collection of González' work can be found at the Museum of Modern Art in Valencia, which holds nearly 400 pieces of his work.

# ARSHILE GORKY

## The most tragic surrealist, who inspired the abstract expressionists in New York



**BORN**: 15 April 1904, Khorgom, Lake Van, Turkey, as Vosdanig Manoug Adoian

**PARENTS**: Father fled to USA in 1908 to avoid draft; mother died of starvation in 1919 while fleeing genocide in Turkey **LIVED**: Turkey, 1904; Russia, 1915; Watertown, Massachusetts, 1920; Boston, 1922; New York, 1925; Connecticut, 1946

**PARTNERS**: Sirun Mussikian (Ruth French) 1929; Marny George, m. 1934; Corinne Michael West, 1935–6; Leonore Gallet, 1938; Agnes 'Mougouch' Magruder, m. 1941 **DIED**: 21 July 1948 in Sherman, Connecticut

Arshile Gorky's life story is the most tragic of any of the surrealists. Born Vosdanig Adoian in a Turkish Armenian village in 1904, he was four years old when his father fled the country to avoid being drafted into the Turkish army. During the First World War, the Turks began a mass slaughter of Armenians and drove the survivors from their land. To escape the onslaught, Vosdanig and his three sisters fled north with their mother, reaching the city of Erevan after a brutal forced march of 125 miles. After several months of living in extreme poverty, both of his older sisters left for America. Their mother, desperate to protect her two younger children, kept moving about seeking some kind of respite until, at the age of only thirty-nine, she died of starvation. This left fourteen-year-old Vosdanig in charge of his twelve-year-old sister, Vartoosh, and the siblings began a long journey on foot in an attempt to find a vessel that would take them to America to join their father. It took them a year to achieve this, but following a period of unspeakable hardship they arrived in the United States in 1920. For the next five years, Vosdanig survived by taking various menial jobs. He changed his name to Arshile Gorky and finally reached New York in 1925, at the age of twenty.

Gorky's adult life begins at this point and, far from having been cowed by the horrors of his childhood, he seems to have been strengthened by them. They had moulded him into a darkly mysterious young man and he was now ready to face the world, fired by a deep-seated anger. He had been making drawings since early childhood and his talent was at last being recognized so that, by the mid-1920s, he made the bold decision to become a full-time artist.

During the Second World War, Gorky married an admiral's daughter called Agnes Magruder; the couple would have two daughters. He was also fortunate during this period in coming into contact with a number of surrealists who had fled the war in Europe and were living as refugees in America. Among them was André Breton, who was deeply impressed by Gorky's work.

With a degree of artistic success in his grasp at last, Gorky and his family moved to the Connecticut countryside, where he set up a large studio. This idyll was, however, short-lived: in 1946, a fire started in his studio and destroyed everything. He then discovered that Agnes was having an affair with his friend, the Chilean surrealist Matta.

It must have seemed as if things could not get much worse, but they did: in 1948 Gorky was involved in a serious road accident, breaking his neck. He sank into a deep depression that proved too much for his wife, who finally left. A few weeks later he went into a barn near his studio, wrote the words 'Goodbye My Loveds' on an old crate, threw a clothesline over one of the rafters, and hanged himself.

Against this catalogue of disasters can be set one major achievement: Gorky's unique form of organic abstractionism served as a pioneering influence. Ultimately, it led to the development of the New York school of abstract expressionism, which was to gain such importance in America in the mid-20th century that it shifted the nerve centre of the modern art world from Paris to New York.

# EUGENIO GRANELL

## The artist who founded a museum devoted to surrealism

**BORN**: 28 November 1912, La Coruña, Galicia  **LIVED**: La Coruña, 1912; Santiago de Compostela (childhood); Madrid, 1928; France, 1939; Dominican Republic, 1940; Guatemala, 1946; Puerto Rico, 1950; Los Angeles, 1955; New York, 1957; Madrid, 1985  **PARTNER**: Amparo Segarra, m. 1940–2001  **DIED**: 24 October 2001, Madrid

There is no censorship in Eugenio Granell's work. He allows poetic invention to act upon him all the time, without any rational intervention. The result is that his paintings have a playful, exuberant quality and his figures are in a state of constant metamorphosis.

Granell was born in La Coruña in the northwest corner of Spain in 1912, but spent his childhood in the cathedral city of Santiago de Compostela, about fifty miles to the south of his birthplace. When he was a boy he was already painting and writing, but then he attended the Madrid Conservatory to study music. His musical career was progressing well until it was cut short by the Spanish Civil War, in which he fought on the losing side against Franco.

Driven into exile in 1939, Granell travelled north to France and eventually reached Paris, where he became friendly with the Cuban surrealist Wifredo Lam. Then, as the Nazis advanced westwards, he, like the other surrealists, fled to the coast. On the train to Le Havre he met Amparo Segarra, the woman he would marry. They sailed to the New World together on the same ship and were married in 1940.

Granell was granted asylum in the Dominican Republic, where his daughter Natalia was born in 1941. It was there that he met the leading surrealist André Breton, en route from Marseille to New York to evade the Nazis. Granell began painting seriously and became a full-blown surrealist. He spent six years in the Dominican Republic, earning a living as a violinist in the local symphony orchestra and exhibiting his paintings, but in 1946 local conditions forced him to move with his family. They relocated to Mexico, and then settled in Guatemala.

In 1947, Granell took part in the major post-war surrealist exhibition in Paris. He managed to acquire a post as a professor of art in Guatemala, but left in 1950 to live in Puerto Rico for a time. From there he moved to Los Angeles and then finally, in 1957, to New York. He would remain there for the next thirty years, until his return to Spain in 1985.

On arrival in New York he developed a close friendship with Marcel Duchamp, further strengthening his ties to surrealism. He also studied sociology, completing a PhD in 1967 with his thesis titled, 'Sociological Aspects of Picasso's *Guernica*: The End of a Spanish Era'. During his time in America he exhibited frequently and in the 1960s also became a professor of Spanish literature at Brooklyn College, remaining in the post until his retirement in 1982.

At the age of seventy-three, Granell finally returned to Spain and settled with his family in Madrid. In 1995, the Fundación Eugenio Granell was established in his hometown of Santiago de Compostela as a permanent home for his work. It held 600 paintings donated by Granell along with others by Picabia, Duchamp, Man Ray, Miró, Esteban Francés and many other surrealist artists.

Physically, Granell was short and slim. A chain-smoker, he was a passionate, humorous conversationalist with a happy personality. At his death in Madrid in 2001, he was survived by his wife Amparo, to whom he had been married for sixty-one years, as well as their two daughters and a son.

# JANE GRAVEROL

## The Belgian surrealist whose work echoed that of Magritte

**BORN**: 29 November 1905, Ixelles, Belgium **PARENTS**: French; father the painter Alexandre Graverol **LIVED**: Ixelles, 1905; Brussels, 1924; Verviers, 1938; Brussels, 1954; Paris, 1967 **PARTNERS**: William Dortu, m. until 1938; Marcel Mariën, 1955–8; Gaston Ferdière, 1967 **DIED**: 24 April 1984, Fontainebleau, France

Jane Graverol was born in Ixelles in the southern suburbs of Brussels. Her father was a well-known illustrator and a symbolist painter, so the visual arts played a dominant role in their family home. She attended the Academy of Fine Arts in Brussels and had her first solo exhibition in 1927, at the age of twenty-two. She married twice when she was very young but both marriages collapsed, the second by 1938.

Although she began as a traditional landscape artist, Graverol's paintings became increasingly unconventional and she described them as 'waking, conscious dreams'. With her interest in surrealism growing, she wrote to René Magritte, and in 1949 she became a member of the Belgian surrealist group.

A few years later, while she was organizing an exhibition of Magritte's work, Graverol met his protégé, Marcel Mariën. They eventually began a passionate affair. Forgetting momentarily his commitment to obscure, surrealist wordplay, Mariën sent her a simple love poem, part of which read: 'Jane sings – Jane laughs – Jane lover in my bed – Jane tall – Jane crazy – Jane haunts my words – Jane night – Jane day – Jane nest of love'. The relationship lasted until 1958, when they separated.

During the 1950s, Graverol's paintings, already influenced by the eeriness of the early de Chiricos, came to closely resemble works by Magritte. They shared a fascination for the device of visual trickery, in which one figure or detail becomes something else. In her painting of an elephant, for example, the animal's head becomes a dark grey swan, with the elephant's raised trunk becoming the swan's neck. A large rose that has fallen down a staircase has left a trail of blood. A gigantic black eagle, standing in an empty room, stares down at a tiny blue parakeet in a golden cage. The bow tying back the hair of a young girl becomes a butterfly. A bird in flight becomes the pubic triangle of a nude figure.

Despite Magritte's clear influence on her work, Graverol somehow made these images her own and managed to avoid the impression that she was plagiarizing the master. Magritte himself certainly felt that her work was important and went so far as to praise it in print, writing: 'Everything that Mme Jane Graverol seeks to represent seems to me to be charged with the symbolic meaning attributed to it by various romantic and dramatic feelings.... The paintings of Jane Graverol are somewhere in this world of feelings in which the relationships between things are contained within precise limits. But sometimes the power of the unforeseen renders their meaning less perceptible. Jane Graverol has no intention of countering this power, as a result of which she is engaged in the only spiritual activity necessary.'

In the 1960s Graverol met André Breton in Paris and then, on a visit to America, encountered Marcel Duchamp in New York. In 1967, a French psychiatrist called Gaston Ferdière visited one of her exhibitions. She met him there, and a bond developed between them. Graverol moved to Paris to live with him, remaining there for the rest of her life, but still exhibiting each year in her native Belgium. In these later years, spent with Ferdière, her imagery became more erotic.

# SAM HAILE

## The promising British surrealist whose life was cut short by a road accident

BORN: July 1909, London, as Thomas Samuel Haile
LIVED: London, 1909; New York, 1939 (as pacifist); Ann Arbor, 1943; Suffolk, 1944; Dartington, 1947
PARTNER: Marianne de Trey, m. 1938–48
DIED: March 1948, Poole, Dorset

Sam Haile was a promising British surrealist whose life was cut short by a road accident when he was only thirty-eight. Sadly, much of the work he completed no longer survives, and as a result he is little known. Nevertheless, he was an important and active member of the surrealist movement in London in the 1930s.

Haile was born in London and left school at the age of fifteen. In 1930 he won a scholarship to the Royal College of Art to study painting, but after a while he became more interested in pottery. In 1938 he married a London-born Swiss art student, Marianne de Trey, who had been studying textiles at the Royal College of Art but who, under his influence, switched to pottery. Haile had a rebellious personality with strongly held views on many topics, which appealed to his new wife. She later said of him: 'He thought all upper-middle-class standards were crazy and was a revolutionary in practically every sense.'

It was in 1938, the year of their marriage, that Haile joined the surrealist group in London and exhibited at the nerve centre of British surrealism: the London Gallery in Cork Street. His daily routine was described as: 'Night time reserved for the interpretation of dreams and surrealist painting and the days for making and teaching pottery.'

When war broke out in 1939, Haile and de Trey left Europe for America. Haile stated baldly that if an artist 'can keep enough freedom to continue his craft, it matters little to him if it is the people's wish to cut each other's throats'. He also remarked: 'I am convinced that surrealism is the only proper and valid interpretation of contemporary reality.'

In New York from 1939, Haile earned a living painting stage sets and teaching. During the next few difficult years he also made a number of surrealist gouaches. In 1943 he was inducted into the American army, but only as a non-combatant – then, the following year, he was transferred to the British army and sent back to Britain, where he became an instructor in the Education Corps.

In 1947 the couple left London and moved to Dartington in Devon, where they set up a pottery. Haile took a job with the Rural Industries Bureau, which meant a great deal of travelling around southern England. It was on one of these trips, in 1948, that tragedy struck and he was killed in a car accident at Poole, Dorset. De Trey, who was pregnant with their first child at the time, stayed on to establish the Dartington pottery they had planned to run together. She managed it herself for the next thirty-seven years, retiring in 1985.

Writing about her husband forty years after his death, Marianne de Trey described his vitality, his 'huge and ribald sense of humour' and his ability to stimulate almost everyone he met. Sam Haile's paintings and drawings appeared in group surrealist shows in England in 1971, 1978, 1985, 1986 and 1987, including the 'Dada and Surrealism' exhibition at the Hayward Gallery, London.

# DAVID HARE

## The handsome American sculptor who stole André Breton's wife

**BORN:** 10 March 1917, New York **PARENTS:** Father a corporate attorney; mother an art collector **LIVED:** New York, 1917; American Southwest, 1927; New York and Paris, 1948; New York, 1953 **PARTNERS:** Susanna Wilson, m. 1938–45; Jacqueline Lamba, m. 1946–55; Denise Browne, m. late 1950s; Therry Frey, m. 1991–2 **DIED:** 21 December 1992, Jackson Hole, Wyoming

David Hare, like his cousin Kay Sage, was one of the rich surrealists. Born in New York City into a family well known among the social elite, he enjoyed a privileged childhood. His mother was an art collector and his father a corporate attorney. His uncle was the architect who designed the Museum of Modern Art, and a trustee of that museum.

Hare studied chemistry and biology for a time before pursuing a career as an experimental photographer. Contact with artists including Calder, Gorky and Tanguy in the late 1930s introduced him to surrealism. In 1938 he married Susanna Wilson, a socialite whose mother was the US Secretary of Labor.

In the 1940s, further involvement with the surrealists who were living in wartime exile in New York led him to move from photography to sculpture. He developed biomorphic sculptural figures which were so successful that he was soon being offered exhibitions at New York galleries.

It was during this period that Hare met Jacqueline Lamba. She and her husband, André Breton, were among the New York émigrés and their relationship was not standing up well to this new environment. Breton refused on principle to speak English, while Lamba was eager to learn; this gave her more freedom than she had ever enjoyed in her marriage back in Paris. When she met the attractive young American sculptor, seven years her junior, it was only a matter of time before Breton's control over her was lost.

At the time that Hare met Lamba he was twenty-five, blonde, handsome and wiry. He had sharp-cut features and an incisive personality; he was self-sufficient and reportedly 'more comfortable nude than clothed'. Breton liked him immediately, but Lamba liked him even more, and they soon fell in love. There is a sad description of a forlorn Breton sitting and watching as she ran joyfully down a beach with the entranced Hare, both of them naked.

In 1945 Breton and Lamba were finally divorced, as were Hare and Susanna Wilson, and the following year Lamba and Hare were married. With the war over, Hare decided he wanted to experience the European art world, and in 1948 he and Lamba moved to Paris, where he remained until 1953 – after which New York beckoned once more. Lamba, however, yearned for Paris life and in 1955 she left Hare for good, returning finally to her home country. In the late 1950s Hare married for a third time, on this occasion to the photographer Denise Browne.

He now began painting, abandoning sculpture for a few years. In the 1970s, however, he returned to sculpture and continued working in both forms for the remainder of his career. In 1985 he moved out of New York and settled in Victor, Idaho, where he built a large studio in the hayloft of a converted barn. He was married for a fourth time in 1991, to Therry Frey, a young Swiss journalist who came to interview him. The following year, he died.

Hare summed up his philosophy with the statement: 'If a work of art appears as an old friend, if we are too much at ease in its presence, it is a failure. Art, like life, is subversive.'

# S. W. HAYTER

## The brilliant technician who taught the surrealists the skills of advanced printmaking

**BORN**: 27 December 1901, Hackney, London **PARENTS**: Father a painter
**LIVED**: London, 1901; Abadan, Iran, 1922; London, 1925; Paris, 1926; New York, 1939; Paris, 1950 **PARTNERS**: Edith Fletcher, m. 1928; Helen Phillips, m. 1940; Désirée Moorhead, m. 1974–88 **DIED**: 4 May 1988, Paris

S. W. Hayter has been described as the greatest printmaker of the 20th century. Atelier 17, his studio in Paris and later in New York, attracted almost all the major avant-garde artists of the day. They went there to learn about the latest developments in advanced printmaking that Hayter was pioneering. Pablo Picasso, Wassily Kandinsky, Alberto Giacometti, Joan Miró, Alexander Calder, Marc Chagall, Jackson Pollock and Mark Rothko all worked with Hayter in his studio at one time or another.

Stanley William Hayter was born at the start of the 20th century in London. His father was a painter but he himself decided to pursue a career in science, obtaining a degree in chemistry and geology. This scientific training would stand him in good stead when he moved into the art world, because it provided him with the necessary technical knowledge to develop new methods of printmaking.

In 1926 he moved to Paris and soon found himself mixing with artists such as Balthus, Masson, Calder, Miró and Giacometti. Realizing that printmaking was badly in need of a technical update, in 1927 he opened Atelier 17, a highly successful enterprise that would run for the next sixty years.

In 1928 Hayter married Edith Fletcher and they had a son, but the marriage was a failure and was dissolved after only one year. Around this time he became part of the surrealist circle, and his paintings and prints began to develop a strong surrealist flavour.

The day after the Second World War broke out in September 1939, Hayter had to abandon Atelier 17 and return to London. When he was declared medically unfit for active duty, he left for New York. Once there, he found himself in the company of a whole group of refugee surrealists from Paris.

It was in New York that Hayter met and married the American sculptor Helen Phillips, with whom he would have two sons. In 1940 he opened a new version of Atelier 17 in the city, and was soon attracting many of the young American artists who would later form the abstract expressionist group.

As in Paris, Hayter's presence at his atelier made a big impression on everyone who worked there. The writer Anaïs Nin commented: 'He always moved about between the students, cyclonic, making Joycean puns.... He was always in motion.... His lines were like projectiles thrown in space.'

A few years later, in 1950, Hayter returned to Paris and reopened the Atelier 17 studio there. His fame as a printmaker was now worldwide and the studio was always busy. Young artists flocked to work with him and he was generous in his advice and guidance. His floppy, unruly hair, hanging over his forehead, his craggy, deeply lined face with its piercing blue eyes, his gravelly voice, and the energetic zeal with which he discussed every small point, made him a commanding figure.

His marriage to Helen Phillips ended in 1973 and the following year he married an Irish poet, Désirée Moorhead; this relationship lasted until Hayter's sudden death of a heart attack in 1988. His Atelier 17 – now renamed the Atelier Contrepoint – continued with his work after his death and is still active today.

# JACQUES HÉROLD

## The surrealist who professed to probe beneath the skin of life

**BORN**: 10 October 1910, Piatra Neamṭ, Romania, as Herold Blumer **PARENTS**: Father made and sold confectionery **LIVED**: Piatra Neamṭ, 1910; Galati, 1913; Marasesti, 1915; Falticeni, 1917; Bucharest, 1923; Paris, 1930; Marseille, 1940; Paris, 1943 **PARTNERS**: Violet Boglio, m. 1936; France Binard, m. 1944; Muguette Haudecoeur, m. 1956 **DIED**: 11 January 1987, Paris

André Breton did his best to capture the essence of the art of Jacques Hérold by saying: 'It is real life that reaches us here after passing through all the filters of sensibility.' Breton was unstinting in his praise for Hérold, going so far as to declare: 'On the artistic level, I believe that it is impossible to over-emphasize the importance of the work of Jacques Hérold.'

Hérold was one of the younger surrealists, born Herold Blumer in Romania in 1910. As a schoolboy he decided that he wanted to be a painter, and he began art studies in Bucharest in 1925. Five years later he moved to Paris and was lucky enough to encounter the two major Romanian artists already working there: Constantin Brancusi and Victor Brauner. They befriended him and it was Brauner who suggested that, to sound more French, he should change his name to Jacques Hérold. Brancusi, who was thirty-four years older, helped the young man by employing him in his studio as an assistant.

Through Brauner, Hérold met the French surrealist Yves Tanguy, and it was Tanguy who would introduce him to Breton and the rest of the Parisian surrealists. In 1934 he became an official member of Breton's group.

Hérold sought in his paintings to go beneath the surface of the natural world. He described his method as 'a systematic skinning of not only the characters, but objects, the landscape, the atmosphere, tearing the skin of the sky'.

Early in 1940, Hérold was among the surrealists who fled from Paris to escape the Nazis, ending up in Marseille waiting for a passage to America. With his Jewish background, he had a better reason to flee than some of the others – and yet, for some reason, he did not accompany them in the end. Instead he eventually joined an artists' community in a village fifty miles north of Marseille. While living there he visited the ruins of the Château de Lacoste, once home to the infamous Marquis de Sade.

A few months later, Hérold was back in Marseille, but again he did not seek a passage abroad. Amazingly, considering the risk, he returned to occupied Paris in 1943. There he joined a small group of other surrealists who had resisted fleeing to America, and in the spring of 1944 he met France Binard, who would become his second wife. After the war ended, he was able to greet André Breton as Breton returned from America.

Remembering the impact that Sade's castle had had on him, Hérold decided to buy a broken-down property lying below it, literally in its shadow. He acquired this house in 1948 and settled there so that he could paint in isolation from the social whirl of Paris.

Hérold's surrealist phase came to an end in 1951, when he left the surrealist group in protest against Breton's growing weakness. In 1955, his wife suddenly left him without explanation – perhaps tiring of the ever-present Sadean atmosphere. The following spring, Hérold met Muguette Haudecoeur, who would become his third and last wife. Their daughter was born in 1963. From this point onward he continued to paint and exhibit internationally – sadly, however, the sharp and often sinister motifs of his early surrealist paintings were no longer in evidence.

# CHARLES HOWARD



## The American artist who was at the abstract end of the surrealist spectrum

**BORN**: 2 January 1899, Montclair, New Jersey  **PARENTS**: Father a New York architect  **LIVED**: Montclair, 1899; Berkeley, California, 1903; Paris, 1922; New York, 1926; London, 1934; Bay Area, San Francisco, 1941; Helions Bumpstead, Essex, 1946; Bagni di Lucca, Italy, 1970  **PARTNER**: Madge Knight, 1934  **DIED**: 11 November 1978, Bagni di Lucca

Charles Howard was that rare thing, an American surrealist who was working in the 1930s. Indeed, he is sometimes credited with having played a key role in introducing European surrealism to the United States. He belongs to the category of artists best described as 'abstract surrealists'.

Charles Houghton Howard, to give him his full name, was born in 1899 in Montclair, New Jersey, the son of well-known architect John Galen Howard. When he was three his family moved to California, where he was raised and attended the University of California at Berkeley. After that, he studied English at both Harvard and Columbia. Despite his extensive education, he never took an art course, and when he began to paint he was entirely self taught.

In 1924, Howard's father financed a trip to Europe for him, and one day he found himself in the small northern Italian town of Castelfranco Veneto. What happened next would change his life. He wandered into the local cathedral, where he saw a painting of the Virgin Mary by Giorgione. For some reason it made a massive impression on him and he stood in front of it, transfixed, for three-quarters of an hour. When he finally managed to drag himself away, its impact had been so great that he started vomiting. What is interesting about this extraordinary response to Giorgione's painting is that we now know it was not a unique occurrence. It even has a name – Stendhal Syndrome.

Howard suddenly knew with great certainty that he would have to become a painter, and he took the next train to Paris. Thanks to his experience in Italy, he would spend the rest of his life creating visual images. After two years in Europe, he returned to America and settled in Greenwich Village, New York City. In 1932 he was included in the landmark exhibition at the Julien Levy Gallery that introduced surrealism to the United States. There were only two other Americans in the show: Man Ray and Joseph Cornell.

In 1934 he met and married the English artist Madge Knight and they moved to London. Howard soon became involved with the group of surrealists who were gathered there and contributed some of his work to the 1936 International Surrealist Exhibition. Three years later, Peggy Guggenheim gave her fellow American a solo show at her London gallery that helped to establish his reputation.

When the Second World War broke out, Howard and his wife moved back to the United States and set up a studio in the Bay Area of San Francisco. He did some war work in a local shipyard, where he was influenced by the streamlined design of the Victory ships, and integrated their shapes into his paintings. At the same time he began studying biology and in his work attempted to blend the metallic shapes of the boats with the organic forms of biological organisms.

At the war's end, Howard and Knight moved back to England, settling in the Suffolk village of Helions Bumpstead. At this point Howard's compositions became more severe, not in their shapes but in their colours – they were now predominantly black, white and grey. In 1970, he retired to Italy, where his long aesthetic journey had begun nearly fifty years earlier. His wife, who was four years his senior, died in 1974, and Howard himself died in 1978.

# GEORGES HUGNET

## The friend of Paul Éluard, whose loyalty saw him beaten unconscious by a surrealist poet

Georges Hugnet was the ultimate collagist. He was born in Paris in 1906, the son of a successful furniture manufacturer, but spent his first seven years living in Buenos Aires before returning to Paris to attend boarding school. He was something of a troublemaker there, and on one occasion played a foxtrot during a religious service. His parents separated when he was fourteen, but his father always encouraged Hugnet's study of the arts.

In 1926 Hugnet began a literary relationship with the American author Gertrude Stein and a few years later, with financial help from his father, he set up his own publishing company. He was accepted into the Breton circle in 1932, and his complex personality both startled and amused his new friends. The American composer Virgil Thomson said: 'His conversation was outrageous, and if you like outrage, hilarious. Rarely have I heard matched the guttersnipe wit with which he can lay out an enemy.'

In the late summer of 1933 an attractive young redhead, Marcelle Ferry, moved into Hugnet's Paris apartment with him. He brought her along to one of the surrealists' group meetings, but as soon as she saw the impressively leonine André Breton, she decided to change lovers and by the end of that evening was busy seducing the great leader. The following day, Breton informed Hugnet that he was madly in love with Marcelle and that she was going to move in with him. Hugnet's great respect for Breton forced him to accept his leader's 'droit de seigneur'.

In 1939, Breton expelled Hugnet from the surrealist group over a political disagreement involving Paul Éluard. This angered many people, and when Breton fled from the Nazis in 1940 and went into exile in America, Hugnet was able to get his revenge, publicly stating that Breton's cowardice had dishonoured surrealism. For his part, Hugnet was taking risks in occupied Paris, where his bookshop and publishing house concealed a secret nerve centre for the French Resistance.

Whatever his faults, Hugnet was a loyal friend and continued to support Éluard for many years, at significant cost to himself. In 1962, knowing full well how many enemies Éluard had made, he wrote warmly of Éluard's role as a resistance poet during the Second World War and made some scathing observations about the late Benjamin Péret, who had ridiculed Éluard. Two weeks after the article appeared, three minor surrealist poets called Schuster, Mayoux and Bounoure knocked on his door late at night and forced their way into his apartment. Hugnet pleaded that he had a heart condition, but they ignored this and Bounoure proceeded to beat him unconscious. As someone cynically remarked, 'poets will be poets'.

Later that year, Hugnet suffered a stroke that may have been aggravated by their assault. Another catastrophe was to come. One winter towards the end of his life, his Christmas tree caught fire and burned out his apartment, destroying his large art collection and his library of rare books. As Hugnet had recently been earning his living as a dealer in rare books, this loss was particularly devastating. He died at the age of sixty-seven in 1974.

# MARCEL JEAN



## The surrealist who became the published historian of the movement

**BORN**: 1900, La Charité-sur-Loire, France
**LIVED**: La Charité-sur-Loire, 1900; Paris, 1919; USA, 1924; Paris, 1926; Budapest, 1938; Paris, 1945
**PARTNER**: Lily, m. 1938
**DIED**: 4 December 1993, Louveciennes

Marcel Jean was born in a small town on the banks of the River Loire in central France at the turn of the 20th century. He was conscripted for war service in 1918, but within a few months armistice had been declared and he escaped the horrors of the trenches. Back in civilian life at the age of nineteen, he moved to Paris to study at the National School of Decorative Arts. There he learned the skills that would enable him to make a living as a textile designer.

In the late 1920s the newly formed surrealist movement was at its peak of activity, and Jean became fascinated by its members' publications and wild proclamations. Having met André Breton, he joined the movement in 1933 and became close to Yves Tanguy and Óscar Domínguez. In 1935 he spent some time in Barcelona with Domínguez, where he introduced Remedios Varo to surrealism.

He began producing surrealist works of art – not only paintings, but also objects – one of which, made in 1936, would prove to be his most memorable creation. Called *Spectre of the Gardenia*, it consisted of the plaster head of a woman covered in a skin of black-painted cloth, with zip-fasteners in the eye sockets. Today it resides in the Museum of Modern Art in New York, one of the icons of early surrealism.

In 1937, through his friend Wolfgang Paalen, he met Lily, a young couturier at a Paris fashion house. They fell in love, and the following year Jean was offered work as a textile designer in Hungary. The young couple could not bear to be parted, so they married hurriedly in September 1938 and boarded a train for Budapest a few days later.

Jean had only planned to spend a year in Hungary, but when war broke out in 1939, he and Lily found themselves stranded, and they had to remain there until peace was declared in 1945.

During his time in Budapest, Jean used his design skills to forge false documents for Jews who were escaping from the Nazis. He became well known in underground networks for people desperately seeking exit papers, and is said to have saved many Jewish lives through his forgery skills.

Back in Paris after the war was over, he found the surrealist movement in disarray and worked hard to get it into action again, participating in the major 1947 exhibition there. In the 1950s he decided to make himself the chronicler of the movement and write a definitive study of surrealist art. It was called *Histoire de la peinture surréaliste* (*A History of Surrealist Painting*) and was eventually published in 1959. Jean sums up his feelings about surrealist art in its final paragraphs, where he says: 'The greatness of surrealist painting lies in its passion for discovery, in its appeal to the Marvellous, in its exact, legible, mysterious content.'

Jean was now viewed as 'the scholar of surrealism' and was invited to give a series of lectures on the subject in the United States. Unlike some surrealists, he was very approachable and cooperative, doing his best to encourage public interest in his subject. He outlived many of his fellow surrealists and at the age of ninety-one, two years before his death, he published a memoir called *Au galop dans le vent* (*Galloping in the Wind*).

# HUMPHREY JENNINGS

## The documentary filmmaker who was also a passionate surrealist

**BORN**: 19 August 1907, Walberswick, Suffolk
**PARENTS**: Father an architect; mother a painter
**LIVED**: Suffolk, 1907; Cambridge, 1926; London, 1934
**PARTNERS**: Cicely Cooper, m. 1929; Emily Coleman, 1936; Peggy Guggenheim, 1937
**DIED**: 24 September 1950, Poros, Greece

Humphrey Jennings was born in 1907, in a small village on the coast of Suffolk in East Anglia, and lived there for the first nine years of his life. His parents gave him a great deal of freedom. He was allowed to smoke, take coffee and drink alcohol from an early age.

By the time Jennings was a young adult, he had developed the sort of strong personality that divided opinion. His admirers saw him as energetic and inquisitive, while his critics viewed him as dogmatic and restless. He was certainly very gifted and graduated with a starred first in English from Cambridge.

In 1929 Jennings held his first exhibition. He was still at Cambridge, with a post-graduate scholarship, studying the poetry of Thomas Gray. This was also the year that he became a married man, aged twenty-two; his bride, Cicely Cooper, was a year younger. The young couple struggled to make ends meet on Jennings' meagre scholarship income, but despite their poverty he always managed to find time to paint. His main influences were said to be Klee, Masson, Ernst and Magritte, which suggests that even in the earliest days of the surrealist movement he was well acquainted with its central figures.

The birth of a daughter in 1933 meant that Jennings had to start thinking seriously about earning a living. The following year, he moved to London and took a job with the GPO Film Unit. This would be the start of a highly successful career as a documentary filmmaker – which did not mean that he abandoned painting, but simply that it was pushed into the background.

Then, in 1936, something happened that brought it back into the foreground. Roland Penrose had just returned to London from Paris and wanted to introduce surrealism to the British public. He needed support in his project, and the person who offered this was Jennings. Together they set up a London surrealist group and gathered a team around them who would help to organize a major exhibition.

Jennings was also busy in his private moments, making surrealist collages, objects, photographs and paintings. Six of his works were included in the International Surrealist Exhibition at London's New Burlington Galleries, which opened in June 1936. Paul Éluard bought one of them, and Jennings himself bought a Magritte.

Jennings' involvement with the surrealist group brought him into contact with the eccentric American heiress Peggy Guggenheim, who was in London in 1937 trying to decide whether she should open a modern art gallery. Jennings was excited by the idea and encouraged her, promising to help in any way he could. They soon became lovers, and when Peggy travelled to Paris, Jennings followed her there and introduced her to André Breton and Yves Tanguy. Peggy, for her part, introduced Jennings to Marcel Duchamp. Peggy ended the affair as diplomatically as she could, telling Jennings that it was her fault, but he was distraught.

During the war years Jennings became more and more involved with his documentary filmmaking, and this continued after the war ended. In the summer of 1950 he set off for Greece with a film crew. On the island of Poros, scouting for locations, he made his way to the top of a cliff to assess the view. About twenty-five feet up, he slipped and fell to the beach below, crashing head first onto rocks; attempts were made to revive him, but he died two hours later. He was forty-three years old.

# FRIDA KAHLO

## The shining star of Mexican surrealism whose life was beset by tragedy

**BORN:** 6 July 1907, Coyoacán, Mexico City **PARENTS:** Father a Lutheran German; mother a Mexican Roman Catholic **LIVED:** Mexico City, 1907; San Francisco, 1930; Mexico, 1931; Detroit, 1932; New York, 1933; San Ángel, Mexico, 1934; Paris, 1939; Mexico City, 1940 **PARTNERS:** Alejandro Gómez Arias, 1925–7; Diego Rivera, m. 1929; div. 1939; m. 1940; Nickolas Muray, 1931–9; Isamu Noguchi, 1934; Heinz Berggruen, 1930s; Josephine Baker, 1930s; Dolores del Río, 1930s; Georgia O'Keeffe, 1930s; Paulette Goddard, 1930s; Jacqueline Lamba, 1930s; Leon Trotsky, 1937 **DIED:** 13 July 1954, Coyoacán

Frida Kahlo was born on the outskirts of Mexico City in 1907, the daughter of a Lutheran German who had married a Mexican girl. Her family wanted her to train as a doctor, but this ambition was cut short in September 1925 when, aged eighteen, she suffered an appalling accident: she was travelling home from the city centre by bus when a tram collided with the vehicle.

The catalogue of Kahlo's injuries is horrific. She had a broken back, a broken collarbone, broken ribs, a broken pelvis and eleven separate breaks to her right leg. In addition, she had a crushed and dislocated right foot and a dislocated shoulder. As if that were not enough, an iron handrail had entered her belly and pierced through her uterus, ending her reproductive life.

The legacy of this dreadful accident was that Kahlo spent much of her life in terrible pain. Her convalescence lasted for three months, during which time she had to wear a full-body cast. She took up painting to pass the time and soon developed a passion for it. Her mother had a special easel made for her so that she could paint in bed, and the activity gave her something to occupy her mind during the long hours of bedridden isolation.

In 1929 Kahlo married the artist Diego Rivera. The marriage lasted ten years, ending when Rivera (despite having been unfaithful himself) could no longer tolerate Kahlo's many affairs. During the 1930s she had liaisons with the sculptor Isamu Noguchi, the art dealer Heinz Berggruen, the exiled politician Leon Trotsky and the photographer Nickolas Muray – not to mention the actresses Dolores del Río and Paulette Goddard, the dancer Josephine Baker, and the artists Georgia O'Keeffe and Jacqueline Lamba.

When André Breton visited Mexico in 1938, he was entranced by the exotic, eccentric Kahlo. He immediately declared her a surrealist, saying: 'The art of Frida Kahlo is a ribbon around a bomb.' He agreed to arrange an exhibition of her work in Paris, and she arrived there in the spring of 1939. As it turned out, she hated the surrealists' endless theoretical discussions, but at the opening of her Paris exhibition she got a hug from Miró, kisses from Kandinsky and a pair of earrings from a smitten Picasso.

In the 1940s Kahlo's health began to decline and in 1953 her body had become so frail that she was told she was too ill to attend a major exhibition of her work in Mexico. Ignoring this, she ordered an ambulance to take her to its opening. She was carried into the exhibition lying on a bed that was placed in the centre of the hall, where she held court surrounded by all the guests.

Sadly, the end was near. After another year of physical misery, Kahlo finally died. Little more was heard of her until the 1980s, when her extraordinary story was rediscovered: a steady stream of biographies, retrospectives and films followed, and the singer Madonna began to collect her work. The remarkable Frida Kahlo had at last achieved the global fame that her stubborn determination and eccentric vision deserved.

# PAUL KLEE

## The forerunner of surrealism, whose brilliant visual games anticipated Breton's movement



**BORN**: 18 December 1879, Münchenbuchsee, Bern, Switzerland **PARENTS**: Father German, a music teacher; mother Swiss **LIVED**: Münchenbuchsee, 1879; Bern, 1880; Munich, 1898; Italy, 1901; Bern, 1902; Munich, 1906; Weimar, 1921 (Bauhaus); Dessau, 1925 (Bauhaus); Düsseldorf, 1931; Bern, 1934 **PARTNER**: Lily Stumpf, m. 1906 **DIED**: 29 June 1940, Muralto, Switzerland

Paul Klee was producing surrealist works as early as 1914 – before the word had been invented, and a decade before the first surrealist manifesto. Although he was never a member of any surrealist group, he was so admired by the early surrealists that they included his work in their very first group show in Paris in 1925. Like de Chirico, Klee had independently found his own way to a new kind of painting. He was quoted as saying: 'Formerly we used to represent things visible on earth…. Today we reveal the reality that is behind visible things.'

Klee was born in 1879, making him two years Picasso's senior and one of the oldest artists to work in the surrealist manner. He was born near Bern in Switzerland and grew up in a family atmosphere that was musical, learning to play the violin well enough to take a place in an orchestra. When he was nineteen he moved to Munich to study at the Academy of Fine Art there, and during his three

years in Germany he started painting seriously.
He also met his future wife, the pianist Lily Stumpf.
In 1905 he visited Paris, where the first fauvist
exhibition was being held. The following year he
married Lily and she would soon give birth to Felix,
their only child.

At this point, in 1907, Klee became a house-
husband. His wife went out to work, giving piano
lessons, while he stayed at home to look after Felix.
This state of affairs lasted for years and enabled Klee
to juggle painting and drawing with his paternal
duties. When he was busy, he would leave the little
boy with a friendly neighbour who was also an artist.
Felix Klee must surely have been the only small boy
to have Wassily Kandinsky as a babysitter.

When the First World War broke out, Klee was
called up for military service. After he war he was
invited to join the Bauhaus, an impressive modernist
art school, at Weimar. He began teaching there in
1921, and his lectures were described as inspirational.
His most widely quoted remark comes from this
period – 'When I draw, I take a line for a walk.'

In 1931 Klee was offered a professorship in
fine art at Düsseldorf, but when Hitler came to
power in 1933, he was forced to resign and move
to Switzerland. Tragically, just as his fame was
beginning to spread, his health started to deteriorate.
He began painting with greater urgency, as if sensing
his time was limited. In 1937 he was visited by
Picasso, who praised 'his mixture of wisdom and
energy, passionate asceticism and intensity'. The
Nazis had a very different view, removing more than a
hundred of his pictures from German museums.

When war broke out in 1939, Klee was still hard
at work painting in his studio; the following year,
as a major exhibition of his work opened in Zurich,
he was moved into a clinic. He died there at the age
of sixty in 1940, leaving behind over 10,000 works –
each one carefully numbered and catalogued by him.
Earlier, he had written: 'I shall die gladly when I have
created a few more good works.'

# FÉLIX LABISSE



## The surrealist whose work was a brightly coloured version of Magritte's

**BORN**: 9 March 1905, Marchiennes, France
**LIVED**: Marchiennes, 1905; Douai, 1905; Ostend, 1927; Paris, 1932; Knokke, Belgium, 1945; Neuilly-sur-Seine, 1951
**PARTNER**: Jony Herlin, m. 1955
**DIED**: 27 January 1982, Neuilly-sur-Seine

Although it is tempting to describe Félix Labisse as a colourful version of René Magritte, that would be unfair. It's close to the truth, but not the whole truth.

Labisse was seven years younger than Magritte, having been born in 1905 in Marchiennes, near Douai, at the northern tip of France near the Belgian border. Although born in France, he was of Polish and Flemish descent and spent a great deal of his life in Belgium. As a child, he was terrified by the bombing in the First World War – the front line was only fourteen kilometres from his home.

In Ostend in the early 1920s, he met the artist James Ensor, who had a major influence on him. In 1932 Labisse visited Paris, and in the following years he divided his time between Paris, Ostend and Knokke. He met his future wife, Jony Herlin, in 1938 and in Brussels in the same year he made the acquaintance of the two major figures in Belgian surrealism: Magritte and Paul Delvaux.

Magritte's impact on Labisse was considerable. Shortly after they first met, he produced his first hybrid figure: *The Green Minotaure*, a human figure wearing a cloak but with the head of a bull. Other hybrid figures followed, and Magritte's influence was consistently clear. Labisse did manage to avoid the famous Magritte example of the 'man with the head of an apple', but came perilously close to it with a figure that had the head of a ripe fig.

Labisse was called up for military duty in 1939, but by 1940 he was back in Paris, where he took over Man Ray's old studio. In 1945 he participated in a surrealist group show in Brussels, but in the following years he spent more time with the Parisian surrealist group. He was friendly with most of the major surrealists, including Dalí, Ernst, de Chirico, Fini, Lam and Domínguez, as well as the Belgians Delvaux, Magritte and Mesens.

His work as a set designer meant he also had a wide circle of theatrical friends, including Leslie Caron, Monica Vitti, Agnès Varda, Jean Seberg, Jacques Tati, Jean-Louis Barrault, Pierre Brasseur and Gérard Philipe – but he did not neglect his surrealist painting while focusing on the design work. In 1962 he invented a form of landscape he called the 'libidoscape', and in 1964 a new obsession of his began: his blue nudes, to which he would return time and again in the following years.

During his life Labisse completed about 800 paintings, and no fewer than a hundred of those depicted a nude female. As soon as he broke free from this preoccupation he was a new man, an inventive surrealist with a fascinatingly dark imagination. In his best work he managed to avoid Magritte's visual jokes, instead creating complex surrealist figures and landscapes of a highly personal nature. It is difficult to forget his image of a hungry young woman eating her own fingers.

Towards the end of his life there were a number of major solo exhibitions of his work, and he was still painting vigorously as late as 1981. This final suite of paintings was of strangely folded bulls' heads – as though the bull and the matador's cloak had become one. The following year, in Neuilly-sur-Seine, he died at the age of seventy-six.

# WIFREDO LAM

## The Cuban master who beckoned us to enter his surrealist jungle

**BORN**: 8 December 1902, Sagua La Grande, Villa Clara, Cuba, as Wifredo Óscar de la Concepción Lam y Castilla  **PARENTS**: Father Chinese; mother Congolese Cuban  **LIVED**: Sagua La Grande, 1902; Havana, 1916; Madrid, 1923; Barcelona, 1937; Paris, 1938; Marseille, 1940; Havana, 1941; Paris, 1952; Albissola, Italy, 1962  **PARTNERS**: Eva Piriz, m. 1929–31; Balbina Barrera, 1935–7; Helena Holzer, m. 1944–50; Nicole Raoul, 1956–8; Lou Laurin, m. 1960  **DIED**: 11 September 1982, Paris

Wifredo Lam was born in a small coastal town in Cuba in 1902. His ancestry was complex. His father, who was eighty-four when Wifredo was born, was a Chinese immigrant labourer. His mother was part Congolese and part Spanish. As a teenager, Lam was already devoted to drawing and persuaded his family to let him attend the art academy in Havana.

In 1923 he gained a grant to travel to Madrid, where he studied at the art school attached to the Prado Museum. In 1927 he met a Spanish girl by the name of Eva Piriz, and two years later they were married. The couple were desperately poor and he was heartbroken when their deprived lifestyle led to tragedy, with Eva and their infant son both dying of tuberculosis in 1931.

During the Spanish Civil War Lam met Helena Holzer, a doctor, who would eventually become his second wife. One of her friends gave him a letter of introduction to Picasso – a letter that would change his life. It was soon clear that the republican cause was being crushed and Lam decided to leave for Paris before it was too late, arriving there in 1938 with the letter to Picasso in his pocket. When Picasso greeted him, he was rather surprised to be taken immediately into a room full of African tribal carvings. Picasso told him that he should be proud of these wonderful works of art because he, Lam, had African blood in his veins.

The following year, Picasso introduced Lam to André Breton, who also had a collection of tribal art. In no time at all, Lam found himself welcomed as a member of the surrealist inner circle in Paris. A solo exhibition of his work was arranged and was well received.

When the Nazis arrived in Paris in June 1940, Lam had to make a hurried exit. He travelled south to Marseille, where, in March 1941, he was able to escape as a passenger on an ancient freighter jam-packed with 350 fleeing intellectuals, including André Breton and his family.

Back in Cuba, he settled down to paint. He produced over a hundred new pictures in 1942 alone and soon began work on his masterpiece, *The Jungle*, now in the Musem of Modern Art in New York. His two decades in Europe had moulded him, and he was about to launch into a forty-year exploration of his unique, highly distinctive style – part tribal and part Picasso, but with these two influences well digested and skilfully transformed into pure Wifredo Lam.

As he settled back into a Cuban existence, Lam married Helena Holzer. Six years later, in 1950, she moved to New York, but Lam was unable to obtain a resident's permit there and the couple were divorced. He remained in Cuba, still painting, until 1952, when he returned to Paris. In 1960 he married for a third time, to Lou Laurin, a Swedish painter, with whom he would have three sons. They moved to Italy in 1962 and made it their main home until Lam's death.

Lam lived long enough to see his fame as an artist spread around the world. He and his family travelled extensively during his later years, until 1978, when he suffered a major stroke. He died in Paris in 1982. At his request, his ashes were taken to Havana to rest on Cuban soil.

# JACQUELINE LAMBA



## The wife of André Breton, whose surrealism was overshadowed by her husband

If the surrealist paintings of Jacqueline Lamba are not well known today, it is because she had both the good fortune and the misfortune to marry André Breton. It was good fortune because it placed her at the very centre of the Paris surrealist movement and all its activities; it was misfortune because Breton dominated Lamba, who had ambitions to be a serious artist.

Lamba was born in Paris in 1910. When she was two the family moved to Egypt, where her father was working as an agricultural engineer. After two years in Cairo he was killed in an accident and little Jacqueline, her sister and their mother returned to France.

She attended art schools in Paris, but when she was seventeen her mother died, and Lamba decided to make her way in the world as a teacher. Later she switched to a very different kind of occupation, earning a living as a naked swimmer at an underwater cabaret in Pigalle. She had been reading Breton's essays and wanted to meet him, so she went to a café where he was holding one of his surrealist meetings. He noticed her immediately, later recalling that she was 'scandalously beautiful'.

**BORN**: 17 November 1910, Saint-Mandé, Paris **PARENTS**: Father an engineer; parents wanted a son and called her 'he' **LIVED**: Paris, 1910; Mexico, 1938; Paris, 1939; New York, 1941; Paris, 1955; Simiane-la-Rotonde, 1963; Rochecorbon, 1988 **PARTNERS**: André Breton, m. 1934–45; Frida Kahlo, 1938; David Hare, m. 1946–55 **DIED**: 20 July 1993, Rochecorbon, France

Lamba's fiery intelligence and authentic attraction to surrealist ideas had an enormous impact on Breton. He took his friends to see her dance in the underwater cabaret and wrote lovingly about his 'water nymph'. They were married three months later, in August 1934, with Paul Éluard and Alberto Giacometti as witnesses.

The following year, they travelled together to Prague to meet the Czech surrealists. Around this time, Lamba accidentally became pregnant – much to Breton's alarm. Family life did not fit in with his role as active leader of the surrealist movement. After the birth of their daughter, Aube, in December 1935, Lamba was saddled with all of the parenting duties and tensions began to show in the marriage.

In 1938 the family visited Mexico, where Lamba enjoyed a brief affair with the artist Frida Kahlo. When war broke out the following year and many Parisian surrealists fled to New York, the Bretons were among them. There, in 1942, Lamba met the handsome young American sculptor David Hare, who was the editor of Breton's surrealist magazine *vvv*. She and Hare fell in love. The following year, she left Breton and moved in with Hare, taking Aube with her.

Now, at last, Lamba was free to paint without Breton's dominant presence crushing her artistic ambition. With Hare's encouragement, she held her first solo exhibition in New York in 1944. She also exhibited in the 1947 International Surrealist Exhibition in Paris, by which time she had divorced Breton and married Hare.

Back in New York in 1948, Lamba and Hare had a son together. Their life was full of excitement and interest, including rewarding trips to the West, where she studied the culture and art of Native American tribes. The marriage lasted nine years, but in 1955 Lamba left her husband and returned to her native France. She would remain there for the rest of her life, painting and exhibiting, but never again associating herself with the surrealists.

# LEN LYE

## The experimental filmmaker who was also a notable surrealist artist

**BORN**: 5 July 1901, Christchurch **PARENTS**: Father a hairdresser; mother a cleaner **LIVED**: Christchurch, 1901; Sydney, 1922; Auckland, 1924; Samoa, 1924; Sydney, 1925; London, 1926; New York, 1944 **PARTNERS**: Liz Johnson, 1926–33; Jane Thompson, m. 1934; Janet Learned, 1945; Louise Ames, 1945; Ann Zeiss, m. 1948–80 **DIED**: 15 May 1980, Warwick, New York

Although he is best known as a maker of experimental films, Len Lye was also a surrealist artist whose work was included in the 1936 International Surrealist Exhibition in London.

Lye was born in New Zealand at the turn of the 20th century. His father died of tuberculosis when he was three and his mother then married a lighthouse keeper, so he grew up on a stormy shore in a wild, isolated marine world of rocks, seaweed and crashing waves. It was during this period that he developed a private passion for creating visual images.

As a young man Lye grew increasingly energetic, independent and restless. He was determined to get closer to the hub of the art world in Europe. Unable to afford the sea fare, he worked his passage as stoker on a liner that was sailing for London. Arriving there in 1926, he found a job working for a sculptor in a Hammersmith studio. At night, he slept in a toolshed. Soon he met other artists and began to lead the kind of creative life he had imagined and hoped for.

Lye was both a filmmaker and a painter. His first film appeared in 1929, and it was followed by twenty-five more between then and 1966. His unique cinematic style consisted of dancing shapes, some abstract, some biomorphic – twisting, turning, reproducing, fighting and evolving.

The first exhibitions of his paintings and constructions took place at the end of the 1920s and in the early 1930s. Meanwhile, he had a busy personal life with multiple affairs. In 1927 he met a young South African woman, Jane Thompson; they were married in 1934 and had their first child, a son called Bix, a few years later. Lye found himself enjoying the infant's explorations of drawing and painting.

It was in the mid-1930s that Lye became actively involved with the London surrealists and, when the Second World War broke out in 1939, he continued to be active in surrealist circles in London. He took part in the 'Surrealism Today' exhibition at the Zwemmer Gallery in 1940, the same year his daughter, Yancy, was born. As the war progressed, he found work helping to make public information films.

In 1944 he was offered the chance to make documentary films in America and, leaving his family behind, he relocated to New York. He was delighted with the city and got to know many of the European surrealists sheltering there. As the years passed, he became less interested in film and more focused on producing his kinetic sculptures, which he exhibited with some success. In 1961 he put on a performance at the Museum of Modern Art called *An Evening of Tangible Motion Sculpture*. In 1977 a collection of his sculptures was exhibited in New Zealand – his first show ever in his native country.

A few months before his death from cancer in 1980, Lye paid homage to his roots in New Zealand, establishing a Len Lye Foundation there and sending it all his archives. In 2015, the Len Lye Centre was opened in the western New Zealand city of New Plymouth. Its exterior is architecturally dramatic, with a convoluted, reflective stainless steel skin. As the first museum in New Zealand dedicated to the work of a single artist, it confirms Lye's place in the history of modern art.

# CONROY MADDOX



## The erudite mastermind of the British surrealist movement

**BORN**: 27 December 1912, Ledbury, Herefordshire **PARENTS**: Father a seed merchant and publican **LIVED**: Ledbury, 1912; Chipping Norton, 1929; Birmingham, 1933; London, 1955 **PARTNERS**: Nan Burton, m. 1948–55; Pauline Drayson, 1960s and 1970s; Deborah (Des) Mogg, 1979–2005 **DIED**: 14 January 2005, London

In its early days, when surrealism was an active movement, there was a special category of surrealist: the group leader. In Paris, of course, it was André Breton. His counterpart in London was Édouard Mesens. And in Birmingham, England's Second City, it was Conroy Maddox. He was a theorist, an activist, a pamphleteer and a writer, as well as an artist – in fact, the total surrealist.

Maddox was born in the market town of Ledbury, about forty miles south of Birmingham, in 1912. His father, a seed merchant, was wounded in the First World War and Conroy's earliest memory was of visiting him in hospital. As with many surrealists, this experience started him off on a lifelong hatred of the establishment. In 1933 the family moved to Birmingham and by 1935 Maddox was working as a commercial designer, but in that year he discovered surrealism in the city library and was fascinated by the possibilities that it offered.

He made two lengthy visits to Paris in 1937 and 1938, meeting, among others, Marcel Duchamp and Man Ray. On his final visit in 1939, he decided to leave when he saw workmen putting sandbags around public monuments. He sailed on the last but one ship to leave France before the Second World War broke out.

Back in England, he had become part of the London surrealist group, attending their meetings and exhibiting with them. It was during the war years that he met a lively, strong-minded young woman by the name of Nan Burton. Although she was married, they began a lengthy affair and had two children together. Eventually, in 1947, Nan obtained a divorce and she and Conroy were married early in 1948. She was more than a match for his waspish tongue and his black humour.

Maddox's work comprised three distinct types. There were his collages, in the classic surrealist tradition established by Max Ernst; his small, colourful gouaches of biomorphic beings parading in simple landscapes; and his major works, all of which were oil on canvas. In these less colourful oils he portrayed meticulous, dreamlike scenes that were stylistically somewhere between de Chirico and Magritte, but with Maddox's own special flavour.

If anyone asked him to explain one of his paintings, he was stubbornly uncooperative: 'You can't explain an image like this and you shouldn't. A surrealist does not know what he is doing. Something happens and it develops, but you don't analyze it. By doing that you destroy a surrealist image.'

One of his passions was attacking religion. A painting of his that is hardly ever shown, called *Short-cut to Calgary*, depicts Christ with his cross getting a ride to his crucifixion in a vintage motor car. Maddox is on record as describing religion as 'a brutal insignia of a slow moral decomposition'.

In 1955, with his Birmingham group having dispersed, Maddox moved to London. His marriage to Nan collapsed, although they remained friendly and she continued to visit his exhibitions. He never remarried but later had two more long-term relationships, the first with Pauline Drayson in the 1960s and the second, from 1979, with Deborah (a.k.a. Des) Mogg, who was fifty years his junior.

For Maddox, surrealism was an act of rebellion that would live forever. He said: 'The work of surrealism can never be conclusive. It is more of an exploration...and a struggle.... I will remain on my quest for surrealism until my last breath.'

# RENÉ MAGRITTE

## The Belgian master of the surrealist visual joke

**BORN**: 21 November 1898, Lessines, Belgium
**PARENTS**: Father a tailor and textile merchant; mother a milliner
**LIVED**: Lessines, 1898; Brussels, 1916; Paris, 1927; Brussels, 1930
**PARTNERS**: Georgette Berger, m. 1922–67; Sheila Legge, 1937
**DIED**: 15 August 1967, Schaerbeek, Brussels

Magritte was an artist addicted to contradiction. Every element in a Magritte painting is realistically portrayed and immediately recognizable; everything is matter of fact. Everything, that is, except the relationships between those elements. These are anything but realistic – they are irrational, illogical and paradoxical. Magritte spent his whole life trying to think up novel ways of insulting the common-sense values of everyday existence.

He used ten main devices:

**The composite** – He combined two different things as one: a nightdress hanging in a wardrobe has a pair of breasts.

**The switch** – He reversed the elements of a subject: a mermaid has the head of a fish and the legs of a girl.

**The see-through** – He painted a solid object as if it were an opening through which we could see: through a flying bird, we can see a cloudy blue sky.

**The out of scale** – He altered the size of a subject: a green apple fills a room.

**The out of place** – He added an element that was completely out of place: a small white cloud creeps into a room through an open door.

**The out-of-time** – He interfered with the time-scale of a subject: an artist paints a portrait of an egg, but the canvas shows a bird.

**The anti-gravity** – He depicted solid objects floating in the air: a giant rock floats above an ocean.

**The misnamed** – He wrote an irrelevant name under a familiar object: a horse is labelled 'the door'.

**The transformation** – He showed one subject changing into another: growing plants develop the heads of birds.

**The substance change** – He showed an object made of another material: a yacht is made of ocean waves.

The titles of Magritte's paintings have puzzled many people. Anyone struggling to find hidden meanings in them should be warned that Magritte would invite his surrealist friends around for the evening to see who could come up with the most outlandishly meaningless titles for his latest paintings.

Magritte was born at the end of the 19th century in Lessines, about twenty miles southwest of Brussels, where his father owned a tailor's shop. When he was fourteen years old, his mother drowned herself in a river. When her body was found, her nightdress had been dragged up by the water to cover her dead face like a mask – it has been said that Magritte witnessed this, and that it left its mark on his imagination. Certainly, cloaked faces would often feature in his work.

The following year he met a beautiful girl called Georgette Berger, who would later become his wife. They were a devoted couple, deeply in love with one another from childhood to the grave.

During the Second World War, to make money, Magritte is said to have painted and sold a number of fakes. According to his friend Marcel Mariën, he produced fakes of Picasso, Braque, Klee, Ernst, de Chirico, Gris and even Titian. What would a Picasso by Magritte be worth today?

Towards the end of his life, Magritte's fame had spread around the world, and in 1965 he was given a major retrospective at the Museum of Modern Art in New York. Although his health was beginning to deteriorate, he attended the exhibition in person. The following year he visited Italy, but the end was near; in 1967 he died from cancer at his home in Brussels, aged sixty-eight.

# GEORGES MALKINE

**The only visual artist among the 19 names listed in the first surrealist manifesto in 1924**

**BORN**: 10 October 1898, Paris  **PARENTS**: Both violinists; father from Odessa, mother from Copenhagen  **LIVED**: Paris, 1898; Odessa (childhood); Ardennes (war service), 1917; Africa, 1919; Paris, 1922; Nice, 1923; Paris, 1924; Tahiti, 1929; Paris, 1930; Haiti, 1937; Paris, 1938; Marseille, 1940; New York, 1948; Woodstock, 1953; Paris, 1966  **PARTNERS**: Caridad de Laberdesque, 1926; Yvette Ledoux, m. 1930; Sonia Niel, m. 1948  **DIED**: 22 March 1970, Paris

Despite being one of the founding figures of the surrealist movement, Georges Malkine is little known today. This is his own doing, as he went to great lengths to avoid any sort of personal publicity.

Malkine's main claim to a place in the history of surrealism is that he was the only painter listed by Breton in the first manifesto of surrealism in 1924. Of the nineteen names mentioned there, all the others were poets, writers or theorists. When the surrealists issued a declaration in January 1925 as a follow-up to the manifesto of the previous year, there were twenty-six signatories. Again Malkine was there, but now he was joined by two other visual artists: Max Ernst and André Masson. However, although there were three of them, they were still outnumbered nine to one by the writers and poets.

Georges Malkine was born in Paris in 1898. His father was Russian, from Odessa, and his mother was Danish, from Copenhagen. Both were violinists and when they met in Paris and married, they became French citizens. In 1913, at the age of fifteen, Malkine started making drawings, but then the First World War intervened. He served in the army and was wounded out in 1918.

Professionally, Malkine's life was varied and restless. He had many occupations: dockworker, violinist, dustbin seller, sailor, tie salesman, elephant hunter, fairground technican, ship's pilot and film actor. His life as an artist began in earnest in 1922, when he met Breton and became involved in the Paris dada group. In 1924, along with Breton, he moved from dadaism to surrealism. His own painting was developing at this stage, and he held a number of solo exhibitions. He was an innovator, introducing the kind of visual trickery that would later be taken up by Magritte.

Then, in 1933, he stopped painting and switched to film acting. When the Second World War broke out some years later, he worked for the French Resistance. Eventually he was arrested by the Gestapo and tortured for information, after which he was sent to a labour camp in Germany.

When the war ended and he was released, his health was poor, but in 1946 he was well enough to start an affair with an anarchist's daughter, Sonia Niel. Two years later they were married, and they went on to have four children. In 1948 they moved to New York, where Malkine started painting and exhibiting again.

In 1953 the family moved to Woodstock, New York, where Sonia was involved in the founding of the Woostock music festival. Malkine's health was still poor, but he managed to remain active in his studio. In 1966 he suddenly reappeared in Paris, much to the surprise of his old friends, who had assumed he was dead.

He was working in his Paris studio in 1970 when – having just completed a painting called *La Mer*, in which the white crests of the ocean waves are reflected in the wings of white seabirds flying above – he died of a stroke.

Although he destroyed his earliest pictures and lost a collection of his paintings and drawings during the war, Malkine managed to leave behind a total of about 500 works. Despite this, he remains a shadowy figure in the history of surrealism. Studying his paintings carefully makes it clear that he deserves to be much better known than he is.

# MARCEL MARIËN

## The surrealist protégé of Magritte who turned against his master

**BORN**: 29 April 1920, Antwerp **PARENTS**: Father a labourer; mother a dressmaker **LIVED**: Antwerp, 1920; Germany (prisoner of war), 1940; Herenthout, 1941; Brussels, 1948; East Asia, 1963; Brussels, 1965 **PARTNERS**: Elisabeth van Loock, 1941–51; Jane Graverol, 1955–8; Sigrid (niece of Elizabeth van Loock), 1962; Hedwige Benedix, 1965–82; Gudrun Steinmann, m. 1968 **DIED**: 19 September 1993, Brussels

Marcel Mariën was the protégé of René Magritte. Magritte, twenty-two years older than his young friend, took Mariën under his wing in 1937.

Mariën was wildly enthusiastic about the surrealist art of Magritte and his companions, but suffered from one major drawback: he could not draw or paint. He overcame this by making photographic collages and surrealist objects. His most famous objects were spectacles with only one central eyepiece, and a tennis racket strung with barbed wire.

Mariën was born in 1920, rather late for a surrealist, and grew up in Antwerp. His parents were poor – his father a labourer and his mother a dressmaker. They encouraged him to leave school at an early age in order to start earning a living, and he became a photographer's assistant at the age of fifteen.

His first encounter with surrealism came in 1935 when he saw works by Magritte at an arts festival.

Two years later he made a trip to Brussels, where he met most of the major Belgian surrealists. Just as he was starting to get close to them, he was called up for army service, and in 1940 he was captured by the Germans and sent to a prisoner-of-war camp.

Released the following year, he returned to Belgium and rejoined the surrealist group. In 1942–3, during the darkest days of the war, with occupied Belgium suffering from many shortages, Mariën and Magritte cooperated in an illegal adventure. Magritte painted fake Picassos, Braques, Klees, Ernsts and de Chiricos, and Mariën carried them off to Paris to sell them on the black market.

In 1953 Mariën met the surrealist artist Jane Graverol, and two years later they began a passionate, tumultuous affair that lasted until 1958. By that time, Mariën was involved in another illegal project, the profits from which he used to finance his surrealist film, *L'Imitation du cinéma*. The film featured a mixture of sexual and religious elements and was so controversial that it was repeatedly banned in Belgium, France and the United States.

In 1962 Mariën perpetrated a major hoax, producing a tract called 'La Grande Baisse' (The Great Decline) to coincide with a major exhibition of Magritte's work in Belgium. Purportedly written by Magritte himself, it offered great reductions on his paintings and stated that they could be ordered in different sizes to suit the buyer. When Magritte found out, he was furious and never spoke to Mariën again. He could not see the joke because, of course, it was a little too close to the truth – for Magritte was not averse to making several examples of a particular composition if he found more than one buyer for it.

There are two contrasting ways of viewing Marcel Mariën: as ungrateful and envious of Magritte's fame, or as a protégé who kept his faith with the principles of surrealism and, when he saw his old mentor succumbing to commercialism, took action against him. Or you can accept both views as representing two sides of a very complex man.

# JOAN MASSANET

The quiet Catalan surrealist whose work was overshadowed by that of his flamboyant neighbour, Salvador Dalí

**BORN:** 24 May 1899, L'Armentera, Girona, Catalonia
**LIVED:** Girona; Barcelona; Madrid; L'Escala
**DIED:** 23 December 1970, L'Escala, Girona

Joan Massanet was one of the early Catalan surrealists, but was overshadowed by his more talented neighbour, Salvador Dalí. He also suffered from the fact that he borrowed quite a few of Dalí's visual devices. Despite this, he was a surrealist artist worthy of respect and should, perhaps, have become better known than he is.

Like Dalí, Massanet was committed to living out his life in a village on the Costa Brava in the extreme northeast corner of Spain. He was based in L'Escala, while Dalí's studio was in Port Lligat, about twenty miles to the north. The big difference was that Dalí was an international figure and Massanet was a stay-at-home. As one critic put it, their art may have been similar, but they were poles apart in their lifestyles: 'Universal, cosmopolitan traveller Dalí; Local, seated, sedentary Massanet.'

Massanet was born at the end of the 19th century in L'Armentera, a few miles inland from the fishing port of L'Escala. He never attended an art school and was entirely self taught. Instead, his education was as a scientist – a pharmacist. He obtained his university degree in Barcelona and then went on to Madrid to acquire a doctorate. While studying, he became a keen collector of avant-garde art publications from Paris, such as *Minotaure* and *Cahiers d'Art*, and made a careful study of the latest developments in surrealist art.

When his mother died Massanet went to live with his uncle, a pharmacist, in L'Escala and remained there for the rest of his life, becoming deeply involved in local affairs. He was elected mayor of the port between 1959 and 1966. Nearby are the ruins of the ancient Greek settlement of Empúries, and Massanet became absorbed in studying the ancient architecture of this idyllic site, a preoccupation that is reflected in some of his surrealist paintings.

Massanet's earliest known surrealist work dates from 1924, but his style was not fully developed until 1927. This was the year that he met his neighbour Dalí for the first time – the start of what one Spanish commentator described as a 'sporadic and symmetrical relationship'.

He was included in a group show in 1936, an important exhibition of Spanish surrealism given the title 'Logicofobista'. Later, in 1950, he founded a local avant-garde group of artists called Indika. Surprisingly, he did not have his own first solo exhibition until 1953, when he was fifty-four years old.

In the 1960s he introduced a third dimension into his work, adding to his canvases a wide variety of substances including sand, shells, roots, resin, rope, fabrics, flotsam and weathered pieces of wood from old boats. He also created a number of sculptures, often in the form of large masks, using old pieces of stone and wood.

Although Massanet may not be as well known as certain other Spanish surrealists, he did have one special honour accorded to him: the central street in L'Escala, which runs through the middle of the village down to its small beach, has been given the title of Carrer Pinto Joan Massanet – Road of the Painter Joan Massanet. His name will now forever be linked with the place where he spent his entire working life.

# ANDRÉ MASSON



## One of the central figures of the surrealist movement from its earliest days

**BORN**: 4 January 1896, Balagny-sur-Thérain, Oise, France  **PARENTS**: Father a wallpaper seller  **LIVED**: France, 1896; Brussels, 1904; Paris, 1912; Army, 1914; Céret, France, 1919; Paris, 1921; Spain, 1934–6; Paris, 1937; New Preston, Connecticut, 1941; Paris, 1945; Aix-en-Provence, 1947  **PARTNERS**: Odette Cabalé, m. 1920; Rose Maklès, m. 1934  **DIED**: 28 October 1987, Paris

André Masson was born in northern France, but when he was seven his family moved to Belgium, so he experienced a Flemish childhood. His early interest in drawing was encouraged by his mother, who fostered in her son a love of the unconventional. With her backing, he gained entry to the prestigious Art Academy in Brussels at the tender age of eleven, well below the official limit.

Masson's precocious start in the world of art was interrupted by the outbreak of the First World War. He served as a private in the French infantry and, in 1917, was severely wounded in the chest. When he was finally discharged at the end of 1918, he moved to the French countryside, where he met and married Odette Cabalé. In 1920 they moved back to Paris, where his next-door neighbour happened to be the young Joan Miró. The two became close friends.

In 1924 Masson held his first solo exhibition. It was visited by André Breton, who bought one of his paintings and invited him to join the official surrealist circle. Under Breton's influence, Masson started making automatic drawings, and he was soon exhibiting in group shows with the other official surrealists. He became a central figure in the movement for several years – until, in 1929, he crossed swords with Breton and left. As Masson had been one of the very first painters to join the circle, this must have hurt Breton; his Second Surrealist Manifesto included a savage verbal attack on his old friend.

Masson's separation from Breton was not the only one he suffered in 1929, for in that year his marriage to Odette also collapsed, ending in divorce. The early 1930s saw him in a troubled state of mind with an underlying sense of 'dereliction and despair'. His paintings and drawings during this phase became increasingly violent, as though his art was an outlet for his pent-up emotions.

In 1934 he visited Spain, where he met and married Rose Maklès. They had two sons together, and Masson's state of mind became calmer. He participated in the 1936 International Surrealist Exhibition in London, showing fourteen of his works, and he and Breton patched up their differences. This meant a great deal to Masson, and there followed a productive phase of painting during which he produced some of his most important work.

This was cut short by the outbreak of the Second World War, when he and his family joined other surrealists in an exodus to the USA. Once safely in America, they settled in Connecticut, where his stimulating neighbours included Calder, Tanguy and Gorky. During this period his relations with André Breton began to deteriorate once again and in 1943 there was another heated disagreement, after which Masson left the surrealist group for good. He summed up his basic disagreement with Breton with the words: 'To indulge in mental chaos is as stupid and narrow as to stick to too much reason.'

In 1945 Masson returned to France and, for the next two decades, exhibited his work both there and internationally with great success. This continued until, in 1977, his health collapsed. He became a wheelchair user but was able to continue painting for another three years – eventually, however, this became impossible, and he spent the final seven years of his life in a frustratingly non-creative state.

# ROBERTO MATTA

## The greatest surrealist to emerge from South America

**BORN**: 11 November 1911, Santiago, Chile, as Roberto Sebastián Antonio Matta Echaurren **PARENTS**: Father Chilean, a landowner and devout Catholic; mother Spanish **LIVED**: Santiago, 1911; Paris, 1933; New York, 1939; Paris and Rome, 1948; Europe and South America, 1950s and 1960s **PARTNERS**: Anne Alpert, née Clark, m. 1937; Patricia Kane, m.; Agnes Magruder, 1948; Angela Faranda; Malitte Pop; Germana Ferrari, m. **DIED**: 23 November 2002, Civitavecchia, Italy

Roberto Matta – known simply as Matta – was the greatest artist to come out of Chile and a key figure in the surrealist movement. Born in Santiago in 1911, he was slightly younger than the founders of the group. When André Breton produced his first surrealist manifesto, Matta was a schoolboy of thirteen, and it would be another decade before he made contact with the group in Paris.

Matta's maternal ancestors were Basques from northern Spain. His Chilean father was a landowner and his Spanish mother was a highly cultured woman who encouraged her son's interest in art, literature and languages. At university he studied architecture, and his mature paintings possess a strong structural quality; like designs for exploding buildings overrun by frantic humanoid biomorphs.

At twenty-two, Matta decided that Paris was where he had to be. He worked his passage across as a merchant seaman. Once there, he found a job in the offices of the great French architect, Le Corbusier.

In time Matta got to know Salvador Dalí and Gordon Onslow Ford, who encouraged his drawing, but his progress within the Parisian surrealist group was soon interrupted by the start of the Second World War. In 1939 he left France for the United States along with other fleeing surrealists. After arriving in New York he began exhibiting his work and was soon in touch with young American artists, who were fascinated by his compositions.

It was in New York that Matta's relationship with André Breton began to deteriorate. The problem was language: Matta spoke English fluently, and Breton did not. Worse still, Matta was university educated, verbally skilful and a good communicator. The surrealist refugees who had gathered in New York fascinated the young American artists and the person who, by rights, should have been at the centre of disseminating the surrealist doctrine was obviously the great leader, Breton himself; but he could not get his message across. Instead it was the eager, intelligent, handsome young Matta who began organizing meetings and seminars. So it was no great surprise to anyone when, in 1948, Breton found an excuse to expel him from the surrealist group. In 1949 Matta moved to Rome and did not return to Paris until 1954. Then, in 1959, during an extraordinary surrealist evening, he was finally reinstated into the group by Breton. The occasion was a celebration of the Marquis de Sade, featuring a masked performer who took hold of a red-hot iron and branded his flesh with the word SADE. He then invited any member of the audience to do the same and Matta rushed up, tore open his shirt and branded his chest in the same way. Breton, who was present, was staggered by this extraordinary act, and two days later issued a formal surrealist communiqué reinstating Matta.

Matta's reputation in the art world was spreading and during the 1960s and 1970s he was awarded major retrospectives. He summed up his life's work succinctly with the words: 'I am interested only in the unknown and I work for my own astonishment.' By the time of his death at the age of ninety-one, Matta had become greatly respected in the country of his birth. On hearing the news, the president of Chile declared three days of national mourning – an honour that few artists have ever received.

# F. E. McWILLIAM

## The best surrealist sculptor
## to come out of Ireland



**BORN**: 30 April 1909, Banbridge, County Down, Northern Ireland, as Frederick Edward McWilliam **PARENTS**: Father a doctor **LIVED**: Banbridge, 1909; Belfast, 1926; London, 1928; India (in RAF), 1944; London, 1946 **PARTNER**: Beth Crowther, m. 1932–88 **DIED**: 3 May 1992, London

The Irish sculptor F. E. McWilliam, known to his friends simply as 'Mac', belongs to that class of artist who produced important surrealist work but rejected any kind of group activity. He admired the surrealists for wanting to let the imagination run freely, but would never have attended any of their meetings.

McWilliam was born in Banbridge, a small town in Northern Ireland. The son of the local doctor, he had an idyllic childhood, the only dark cloud being the sectarian disputes between Catholics and Protestants. It was this needless violence that gave him his lifelong hatred of group allegiance, and for the rest of his life he would remain a loner – a devoted non-joiner.

A by-product of this was that, once he had developed a particular style of sculpture, he felt restricted by it and had to switch to something different. It was as though he had to 'un-join' himself, even from his own work. This creative restlessness meant he never reached the level of fame enjoyed by some other sculptors of his generation, such as Henry Moore or Barbara Hepworth.

After studying at the Belfast College of Art, McWilliam left Ireland and, still a teenager, moved to London in 1928. There he attended the Slade School of Art, where he met Moore, who would become a lifelong friend, and Beth Crowther, who would later become his wife – they would remain together until her death in 1988. McWilliam won a scholarship that enabled him to spend time in Paris in 1931, at the height of the surrealist explosion.

In 1936 he visited the International Surrealist Exhibition in London and was fascinated by what he saw there. In 1937 he began exhibiting with the surrealists, saying 'I chose the surrealist camp because of its more liberal, non-doctrinaire attitude.' He continued to show with them until the Second World War broke out, when he joined the Royal Air Force. After the war he returned to London and ended up in charge of the sculpture department at the Slade School, a post he would retain for twenty-one years.

In the 1980s, during a severe storm, an ancient mulberry tree was uprooted in the McWilliams' garden. Its trunk was twisted into all kinds of exciting knobs and lumps; McWilliam cut it into pieces and converted them into tortured sculptural shapes unlike anything he had done before. Once again, in his restless way, he had moved on and adopted a new style.

F. E. McWilliam's life's work can be divided into seven main periods, each quite different from the others, thanks to his restless curiosity. These were: his wood carvings of the mid-1930s; his stone carvings of the late 1930s and the late 1940s; his rough-surface bronze figures of the 1950s; his sharply pointed compositions of the early 1960s; his playful bean figures of the mid-1960s; his disembodied, elongated bronze legs of the late 1970s and early 1980s; and finally, his mulberry tree-trunk wood carvings of the late 1980s.

In 2009, his hometown of Banbridge in Northern Ireland honoured him by opening a McWilliam Gallery and Studio – complete with a sculpture garden, a reconstruction of his workshop, a permanent display of his work, and a large exhibition space.

# OSCAR MELLOR

## The very private surrealist with a persistently erotic imagery

**BORN**: 7 June 1921, Manchester **LIVED**: Manchester, 1921; Birmingham, 1939; Oxford, 1948; Swinford, near Oxford, 1959; Exeter, 1969 **PARTNERS**: Iris Poulton, m. 1948–67; Yvonne Taylor, m. 1969–78; Maureen Sandford, m. 1983–2005 **DIED**: 24 October 2005, Exeter

Oscar Mellor was born in 1921 and grew up in Manchester, where his father had his own business in the cotton industry. Mellor's earliest surviving painting dates from 1936, when he was fifteen years old, and already shows strong surrealist influences. The approach of war hit the already ailing cotton industry hard and in 1939 the family moved to Birmingham, where Mellor's father found employment in a firm making shrouds.

Mellor volunteered to serve in the Royal Air Force in 1940 and was accepted in 1942, training at various locations in England and Canada. Demobbed in 1946, he joined the surrealist circle that had gathered around Conroy Maddox in Birmingham, and by the late 1940s he was fully engaged with surrealist activities. His paintings were skilfully executed in meticulous detail, depicting human figures – often nude women – engaged in dreamlike rituals.

Mellor was one of the founder members of the Birmingham Artists Committee, an avant-garde organization set up in opposition to the conservative Royal Birmingham Society of Artists. He exhibited in their annual group shows between 1947 and 1951, alongside other Birmingham surrealists.

He married Iris Poulton in 1948 and they moved from Birmingham to Oxford, where Mellor studied at the Ruskin School of Art from 1948 to 1951. He and Iris then established the Fantasy Press, publishing surrealist poetry and other documents, carrying out all the printing and binding work themselves. Mellor's paintings during the 1950s included a strange series of portraits of women with large, winged insects. His landscapes were often bleak and the mood of his pictures at this time was usually haunted – and haunting. Around this time he also began working as a professional photographer, and in 1966 he was elected an Associate of the Royal Photographic Society.

Mellor's paintings now began to focus more and more on the female form. He was led astray from pure surrealism by his association with the Nicholas Treadwell Gallery in London. Treadwell was obsessed with erotic images and encouraged his stable of artists to make their paintings more and more sexually explicit. Mellor was swept along by this trend and it distracted him from his serious work. It was a relief to his friends when he eventually broke free of Treadwell's influence and, later in life, returned to mainstream surrealist works once again.

He and Iris were divorced in 1967 and he then moved from Oxford to Exeter in Devon, where he became senior lecturer in photography at the Exeter College of Art. In 1969 he married Yvonne Taylor, whom he had met while she was a student at St Anne's College in Oxford.

He and Yvonne were divorced in 1978. In the 1980s, following his retirement from college teaching, Mellor was able to devote much more time to his canvases. He pulled together, again in meticulous detail, all the various elements and symbols that had fascinated him over the years. Strange light bulbs, candles, lions, lamps, mirrors, lobsters, waterfalls, butterflies, brides and bulls milled around in dreamlike scenes, rendered with the academic precision of traditional art.

Mellor married for a third time in 1983, to Maureen Sandford. In 1996, at the age of seventy-five, he suffered a serious stroke that ended his painting career. Following a long illness, he died in 2005.

# JOHN MELVILLE

## One of the forgotten surrealists whose involvement, although brief, produced some major works

**BORN**: 25 August 1902, London
**LIVED**: London, 1902; Birmingham, 1913
**PARTNER**: Lily Beatrice (Betty) Samuel, m. 1929
**DIED**: 8 December 1986

John Melville is one of the forgotten surrealists of British art. Although he did produce some important surrealist paintings in the 1930s, for him it was only a passing phase. Also, he did not live in London, where most of the British surrealists were gathered, and he was not represented at the major International Surrealist Exhibition in London in 1936. This had the effect of sidelining him.

Melville was born in London but when he was a teenager his family moved to Birmingham, where he spent the rest of his life. He was largely self taught, although he did attend some classes at the Birmingham College of Art. His brother Robert shared his feelings about modern art and would later become an important author and critic, specializing in surrealist work.

In 1938, at the height of his surrealist phase, six of John Melville's paintings were banned from inclusion in an exhibition in Birmingham on the grounds that they were 'detrimental to public sensibilities'. Melville tried to defend himself in the local press, but to no avail.

His most famous work, *The Museum of Natural History of the Child*, described as one of the key paintings of British surrealism, labels him clearly as one of the paradoxical surrealists, with a realistic portrayal of a bizarre event in which a child, bent forward, is seen carrying a heavy wooden chair upside down on her back. She is approaching an outsized apple, sliced in half, out of which a phallic blue caterpillar is emerging and aiming itelf at her body. In the background, insects and bits of floating vegetation drift through a window. The atmosphere of this haunting scene is oppressive and strangely sinister, despite its attractive colours. It shows that Melville had grasped one of the central ideas of surrealism – the disturbing power of an irrational arrangement of familiar figures and objects, presented in a realistic, conventional style.

Melville had a reputation as something of a purist, intolerant of those who did not become totally immersed in the principles of surrealism. It has often been said that he refused to exhibit at the 1936 International Surrealist Exhibition in London because too many non-surrealists had been included in the show. This criticism was certainly justified, but was it the real reason for Melville not participating? When David Gascoyne, who had helped to organize the exhibition, was asked why Melville had not been included, he replied rather sheepishly 'We didn't know about him.' In other words, Melville could not have refused to exhibit, because he was not asked in the first place.

Whatever the truth, the fact remains that the Birmingham enclave were out of the limelight in 1936, so it is not surprising that in 1938 Melville joined the London group of surrealists in the hope of becoming better known. Unfortunately, his hopes were derailed by the start of the Second World War in 1939. After the war, his art was negelected for many years and the important surrealist paintings he had done in the 1930s were overlooked. He himself had seemingly had enough of the surrealist crusade and moved on to other types of work.

Melville's reputation was eventually revived when, fifty years after the 1936 exhibition, that seminal event was commemorated with a number of anniversary shows. This time he was included among the exhibitors and his work was, at last, singled out for the praise it deserved.

# E. L. T. MESENS

## The inspirational Belgian martinet who ruled British surrealism

**BORN**: 27 November 1903, Brussels, as Édouard Léon Théodore Mesens **PARENTS**: Father a druggist selling patent medicines **LIVED**: Brussels, 1903; London, 1938; Brussels, 1951 **PARTNERS**: Norine van Hecke, 1920s; Peggy Guggenheim, 1938; Sybil (née Fenton) Stephenson, m. 1943–66 **DIED**: 13 May 1971, Brussels

Édouard Mesens was to London what André Breton was to Paris – the leader of the pack, the alpha surrealist. He was born in 1903 in Brussels, where his father owned a pharmacy. As a boy he seemed destined for a musical career, and he did become an accomplished musician; however, at the age of twenty he abruptly gave up music and turned his attentions to surrealism. The moment of truth for him was a visit to Magritte's first exhibition in 1920. They became lifelong friends; Magritte would even let Mesens watch him painting. As time passed, Mesens began making collages. He never had the technical skill to become a painter, but his collages did show a remarkably poetic imagination.

In 1936 he was brought over to London to help organize the important International Surrealist Exhibition of that year. On arrival, he took one look around and immediately began to rehang the entire show. Recognizing the strength of his surrealist credentials, Roland Penrose decided to set him up with his own gallery – the London Gallery – which Mesens ran from 1938 to 1940 and again, after the Second World War, from 1946 to 1950. Throughout this period, Mesens was the nerve centre of the movement in Britain, and when he lost his gallery the movement died. Surrealist art continued, of course, and still does; but as an active art movement with official meetings, tracts, declarations, disputes and expulsions, it ceased to exist.

Once the London Gallery was up and running in 1938, Mesens started to gather around him all the British surrealists still working in the field. At one of these meetings he insisted that official members of his group must obey Breton's strict rules of behaviour. This meant that, among other things, they could not exhibit their paintings alongside non-surrealist work, could not engage in any kind of religious behaviour, and could not belong to any non-surrealist organizations. These rules excluded a number of members and Mesens found himself with a greatly reduced team.

At the end of the war Mesens relaunched the London Gallery, now at a new address in Brook Street, with an exhibition of the work of Wifredo Lam. As before, the gallery became the centre of all surrealist activity in London, but in April 1950 it was forced to close down. In the exhausted mood of post-war austerity, surrealist painting was simply not selling, and the gallery was losing too much money to continue.

In the years that followed Mesens busied himself with organizing exhibitions in Belgium and, in 1954, began to devote much more time to making his own collages. In the 1960s he held a number of solo exhibitions of his work, but it was a sad decade for him; his wife, Sybil, died of leukaemia in 1966, and his lifelong friend Magritte died the following year.

Mesens himself did not live much longer. He died in a Brussels nursing home in 1971 – a rich man because of his collection of surrealist masterpieces, assembled over many years. His final weeks were painful, and he did his best to shorten them by consuming large quantities of alcohol when it was expressly forbidden by his doctors. A friend described his death as 'suicide by absinthe'.

# JOAN MIRÓ

## The unrivalled Catalan genius of the surrealism movement

**BORN**: 20 April 1893, Barcelona  **PARENTS**: Father a watchmaker  **LIVED**: Barcelona, 1893; Montroig, Tarragona and Barcelona, 1910; Paris, 1920; Barcelona, 1932; Paris, 1936; Normandy, 1939; Palma, Majorca, 1940; Barcelona, 1942; Palma, Majorca, 1956  **PARTNER**: Pilar Juncosa, m. 1929  **DIED**: 25 December 1983, Palma

Born in Barcelona in 1893, the grandson of a blacksmith and the son of a goldsmith who was also a watchmaker, Joan Miró was, by his own admission, a poor pupil at school. He described himself as a daydreaming misfit. By the age of eight he was already busy making drawings. In 1912, when he was nineteen, he encountered modern art for the first time when he visited an exhibition of cubist art in Barcelona.

In 1920 he moved to Paris, where he visited Picasso in his studio and explored the city's museums and galleries. From this point on he developed an annual pattern of winters in Paris and summers at the family farm in Montroig, south of Barcelona. It was there in 1921 that he produced his first major work – called simply *The Farm* – which he sold to Ernest Hemingway.

In Paris, his neighbour was André Masson, who became a close friend and introduced him to the Parisian avant-garde. By 1923 Miró was creating works that involved wild visual distortions and dramatic modifications of the natural world, and by 1924 he had somehow managed to fling off all traditional influences.

Miró was happy to participate in surrealist exhibitions but he did not care for Breton's rules and regulations, and he never signed any manifestos or attended any group meetings. In an interview in 1931 he said: 'I consider surrealism an extremely interesting intellectual phenomenon...but I don't want to subject myself to its severe discipline.' Whether he liked it or not, though, his work placed him at the very core of the surrealist movement – and to be fair to Breton, he did recognize this. When Miró produced his brilliant *Constellations* series in the 1940s, Breton found them very moving, calling them 'these superb paintings that appeared quite naturally as floodgates from which love and liberty gushed forth in a single stream'. Miró may have rejected Breton's leadership, but Breton could not bring himself to reject Miró.

When the Second World War began, Miró decided to return to Spain even though Franco was in power. He avoided the mainland and settled on the island of Majorca. Later, in 1956, he moved into the house that would remain his home until his death in 1983. Called So N'Abrines, it was on a hill above Palma. All his life he had dreamed of owning a large studio and now, at last, he had one. Perhaps because of its size, his later work was much more powerful, largely lacking in the refined figures he had perfected in the forties and fifties.

Miró's personal life was largely uneventful. Unlike many other surrealists, he was not interested in drunken parties, sexual adventures or other typical forms of surrealist decadence. His wild acts of rebellion were reserved for his canvases. At home, his family life was very ordinary. He had married in 1929 and his cheerful wife, Pilar, hailed from Palma, so for her, settling there was a matter of coming home. They had one daughter, who gave them three grandchildren. Joan and Pilar Miró remained happily married for fifty-four years, until his death from heart failure on Christmas Day in 1983 at the age of ninety.

After his death, two Miró Foundations were established: one in Barcelona and another in Palma. In Palma it is possible to visit Miró's large studio, still arranged exactly as he left it on the day he died.

# PIERRE MOLINIER



**BORN**: 13 April 1900, Agen, France  **PARENTS**: Father a house painter and decorator; mother a dressmaker  **LIVED**: Agen, 1900; Paris, 1920; Bordeaux, 1923–76  **PARTNERS**: Andrea Lafaye, m. 1931–6; Emmanuelle Arsan (Marayat Rollet-Andriane); Hanel Koeck  **DIED**: 3 March 1976, Bordeaux

Pierre Molinier's whole existence was a surrealist work of art. He devoted himself to elevating depravity to the level of an art form. Every kind of sexual excess was like a magnet that he had to explore; actions which would have been most men's darkest secrets were for him events to be shared proudly with others. He defined eroticism as 'a privileged place…where the most profound moments of life make sport'.

The son of a house painter, Molinier began working for his father when he was thirteen and attended art school in the evenings. After a period of military service from 1920 to 1922 he spent several years in Paris, but eventually he moved to Bordeaux, where he would remain for the rest of his life. He lived in the same cramped apartment from 1931 until his death in 1976.

In 1950 he built his own 'Premature Tomb', on which he engraved the words:

*Here lies Pierre MOLINIER – born on 13 April 1900 – died around 1950 – he was a man without morals – he was proud of it – and gloried in it – no need to pray for him.*

The following year, after one of his explicit paintings caused a scandal in Bordeaux, he decided to switch his attention to Paris. In 1955 he sent a portfolio of his work to André Breton, who was immediately captivated by his outrageous imagery and organized a Paris show of his paintings and drawings.

Molinier continually pushed the boundaries of socially acceptable behaviour in his day-to-day life as he developed his artistic practice. In 1960 he was imprisoned for assaulting his estranged wife when she visited the family home, and in 1961 she was finally granted a divorce.

Excited by the controversial novel *Emmanuelle* – which would later be made into a series of famous erotic films – in 1964 he contacted its author, Emmanuelle Arsan. This was, it turned out, a pen name used by Marayat Rollet-Andriane and her diplomat husband – Molinier then developed a passionate relationship with Marayat. He also became better acquainted with other surrealist artists during this period, notably Clovis Trouille and Hans Bellmer.

Molinier's excesses continued to appeal to Breton. In the 1965 edition of *Surrealism and Painting*, Breton devotes a whole chapter to his work and heaps praise upon him: 'I have no fear in saying that, with Molinier, things will be different now. A silken ladder has at last been thrown from the world of dreams to the other world, which proves conclusively that this other world could only be that of carnal temptation.'

Molinier met Hanel Koeck, a German art student and leg fetishist, in 1967 and once again began a passionate relationship, with the much younger Koeck offering herself as a model for some of his more outlandish paintings and photomontages.

In 1975, Molinier's adult son died in an accident while handling explosives. Molinier's own death the following year was as bizarre as his life. Having left his body to medical science, he prepared by painting his toenails bright red to amuse the students who would be dissecting his corpse. He then stood in front of a mirror, placed a gun in his mouth and watched himself as he pulled the trigger, hoping to last long enough to see the back of his head explode. Whether he fulfilled this final, depraved desire, if only for a fraction of a second, we will never know.

# HENRY MOORE



## The greatest surrealist sculptor of the 20th century, foolishly expelled by the movement

**BORN**: 30 July 1898, Castleford, West Yorkshire
**PARENTS**: Father a colliery under-manager, of Irish origin
**LIVED**: Castleford, 1898; Leeds, 1919; London, 1921; Hampstead, 1929; Perry Green, Hertfordshire, 1940
**PARTNER**: Irina Radetsky, m. 1929
**DIED**: 31 August 1986, Perry Green, Hertfordshire

Henry Moore was born in a Yorkshire mining town, the sixth of seven children of a tough coal miner. The family lived in a house so small that the children always had to sleep three or four in a bed, but Moore was lucky because his father, whose word was law, respected learning and wanted his children to be well educated.

Moore was also encouraged to go out into the local countryside, where he became fascinated by piles of rocks he came across in the woodlands. One pile in particular looked like a sphinx worn smooth by time, an image he never forgot. When he was eleven he decided that he wanted to be a sculptor, but first he became a school teacher. This career was interrupted by the First World War, in which he served and was lucky to survive. After one battle, he was one of only forty-two left alive from a group of 400 men.

After the war, Moore was given a grant that enabled him to attend Leeds School of Art and pursue his sculptural work in earnest. Later, he moved to London and the Royal College of Art. There he lived in Chelsea in a room that was only eight by nine feet – but he loved it, because he didn't have to share it.

At college, he hated still life classes and would sneak off if he had the chance. One day, he idly opened some old drawers in the corner of an art room. Inside he found some dusty animal bones that had long ago been used for drawing lessons. Fascinated by their shapes, he began sketching them. These biomorphic shapes would become the very basis of his later work, in which he saw beneath the surface of human and animal forms to get at their structural essence.

It was later, when he was teaching at the Royal College of Art, that Moore met the Russian/Polish art student Irina Radetsky, who became his wife and his lifelong partner. They moved out of London and bought a farmhouse near Much Hadham, Hertfordshire, where they would live for the rest of their lives.

When Moore first visited Paris in the early 1930s, he met André Breton and encountered the work of sculptors like Arp and Giacometti. He disliked some aspects of the movement but admired the openness of its ideas and its encouragement of unconscious experimentation. The way he was starting to play with the human form, metamorphosing it in various ways in his sculptures, fitted well with the surrealist approach. He became seriously involved with the movement in 1936, when Roland Penrose began organizing the major International Surrealist Exhibition in London. Moore was elected the treasurer of the British Organizing Committee and contributed four pieces to the exhibition.

In 1944 Moore accepted a commission to make a Madonna and Child for a church in Northampton, breaking one of the cardinal rules of surrealism. This led to his expulsion from the group. But he had taken what he wanted from the movement and enjoyed the release it had given him, freeing him from conscious control to create excitingly novel forms. Today, he is regarded as the most original sculptor of the 20th century.

# PAUL NASH



## The pastoral landscapist who had a brief but significant affair with surrealism in the 1930s

**BORN:** 11 May 1889, Kensington, London **PARENTS:** Father a barrister; mother mentally unstable **LIVED:** London, 1889; Western front in the First World War, 1917; Dymchurch, Kent, 1921; Rye, 1925; Swanage, 1934; London, 1936; Oxford, 1939 **PARTNER:** Margaret Odeh, m. 1914–46; Eileen Agar, 1935–44 **DIED:** 11 July 1946, Boscombe, Dorset

Paul Nash is something of a contradiction. He was a leading light in the British surrealist movement but at heart he was a pastoral landscape artist. He seems somehow out of place in the rebellious world of the true surrealists, and yet his mysterious images of the 1930s demand that we consider him in their company.

Nash was born in London, the son of a barrister. When he was thirteen the family moved out of the city and he was able to grow up in the countryside, becoming absorbed in the English rural scene. His mother suffered from severe mental illness and died young, in an institution, when Nash was twenty-one. He studied at the Slade School in London and his year was a remarkable one, with his fellow students including Edward Wadsworth, Ben Nicholson and Stanley Spencer.

He was twenty-five when war broke out in 1914 and he joined the army, where he was given the rather strange duty of guarding the Tower of London. Before the end of that year he had married Margaret Odeh, an Oxford-educated suffragette. In 1917 he was sent to the Western front, where he started making sketches of the terrible scenes he encountered there. He was lucky to survive, nearly his entire unit being killed in fierce fighting. Back in London, he applied to become an official war artist and returned to France to begin the gruesome task of portraying the horrors of trench warfare. It was his disgust at the appalling slaughter that probably primed him to join the anti-establishment surrealists in the 1930s.

After the war, his paintings of the devastated landscape of the trenches brought him national fame, and he went on to become a successful landscape artist. Then, in 1928, he made a deliberate change, moving towards surrealism. It was in that year that he visited an exhibition of the early work of de Chirico in London, and the Italian's haunted compositions made a big impact on him.

In the years that followed Nash became obsessed with prehistoric standing stones and other ancient monuments. He began to collect surrealist objects – strangely shaped flints and flotsam from the south coast of England. At Swanage in 1935 he met the surrealist artist Eileen Agar and fell in love with her. They began a lengthy affair that caused trouble for both of their marriages.

In 1936 Nash and his wife moved to Hampstead in north London, and it was there that he at last became fully engaged with the world of the surrealists. His new neighbour, Roland Penrose, was busy organizing the big International Surrealist Exhibition, and Nash joined the committee and helped with the selection of contributing artists. His own work was also shown – four oils, five collages and three surrealist objects. His work was praised by such major figures as André Breton, Max Ernst and René Magritte. Magritte called him 'The Master of the Object' – which, coming from him, was praise indeed.

By the mid-1940s it was clear that Nash was beginning to lose a long battle with asthma, and his poor health was causing increasing concern. In 1946, while on holiday on the south coast, he suffered a heart attack and died at the early age of fifty-seven.

# RICHARD OELZE



## The gloomiest of all the surrealists, whose skilful work is so depressing that he remains little known

**BORN**: 29 June 1900, Magdeburg, Germany **LIVED**: Magdeburg, 1900; Bauhaus at Weimar and then Dessau, 1921; Dresden, 1926; Ascona, Switzerland, 1929; Berlin, 1930; Paris, 1932; Switzerland and Italy, 1936; Germany, 1938; Worpswede, Germany, 1939; German army, 1941; Worpswede, 1946; Posteholz, 1962 **PARTNER**: Norma Pflugstert, m. late 1920s–32 **DIED**: 27 May 1980, Gut Posteholz, near Hameln

Richard Oelze was a highly inventive German surrealist with exceptional technical skill, and yet he remains virtually unknown. He was a biomorphic surrealist who created an imaginary world of sinister landscapes peopled with shapes that hint at human qualities, but are confused and ambiguous. One reason Oelze is not more popular may be that his palette is so gloomy – almost always ranging from dull browns to dull greys – and the atmosphere he creates in his 'other world' is relentlessly dark and depressing.

Richard Oelze was born in the German city of Magdeburg at the start of the 20th century. His date of birth condemned him to fight in the German army in both world wars, a fact that may have contributed to the gloomy nature of his art. After the First World War he enrolled at the Bauhaus in 1921, where he was lucky enough to be taught by Paul Klee; Klee also gave him private tuition. In 1926 Oelze moved to Dresden, where he became actively involved in the local art world and met the surrealist filmmaker

Hans Richter. They worked together on experimental projects. Oelze moved to Switzerland in 1929, where he met up with the surrealists there. In 1930 he returned to Germany, living in Berlin until, in 1932, following a divorce, he decided that Paris was where he had to be.

In the French capital, he became involved with André Breton, Max Ernst, Leonor Fini, Victor Brauner and Salvador Dalí and started exhibiting his work in major surrealist group shows. He had five pieces in the 1936 International Surrealist Exhibition in London and was also represented at the 'Fantastic Art, Dada, Surrealism' show at the Museum of Modern Art in New York that same year.

His most famous painting, *The Expectation* (1936), ended up in the permanent MoMA collection and is the one by which most people know his name. It has been interpreted as a warning of the looming conflict in Europe. As the Second World War approached, Oelze did not flee to America like the other surrealists, but instead served in the Germany army. He was captured and held as a prisoner of war by the Allies. When he was released at the end of the war, he returned to Germany. From the early 1960s onwards he made his home in Posteholz in central Germany and lived a quiet, reserved life, although he still exhibited regularly, including a major retrospective at Hanover in 1964.

Oelze remains a mysterious figure. He was intensely private, quietly transferring his haunted dreams to canvas in his studio. While with the surrealists in Paris during the 1930s, he had reportedly been very introverted – as well as addicted to opium and living in misery, all of which fits with the general mood of his paintings. Towards the end of his life he became too weak to paint and developed agoraphobia, so that he completely stopped leaving his house.

He died in 1980, one month short of his eightieth birthday. He received several posthumous honours in Germany, and in his birthplace of Magdeburg they named a street after him: the Oelzeweg.

# GORDON ONSLOW FORD

## The British artist who referred to his work as spontaneous abstract surrealism

Gordon Onslow Ford was born into a family of artists in southern England before the First World War. His grandfather was the well-known Victorian sculptor Edward Onslow Ford, and both of his parents were artists; he himself knew from a very early age that he wanted to be a painter. Reminiscing, he said that the great advantage of being a painter was that you didn't have to know anything – if you were stuffed with too much knowledge it could interfere with the directness of your visually creative actions.

When Onslow Ford was fourteen, his father died and he was packed off to the Royal Naval College at Dartmouth. The visual impact of the ocean had a deep effect on him, but after some years as a naval officer he decided to pursue his first love of painting, and in 1937 he resigned his commission and moved to Paris.

He made friends with the Chilean surrealist Matta, and they spent a whole summer discussing surrealism. Together they began attending Breton's gatherings at Les Deux Magots in Montmartre. After a while, Breton took notice of Onslow Ford and visited his studio. In 1938 he invited him to become an official member of his surrealist group. Through Breton's introduction, Onslow Ford was then able to make contact with other important surrealists including

**BORN**: 26 December 1912, Wendover, Buckinghamshire
**PARENTS**: From an artistic family
**LIVED**: Wendover, 1912; Dartmouth, 1926; Paris, 1937; New York, 1939; Erongaricuaro, Mexico, 1941; San Francisco, 1947; Inverness, California, 1957
**PARTNER**: Jacqueline Johnson, m. 1941
**DIED**: 9 November 2003, Inverness, California

Tanguy, Ernst, Brauner, Miró and Masson. Breton admired what Onslow Ford was doing, saying that he depicted 'a kind of world in which the last clear angles of cubism are fragmented'.

Just before the Second World War broke out, Onslow Ford rented a château in eastern France and entertained his friends there – a last summer idyll before hostilities began. Breton and his wife, Tanguy and Kay Sage, Matta and Esteban Francés were all guests, painting and discussing the future of surrealism. A few months later, that future became a group exile in America as they all fled the Nazi invasion.

In New York, some of the surrealist émigrés struggled with the language barrier, but English-speaking Onslow Ford found himself suddenly at a social advantage and was invited to give a series of lectures on surrealism. It was at one of these that he met an American writer called Jacqueline Johnson. They were married in 1941 and moved to Mexico, settling in a remote Tarascan Indian village. There they were visited by many of their surrealist friends, including Wolfgang Paalen, who was also a near neighbour, Matta, Remedios Varo and Esteban Francés.

After six years in Mexico, Onslow Ford and his wife moved to California in 1947 and he became an American citizen. They settled in the artists' colony of Sausalito, across the bay from San Francisco, converting an old ferryboat into a studio. In 1948 the San Francisco Museum of Art gave Onslow Ford a major retrospective.

During the second half of his life he became immersed in eastern religions, and the quality of his painting deteriorated. He himself saw it as a natural progression, saying, 'We are continuing surrealism on a deeper level.' To his critics, however, his work seemed to have become shallower. This unfortunate state of affairs persisted late into his life – a sad end to what had been such a promising beginning – but his early work survives to remind us of his considerable achievements.

Onslow Ford died of a stroke at the age of ninety, in 2003.

# MERET OPPENHEIM

## The surrealist whose life was dominated by her iconic fur-covered cup and saucer

**BORN**: 6 October 1913, Charlottenburg, Berlin **PARENTS**: Father a German Jewish doctor; mother Swiss **LIVED**: Berlin, 1913; Delemont, Switzerland, 1914; Steinen, Germany, 1918; Basel, 1929–30; Paris, 1932; Basel, 1937; Bern, 1954 **PARTNER**: Man Ray, 1933; Max Ernst, 1934–5; Wolfgang La Roche, m. 1949–67 **DIED**: 15 November 1985, Basel

Meret Oppenheim was born in a wealthy suburb of Berlin just before the outbreak of the First World War. Her German father was a Jewish doctor, her mother Swiss. During her childhood, from the age of seven, she showed a passion for drawing and painting. As she was growing up, she encountered the work of the Swiss master Paul Klee, which impressed her greatly. Her parents were worried that she was neglecting her other studies and sent her to Carl Jung for analysis – once he had reassured them that there was nothing to worry about, they agreed to let her go to art school.

In 1932, when she was eighteen, the rebellious, free-spirited Oppenheim moved to Paris. It was there that she met Giacometti and, through him, Arp. The two of them visited her studio, and were so impressed by her work that they invited her to exhibit with them. Soon, Oppenheim was meeting with André Breton and joining in the notorious surrealist gatherings in local cafés. She impressed the surrealists with her uninhibited behaviour and was celebrated by them as the 'fairy woman whom all men desire'.

Oppenheim's first moment of real notoriety arrived with a photographic session arranged by Man

Ray in 1933. He had her pose next to a large printing press, stark naked and with a long smear of printer's ink down the underside of her left forearm and hand. She was not happy with the resulting photographs, but the two of them still ended up in bed.

There was another male surrealist that Oppenheim could not resist: in 1934 she began a year-long, passionate love affair with the charming, charismatic Max Ernst. He had just ended a relationship with the artist Leonor Fini and was now captivated by the free-spirited Oppenheim. Soon, however, she felt stifled by him, and she ended things in 1935.

Her rise to international fame was the result of a passing remark made by Pablo Picasso. Early in 1936, they were drinking coffee together in a Paris café and Oppenheim happened to be wearing a fur-lined metal bracelet that she had designed herself. Picasso, intrigued by the unusual combination of fur and metal, jokingly commented that one could cover anything with fur. Oppenheim picked up her cup and saucer and said 'Even this?' On leaving the café she went straight to a department store and bought a cup, saucer and spoon, which she then carefully lined with the fur of a Chinese gazelle. This disconcerting object was exhibited in May 1936 in Paris, causing a sensation. It was described as the 'quintessential surrealist object'. Later it was acquired by the Museum of Modern Art in New York and became one of the most famous of all surrealist images, along with Dalí's soft watches and Duchamp's urinal.

In 1937, after five years in Paris, Oppenheim was forced to abandon the city for financial reasons and return to Switzerland. A black cloud descended over her at this point and she sank into a depression that would last for seventeen years, until 1954. She was quoted as saying that she had experienced a 'suffocating sense of inferiority' – but then, as suddenly as it had arrived, her depression lifted and she was able to enjoy an active, creative existence for the last thirty years of her life.

# WOLFGANG PAALEN

## The only surrealist to be eaten by wild animals



**BORN**: 22 July 1905, Baden, near Vienna **PARENTS**: Father an Austrian Jewish merchant and inventor; mother a German actress **LIVED**: Baden, 1905; Rochusburg in Sagan, Silesia, 1913; Rome, 1919; Berlin, 1921; Paris, 1924; La Ciotat, Cassis, 1927; Paris, 1929; New York, 1939; Mexico, 1939; Paris, 1951; Mexico, 1953 **PARTNERS**: Helene Meier-Graefe, 1922; Eva Sulzer, 1929–1950s; Alice Rahon, m. 1934–47; Luchita Hurtado del Solar, m. 1947–50; Isabel Marin, m. 1957–9 **DIED**: 24 September 1959, Taxco, Mexico

Wolfgang Paalen has the dubious distinction of being the only surrealist to have been eaten by wild animals.

Paalen was born near Vienna in 1905. His father, Gustav, was an inventor and his mother, Clothilde, was a German actress. Gustav had made a fortune by developing and patenting the Thermos flask. The family lived in a castle that he had restored, among an impressive collection of old masters including works by Goya, Titian and Cranach.

Young Wolfgang was educated at home by a private tutor. When the First World War ended, the family decided to move to Italy, and in 1919 they acquired a palatial villa near Rome. It was there that Paalen started taking painting lessons from visiting artists. In 1929 he clashed with his father, who hated the kind of modern art that his son was now producing. Wolfgang refused to give it up and was promptly disinherited. Fortunately for him, in the same year he met Eva Sulzer, heiress to a vast Swiss industrial fortune, and she took over as his sponsor.

Paalen settled in Paris, where in 1934 he married the poet and artist Alice Rohan. He started exhibiting with the surrealists and soon began his so-called

Totemic Period, creating a fascinating world of spiky figures in alien landscapes that would make his reputation as a major surrealist artist.

In May 1939, ahead of all the other surrealists, he and Rohan decided to leave Europe. At the invitation of Frida Kahlo, they moved to Mexico. Part of the appeal was the country's wonderful pre-Columbian art; Paalen began to make a collection of ancient figures, which he studied closely. The abstract paintings he created during this period were exhibited in New York and would serve as an important stimulus to the young American artists who later formed the abstract expressionist group. As the painter Fritz Bultman said: 'It was Wolfgang Paalen who started it all.'

When the war in Europe ended, Paalen became a Mexican citizen. Around the same time, his marriage to Alice began to disintegrate, and in 1947 they were divorced. He would marry twice more, the final time to Diego Rivera's sister-in-law, Isabel Marin, in 1957; but their marriage would be short-lived, because in 1959 Paalen dramatically ended his life. In the relative isolation of Mexico he had turned to illegal activity, becoming a major smuggler of pre-Columbian antiquities. Rumours about his crimes were starting to circulate and he must have felt that the world was closing in on him. On top of that, he had taken to excessive alcohol and drug use, and his waves of depression were getting worse.

One September night, he took a gun and climbed a hill south of Mexico City, heading for a favourite spot of his where he had often gone to meditate. When he reached it, he put the gun to his head and shot himself. His body was not found for days – except by some hungry wild pigs, who reportedly made a meal of him.

It was a troubling end to a life that had brought him great praise, not least from André Breton, who wrote of his work: 'I believe that no more serious effort has ever been made to apprehend the texture of the universe and make it perceptible to us.'

# GRACE PAILTHORPE

## The artist known as the ogre, who was obsessed with the therapeutic value of surrealism

**BORN**: 29 July 1883, St Leonard's-on-Sea, Sussex **PARENTS**: Members of the Plymouth Brethren, a puritanical religious sect; father a stockbroker, mother a seamstress **LIVED**: St Leonard's-on-Sea, Sussex, 1883; Redhill, Surrey; Southport, Lancashire, 1904; London, 1908; Durham, 1912; War service in France, England and Malta, 1914–18; Australia and New Zealand, 1919–21; Birmingham, 1922; London, 1930s; New York, 1940; Vancouver, 1941; London, 1948; Dorking, 1949 **PARTNER**: Reuben Mednikoff, 1935–71 **DIED**: 19 July 1971, St Leonard's-on-Sea

Grace Pailthorpe and her partner, Reuben Mednikoff, have been described as the eeriest couple in British art. They met in 1935 at a debauched party given by a friend of Aleister Crowley, the occultist known as 'the Great Beast'. While others present were busily engaged in satanic rituals, Pailthorpe and Mednikoff huddled together in a corner discussing how art could be used in the treatment of mental illness.

Within a few years Pailthorpe had written an essay that summed up their approach, called 'The Scientific Aspect of Surrealism'. In it, she drew a comparison between surrealism and psychoanalysis. She mistakenly saw surrealist art as some new kind of visual therapy – what she overlooked was that its true goal was the celebration of intuitive, irrational thought processes, not the curative value of those processes.

Grace Pailthorpe was a Victorian, born in 1883. Her father was a stockbroker and both parents were members of the Plymouth Brethren, a strict religious cult. She grew up with a strong sense of her duty to serve mankind and ended up as a field surgeon in France during the First World War, attending the wounded on the front lines.

In 1923 she joined the British Psychoanalytical Society and was in private practice when she met

Reuben Mednikoff at the satanic party in 1935. Mednikoff, a professional artist from a Russian Jewish family, was twenty-three years her junior, but they became an inseparable couple and remained so for the rest of their lives.

In the late 1930s Pailthorpe and Mednikoff both painted many 'experimental compositions' and they each had several paintings included in the important 1936 International Surrealist Exhibition in London, where their work was singled out for special praise by André Breton. After this they participated in a number of surrealist group shows in Europe, North America and Australia.

All was going well until they organized a meeting in 1940 of the British surrealist group, for the purpose of 'planning the reformation of the Surrealist group in England'. Édouard Mesens, leader of the group, pointed out that no member was allowed to belong to any other group or association – and on this basis Pailthorpe, as a member of the British Psychoanalytical Society, was automatically excluded.

Pailthorpe and Mednikoff were outraged to find themselves formally expelled. A month later they left England for America and then moved on to Canada, where they remained until the Second World War was over. During this period they exhibited their work at the Vancouver Art Gallery, and Pailthorpe delivered a major lecture on the subject of surrealism and psychology. They returned to England in 1946.

In the years that followed they would occasionally show their paintings together and they also started a School of Art Therapy. Pailthorpe died in 1971 at the age of eighty-seven. Within a few months, Mednikoff had also died.

Pailthorpe was a woman of contradictions. In 1939 she remarked, 'One overhears many reactions to Surrealist art, but the most pathetic of all is from those who ask, "What am I supposed to see and feel from this?"' In other words, she was saying that one should experience the work but not ask questions about it – and yet, it was to the consideration of these very questions that she devoted most of her adult life.

# MIMI PARENT

## The rebellious Canadian surrealist, whose ashes were scattered at the home of the Marquis de Sade

BORN: 8 September 1924, Montreal, as Marie Parent

PARENTS: Father an architect

LIVED: Montreal, 1924; Paris, 1948

PARTNER: Jean Benoît, m. 1948

DIED: 14 June 2005, Switzerland

The Canadian artist Mimi Parent was a second-generation surrealist, born in Montreal at the very moment that André Breton was publishing his first manifesto in Paris. Her father was an architect and she was the eighth of his nine children. She attended the School of Fine Arts in Montreal but was expelled in 1947 for rebellious behaviour. Later in her life, she wrote about her moment of rebellion: 'My own discovery of surrealism coincided with my growing awareness of the enemies of my freedom: Family, Fatherland, Religion.'

Her expulsion did not hold her back: she held her first solo exhibition in Montreal later in the same year. The following year, she married fellow artist Jean Benoît. Finding the Canadian art world too restrictive, the couple left Canada in 1948 to live and work in Paris, never to return to Canadian shores.

Soon they were meeting members of the surrealist movement and coming under their influence. In 1959, Parent met André Breton himself and became an official member of his circle. In the years that followed she participated in surrealist group exhibitions in addition to having solo shows of her own.

Breton welcomed her warmly, describing her as one of the 'vital forces' of surrealism. He was especially impressed by an event that she and Benoît presented on 2 December, 1959, the 145th anniversary of the Marquis de Sade's death. It was performed in front of an audience of about 200 people, all associated in some way with the surrealist movement. The evening began with a recording of Breton reading from Sade's *Justine*, accompanied by the soundtrack of an erupting volcano. Then Benoît entered, dressed as a devil and pulling behind him a black coffin with an erect penis protruding through its lid. Parent came forward and slowly removed Benoît's elaborate costume, piece by piece. Finally, when Benoît was naked except for a gigantic, erect wooden penis hanging around his waist, he took hold of a red-hot iron and branded himself with the word SADE above his heart.

With extreme surrealist performaces of this kind, it is little wonder that Parent and Benoît were welcomed into the fold by Breton. They gave the surrealist movement the vital boost that it badly needed in its final years, right up to its official demise in 1969, three years after Breton's death.

In 1970, Parent proclaimed that although the active movement in Paris had finally come to an end, she herself was not going to give up. She kept working and, in addition to her surrealist paintings, during her later years specialized in creating small glass-fronted boxes similar to the ones Joseph Cornell had made famous in New York.

Parent was a vibrant, passionate, vivacious woman with a wicked sense of humour, and her art has been called 'incorrigibly wild and absolute'. When she died in 2005, Benoît made a special pilgrimage to scatter her ashes in the grounds of the castle that had been the home of the Marquis de Sade – the Château de Lacoste – fifty miles north of Marseille in southern France.

André Breton summed up Mimi Parent with the words, 'In Mimi's thistle eyes shine Armida's enchanted gardens at midnight.'

# ROLAND PENROSE

**Joined the surrealist group in Paris, 1928; British surrealist group, 1936**

**BORN**: 14 October 1900, St John's Wood, London  **PARENTS**: Strict Quakers; father an Irish portrait painter, mother the daughter of a wealthy banker  **LIVED**: London, 1900; Oxhey Grange, Watford, 1908; Italy, 1918, with Red Cross; Cambridge, 1919; Paris, 1922; London, 1936; East Sussex, 1949  **PARTNERS**: Valentine Boué, m. 1925–39; Lee Miller, m. 1947–77; Diane Deriaz, 1979–84  **DIED**: 23 April 1984, East Sussex

Roland Penrose produced some major surrealist works, but they were somewhat overshadowed by his other high-profile activities. In addition to being an artist, he was also a highly motivated exhibition organizer, art collector, gallery owner and art historian – and very rich. He bankrolled the surrealist movement to such a degree that it is probably true to say it would have floundered without him.

Penrose was born while Queen Victoria was still on the throne. His mother, who had inherited a fortune from her banking ancestors, married an Irish artist; Roland and his brothers grew up in a strict Quaker household on a large estate. This background gave him his good manners and his kindness – and it also fuelled his rebellious spirit. The Penroses' home life was too rigidly puritanical for a small boy with a lively imagination. There were endless prayer meetings, which young Roland survived by daydreaming and enjoying wild, private fantasies.

During the First World War, while serving with the Red Cross in the field, Penrose encountered roads strewn with rotting corpses. It was a shocking experience for a teenager who had enjoyed such a sheltered upbringing, and left a deep mark on him.

After the war he gained a first in architecture at Cambridge, then moved to Paris to study modern art. Before long he had met and fallen in love with a wild surrealist poet called Valentine Boué. They were soon married and joined the close circle of surrealists gathered around André Breton. In 1930, after receiving his family inheritance, Penrose bought a château in Gascony and lived there with Valentine. He moved back to England in 1936, bought a house in London, and began organizing the first major surrealist exhibition there. It was a huge success, attracting more than 1,000 visitors every day, and established the movement firmly in the British art world.

By now, the Penroses' marriage was nearing its end. In 1939 they were divorced and Penrose took himself off to Paris. There he encountered a blonde, blue-eyed American model called Lee Miller, ex-lover of the American surrealist Man Ray. It was the start of a forty-year relationship that would only end with Miller's death in 1977.

During the Second World War, Penrose became an air raid warden and Miller a war photographer. After the war, Penrose was involved in discussions about opening a Museum of Modern Art in London to rival the one in New York. Instead, in 1946, he ended up founding the Institute of Contemporary Arts (ICA) – fostering anything that was new and outrageous in the world of fine art. He and Miller were married and welcomed their only child, a son called Antony. Two years later, the young family moved out of London to Farley Farm in Sussex, which would remain their home for the rest of their lives – frequently visited by the good and the great, including both Picasso and Miró.

In the 1960s Penrose was kept busy organizing massive retrospectives of work by Picasso and Miró, both good friends of his. His Picasso retrospective at the Tate was the most successful exhibition ever staged in Britain, attracting over 500,000 visitors.

Penrose's two dearest friends, Max Ernst and Man Ray, both died in 1976, and the following year it was Lee Miller's turn. Penrose was inconsolable. He lived on until 1984, saying before his death at Farley Farm, 'I want to go.'

# FRANCIS PICABIA

## The ex-dadaist who turned pieces of machinery into surrealist beings

**BORN**: 22 January 1879, Paris, as Francis-Marie Martínez de Picabia
**PARENTS**: Father a Cuban-born Spanish aristocrat, chancellor to the Cuban Embassy in Paris; mother French haute bourgeoisie **LIVED**: Paris, 1879; New York, 1915; Barcelona, 1916; New York, 1917; Paris, 1918; South of France, 1925; Paris, 1937; South of France, 1939; Paris, 1945 **PARTNERS**: Ermine Orliac, 1897–1909; Gabrielle Buffet, m. 1909–19 (div. 1931); Germaine Everling, 1917–33; Olga Mohler, 1927–53 (m. 1940) **DIED**: 30 November 1953, Paris

If you went to a retrospective of the work of Francis Picabia, you could be forgiven for thinking that you were viewing a group show. No other surrealist had so many completely different styles. One of the reasons for his lack of direction was that he was rich, having been left a fortune by his grandmother.

Picabia was born in Paris in 1879. His Spanish Cuban father was an attaché at the Cuban legation in Paris whose duties inevitably made him rather remote. The small boy, an only child, grew up in a fantasy world of his own. Between the ages of sixteen and eighteen he attended art school in Paris and showed remarkable potential. By the age of twenty-five he was a budding impressionist and could paint like Monet. By thirty he was a pointillist and could paint like Sisley. By thirty-one he had become a fauvist, only to abandon that in favour of experimenting with futurism and orphism. During this early phase, his painting was always derivative, but then, in 1914, he moved into his first original phase – generally known as his 'machine period'. This coincided with his involvement in the dada movement in New York and Paris.

Picabia's mechanomorphic paintings were a remarkable series of portraits of imaginary machine parts, as though he were portraying people. During this phase he also introduced the idea – original at the time – of writing words on paintings: sometimes a few, sometimes many.

In 1921 Picabia began to feel that the dada movement had done all it could, so he abandoned it. His uncle died two years later, leaving him another fortune, and his reaction was to build a château in the South of France and buy a yacht. When the château was completed in 1925, he moved into it. He would spend the next ten years of his life based there, on the Côte d'Azur, before eventually returning to Paris.

In the mid-1920s he made the weird decision to start painting realistic portraits of Spanish senoritas, as if cocking a snook not just at the dadaists but at all forms of modernism. Towards the end of the decade he began to corrupt these images, painting one on top of another in a series of 'transparencies'. These pictures, painted between 1928 and 1931, were enjoyed by the surrealists and regarded by them as surrealist works.

By the late 1930s Picabia's wild spending had almost exhausted his fortune. He is said to have owned no fewer than 127 luxury cars and boats. He was obliged to sell the château and in 1937 he moved back into his family home in Paris.

In the late 1940s he produced a series of crudely finished surrealist images. Then, in 1949, on the eve of a major retrospective of his work, he ran into further money troubles when his apartment was burgled, leaving him almost penniless. During the 1950s he became seriously ill and was hardly able to paint. All he could produce were minimalist works in which a painted canvas would be adorned with just a few coloured spots.

Finally, in 1953, Picabia died at the house in Paris where he had been born. At his funeral in Montmartre André Breton paid him a final tribute, calling his paintings 'an oeuvre based on the sovereignty of caprice.... Only a very great aristocrat of the spirit could dare what you have dared.'

# PABLO PICASSO

## The visual giant who invented the word surrealism and transformed the world of modern art

**BORN**: 25 October 1881, Malaga, as Pablo Diego José Francisco de Paula Juan Nepomuceno María de los Remedios Cipriano de la Santísima Trinidad Ruiz y Picasso **PARENTS**: Father an art professor; mother a minor aristocrat **LIVED**: Malaga, 1881; La Coruña, 1891; Barcelona, 1895; Madrid, 1897; Barcelona, 1898; Paris, 1900; Madrid, 1901; Paris, 1901; Barcelona, 1903; Paris, 1904; Avignon, 1914; Paris, 1914; South of France, 1946 **PARTNERS**: Rosita del Oro, 1896–9; Odette Lenoir, 1900; Germaine Pichot, 1901; Fernande Olivier, 1904–12; Madeleine, 1904; Eva Gouel (Marcelle Humbert), 1912–15; Gaby Lespinasse, 1915–16; Hélène Oettingen, 1916; Elvira Paladini (You-You), 1916; Emilienne Pâquerette, 1916; Irène Lagut, 1916–17; Olga Khokhlova, m. 1918–35; Marie-Thérèse Walter, 1927–36; Alice Mahon, 1935; Dora Maar, 1936–44; Nusch Éluard, 1936; Françoise Gilot, 1943–53; Geneviève Laporte, 1951–53; Jacqueline Roque, m. 1955–73 **DIED**: 8 April 1973, Mougins, France

Picasso's involvement with the start of the surrealist movement has already been discussed in the Introduction.

Picasso was born in Malaga, in the south of Spain, in 1881. His father, a professor of art, started teaching the boy how to paint when he was seven years old. By the time he was thirteen, Picasso had already surpassed him in technique; by fifteen, he was painting like an old master. Later in life, he joked about his precocious skills: 'It took me four years to paint like Raphael, but a lifetime to paint like a child.'

At the turn of the century, Picasso moved to Paris and his art started to go through a number of distinct phases. First came his Blue Period (1901–4); followed by his Rose Period (1904–6); his African Period (1907–9); his Analytic Cubist Period (1909–12); his Synthetic Cubist Period (1912–17); his surrealist period (1917–35); and finally his mature period, which lasted until his death in 1973.

He was one of the most prolific artists of all time. His twin addictions were his paintings and his lovers. Sex was very important to him, and his virility in the bedroom was echoed by the vigour of his brush when he stood in front of the easel.

When he arrived in Paris in 1900, aged nineteen, he explored the French brothels for a while and eventually contracted a venereal disease, a condition that brought on his Blue Period. The doctor who cured him was paid with one of his Blue Period paintings – which, viewed in retrospect, represents possibly the highest fee ever paid for a medical treatment.

In Rome in 1917 he met a Russian ballet dancer called Olga Khokhlova. They married in 1918 and in 1921 had a son, Paulo. As the years passed, they grew apart and eventually separated. They never divorced, however, and remained married until her death in 1955. During this period Picasso had many affairs and sometimes they overlapped. During the Second World War he had three lovers simultaneously. His painting thrived on this situation, and the work he did during the dark days of the war was immensely powerful.

In 1943 a new phase would begin for the now sixty-two-year-old Picasso. He met and fell in love with a twenty-one-year-old French virgin called Françoise Gilot. Their life together was chaotic and she eventually left him, but not before they had two children together, Claude and Paloma.

Now in his seventies but still sexually insatiable, Picasso began one last major relationship in 1953. He had been making ceramics at a local pottery when the attractive salesgirl there, Jacqueline Roque, caught his eye. She became the last great love of his life, moving in and taking over the household. When Picasso's first wife, Olga, finally died in 1955, he was at last free to marry again and he made Jacqueline his second wife in 1961. They had no children, but she stayed with him for the rest of his life, protecting him and caring for him until he died in 1973 at the age of ninety-one.

# ÀNGEL PLANELLS

## The Catalan surrealist who was a cross between Dalí and Magritte

**BORN:** 2 December 1901, Cadaqués, Spain, as Àngel Planells i Cruañas

**LIVED:** Cadaqués, 1901; Barcelona, 1918; Cadaqués, 1920; Blanes, Girona, 1929

**DIED:** 23 July 1989, Barcelona

Àngel Planells was born in the small Costa Brava town of Cadaqués, in the extreme northeast corner of Catalonia. At seventeen he went to Barcelona to study art but two years later, in 1920, was called home to take charge of the family bakery. It was at about this time that he first met Salvador Dalí, whose family had a seaside home in Cadaqués, and began a friendship with him that would last for many years.

Planells' earliest canvases were traditional landscapes in a conventional style. When he encountered Dalí again in 1929, just at the point when Dalí had at last found his mature surrealist style, he was inspired to change direction. Abandoning his landscapes, he turned his attention to surrealism. Around the same time he met René Magritte when the Belgian came to visit Dalí for a holiday in Spain. Both Dalí and Magritte made a strong impact on Planells, who seems to have borrowed liberally from them – unless, of course, it was they who borrowed from him.

One of the devices to which Planells returned repeatedly was also favoured by Magritte, in which part of the background becomes part of the foreground. In one example in Planells' work, the face of a female nude standing on a seashore is made of ocean waves. In another, a hand opens the drawer of a desk and, inside it, ocean waves are lapping. In yet another, a woman has hung up the ocean to dry on a clothesline. Planells' backgrounds often show rocky coastal outcrops that look remarkably like some of Dalí's – but rather than one artist imitating another, this may be to do with the fact that both were painting in Cadaqués and naturally saw similar seascapes.

In 1929, Planells moved down the coast to settle in Blanes, where he published a manifesto attacking 'infallible critics'. In the following year he held a solo exhibition of his work in Madrid, which was followed by other shows in Barcelona.

Said to be a shy, introverted man, Àngel Planells was completely overshadowed by his extrovert, showman friend Dalí. Planells was described as 'a genius in the shade, with tireless imagination and prodigious vitality', and he never gained the wide recognition he deserved. He did, however, have one chance of maximum exposure, when three of his paintings were selected for inclusion in the 1936 International Surrealist Exhibition in London.

Little is known about his private life. A friend summed him up as a 'man full of angst', driven by visions from both dreams and daydreams. Planells himself described the way in which unconscious, surreal images would suggest themselves to him. He could be walking down a street and would see a normal woman, but then, when she moved, 'a surreal transformation would occur'. This seemed to happen to him all the time, and he had no control over it. He asked plaintively, 'I do not know – is this a disease?' Perhaps so, but judging by his extraordinary compositions, it was as much a gift as an ailment.

# PETER ROSE PULHAM

## The forgotten surrealist who may have influenced his friend, Francis Bacon

**BORN**: 26 June 1910, Hampstead Garden Suburb, London
**LIVED**: London, 1910; Oxford, 1928; London, *c.* 1931; Paris, 1936; London, 1939; Conives, France, 1953
**PARTNER**: Theodora Rosling (later FitzGibbon), 1938–42
**DIED**: 18 May 1956, Conives

Peter Rose Pulham is one of the forgotten surrealists. This is unfortunate because, at his best, he created some hauntingly powerful images: human limbs and body parts stretched into abstracted compositions that transmit an intense, almost painful eroticism. He was a friend of Francis Bacon's and there has been some debate as to whether Bacon influenced Pulham or whether Pulham's distorted limbs had, perhaps, a somewhat under-acknowledged influence on Bacon.

Originally, Pulham had intended to become an architect, but he switched his focus to photography and was offered a position as a fashion photographer at *Harper's Bazaar*. When they sent him to Paris in 1936 to cover fashion events, he found himself more interested in the great artists who were working there. His photographs of Picasso, Max Ernst and other surrealists in their studios have become collector's items.

Pulham was so inspired by the atmosphere in 1930s Paris that he remained there until the outbreak of war in 1939. Under the influence of his surrealist friends, he started to paint.

His personal life would have remained unknown if not for a memoir published by his partner Theodora Rosling, later a well-known cookery writer. In it, she describes her first encounter with Pulham. One day at the Café de Flore, they were sitting at adjacent tables and she found herself watching him so intently that Pulham suddenly said, 'I wonder if you would mind sitting at my table, as you distract me sitting where you are.' Later that night, they became lovers. Pulham took her into the bohemian life of Paris, where she met Picasso, Max Ernst, Balthus, Salvador Dalí, André Breton and Jean Cocteau.

When war broke out in 1939, they were forced to abandon Paris and flee to England. Back in London, Pulham set up a studio in Chelsea and worked steadily there on his surrealist paintings for two years before, in 1941, the studio was hit by a German bomb. Almost all of his surrealist work was destroyed.

It was during this period that he and Theodora became friendly with Francis Bacon, Lucien Freud, Henry Moore and Dylan Thomas. They had replaced the avant-garde of Paris with that of London.

Then, one night, Theodora met the Irish American writer Constantine FitzGibbon in a local pub and fell 'passionately, irrevocably in love'. All Pulham said was, 'I always thought he was just the chap for you.' After she had left him, Pulham wrote to her, 'You rescued me and put me on my feet...and I shall always be grateful to you. I'm not in love with you...but I do love you very much.'

Pulham continued painting throughout the dark period of the war and, when it was over, held an exhibition at the Redfern Gallery in 1947. The following year, he moved to Édouard Mesens' London Gallery, the beating heart of surrealist activity in London. Mesens gave him another show in 1949 and this was followed by one at the Hanover Gallery in 1950; however, despite his best efforts, sales were poor. Discouraged, Pulham decided to return to photography.

In 1953, something mysterious happened to make him give up photography and destroy all his negatives. He moved to Conives in central France and died there in 1956, still only in his mid-forties.

# MAN RAY

## The multi-talented American artist at the centre of the surrealist world

**BORN**: 27 August 1890, Philadelphia, as Emmanuel Radnitzky **PARENTS**: Russian Jewish immigrants; father a tailor **LIVED**: Philadelphia, 1890; New York, 1912; Paris, 1921; Los Angeles, 1940; Paris, 1951 **PARTNERS**: Adon Lacroix (Donna Lecoeur), m. 1914–19 (div. 1937); Kiki de Montparnasse (Alice Prin), 1921–9; Lee Miller, 1929–32; Meret Oppenheim, 1933; Ady (Adrienne) Fidelin, 1936–40; Juliet Browner, m. 1946–76 **DIED**: 18 November 1976, Paris

The enigmatic Man Ray was a man of endless talents: a painter, photographer, filmmaker and builder of objects. As one of his biographers puts it, 'he was dedicated to the creative idea rather than any particular style or medium'.

Man Ray was born in Philadelphia in 1890, the eldest son of Russian Jewish immigrants. His father was a tailor and his mother a seamstress. In 1911 his family officially shortened their name from Radnitzky to Ray. The following year, Man Ray started studying at an art school in New York, and in 1913 he visited the famous Armory Show, where he saw the work of Picabia and Duchamp.

In the summer of 1921 he went to Paris, where he met André Breton, Paul Éluard and the Paris dadaists. He also met a nightclub singer called Kiki de Montparnasse, and before long they began a wild affair that would last for six years. During that time she posed for some of his most iconic surrealist photographs.

In 1929 he was enjoying a drink in his favourite Paris bar when a strikingly beautiful American fashion model approached him and announced that she was going to be his photographic student. He refused, saying he did not take on students, but she managed to convince him to let her become his darkroom assistant. Her name was Lee Miller and she and Man Ray soon became lovers.

Three years later, in 1932, Miller returned to New York to open her own photographic studio. Man Ray was distraught at losing her, but rapidly recovered and was soon in the midst of an affair with the Swiss surrealist Meret Oppenheim. His photographs of her naked, standing beside the heavy machinery of a huge printing press with her white skin smeared with black printing ink, would become some of his most famous images.

When the Nazis invaded France in 1940, Man Ray had to flee. He took his precious cameras with him, but on the way to New York they were stolen. Back in his home country, the loss of the cameras, his Paris studio and his network of friends in France turned him briefly into a wounded recluse; but after a while he rallied and travelled to the West Coast, where he met Juliet Browner, a dancer and artists' model. They soon became a couple and he began painting again in earnest. By the end of the war, his spirits had been fully revived and he was able to enjoy a retrospective exhibition of his work in Pasadena.

In 1945 he was briefly back in New York for another exhibition when Germany surrendered, and he was able to celebrate in the company of Marcel Duchamp and André Breton. The following year, he and Juliet married in Beverly Hills at a double ceremony with his old friend Max Ernst and Dorothea Tanning. Bearing in mind the active love lives of both men before this point, it seemed unlikely that these Hollywood-style nuptials would lead to lasting relationships, but surprisingly both marriages lasted for thirty years – until the deaths of both Ernst and Ray, a few months apart, in 1976.

In the spring of 1951, Man Ray finally achieved his dream of returning to Paris. He and Juliet were seen off at the docks in New York by Marcel Duchamp. On arrival they settled into a studio in St-Germain-des-Prés, where they would live for the rest of Man Ray's life.

# CERI RICHARDS

## The scholarly Welsh artist who created some of the greatest surrealist relief-works

**BORN**: 6 June 1903, Dunvant, near Swansea **PARENTS**: Father a tinplate foundry worker, active in the local church, wrote poetry and conducted the local choir **LIVED**: Dunvant, 1908; Swansea, 1921; London, 1924; Cardiff, 1940; London, 1945 **PARTNER**: Frances Clayton, m. 1929 **DIED**: 9 November 1971, London

The Welsh artist Ceri Richards was responsive to many influences, passing through one phase after another, but his involvement with surrealism in the 1930s was perhaps the most impressive period of his career. Some of the surrealist works he created during that decade bear comparison with anything the genre has to offer.

Richards was born in a small mining village near Swansea in South Wales, at the beginning of the Edwardian period. His father, who worked in a tinplate factory, was a cultured man who wrote poetry and directed local theatre productions. At school, Ceri's drawings won competitions, and in 1924 he won a scholarship to the Royal College of Art in London. His teachers there included Paul Nash and Henry Moore, and it was Moore who later described Richards as 'the finest draughtsman of his generation'.

Richards rarely returned to Wales, spending most of the rest of his life in London. In 1929 he married a fellow artist, Frances Clayton, and they had two daughters. Among their friends were the artists Victor Pasmore and Julian Trevelyan, as well as a young designer called Francis Bacon who said that he too hoped to be a painter one day.

By the early 1930s Richards' work was beginning to show marked surrealist tendencies. When he visited the International Surrealist Exhibition in London in 1936, he said it helped him 'to be aware of the mystery, even the "unreality" of ordinary things'.

Richards produced his best surrealist work during the late 1930s. In 1937, his friend Julian Trevelyan brought Hans Arp to Richards' London studio to see his reliefs. Arp must have been impressed to see the impact that his own reliefs had had on Richards and the way in which his earlier simplified, embryo reliefs had grown into more complicated, adult forms in Richards' hands.

The following year, Richards visited an exhibition of Max Ernst's work at the London Gallery and bought an important painting called *The Bride of the Wind*. It is a sinister, turbulent, dynamic composition and it is noticeable that at this point Richards' own paintings also became more turbulent and restless. They matched the mood of the times, as Europe was being plunged into the Second World War. Richards and his wife fled from blitzed London to a village in the country, and in 1940 he was offered a post as head of painting at the Cardiff School of Art. This left him little time for his own work, but the paintings he did manage to complete reflected the restlessness of the period and some of them still retained a strong surrealist quality.

He remained in Cardiff for the duration of the war, returning to London when it was over to teach at the Chelsea School of Art. In the 1960s his painting became more abstract, although it was an organic abstraction. In 1965, one critic wrote of his work that 'he wanders between the worlds of figuration and abstraction with a cheerful ignoring of frontiers'.

Perhaps the best way to think of Richards is as a knowledgable explorer with a high level of curiosity, capable of throwing himself into one visual or symbolic exploration after another. After his death in 1971, Henry Moore wrote of him: 'More than any other British painter of his time he understood three-dimensional form and knew how to express it on a flat surface.' This, coming from Moore, was praise indeed.

# EDITH RIMMINGTON

## The shadowy figure of British surrealism who created some unforgettable images

**BORN**: 1902, Leicester
**LIVED**: Leicester, 1902; Manchester, 1920s; London, 1937, Bexhill-on-Sea, Sussex
**PARTNER**: Robert Baxter, m. 1926
**DIED**: 1986, Bexhill-on-Sea, Sussex

Edith Rimmington played an important role in the history of British surrealism, creating some iconic images, but she herself remains a shadowy figure; little is known about her personal life. Surviving works by her are extremely rare, but it is not clear whether this is because her output was limited or because much of it was lost.

Her most famous painting, called *Oneiroscopist* (or *Transcriber of Dreams*), shows a cloaked, seated figure with the feet of a giant bird, human hands, an insect head and a long, skeletal avian beak. Around its neck is a deep-sea diver's collar, and the diving helmet itself is on the ground beside the figure. This strange hybrid being, a surrealist chimera, sits serenely on a platform high above the clouds, as if it is waiting patiently to perform some sort of rescue operation when an emergency occurs below. Unfortunately, this is going to be a disaster, because its long beak will not fit into the diving helmet.

Rimmington was born in Leicester at the beginning of the Edwardian period, and after the First World War she attended the Brighton School of Art. In the early 1920s she met the surrealist artist Robert Baxter, whom she married in 1926; they moved to Manchester, where he had a teaching post. In 1936 Rimmington made a visit to London to see the International Surrealist Exhibition at the New Burlington Galleries. It made a deep impression on her, and she realized that this was the form of art she felt compelled to pursue in future. The following year, she left Manchester for London, where she found a studio in Camden and set about making contact with the surrealists who were gathered in the capital.

In 1939 Gordon Onslow Ford introduced her to the self-styled leader of the British surrealists, Édouard Mesens, and in 1940 she became an official member of his surrealist group, regularly attending their weekly meetings at the Barcelona Restaurant in Soho.

Rimmington's closest friends during this period were Emmy Bridgwater and Conroy Maddox. She and Bridgwater occasionally had sessions of automatic drawing in the surrealist tradition. In a letter to a friend she complained that her wartime work as a secretary to Stanley Lief, founder of the famous Champneys Spa at Tring in Hertfordshire, was interfering with her painting activities, but there may have been more to it than that; it was rumoured that when Rimmington's marriage ended she had an affair with Lief.

Her surrealist writings during the war reveal how obsessed she had become with the violence of the period and the ever-present threat of death: 'Death is alive in rhythm at the screech of the siren like a calm box pouring out music, projecting a lifetime through endless rooms...' After the war, she exhibited in the 1947 International Surrealist Exhibition in Paris.

Rimmington abandoned her easel in 1967, shifting her focus of interest to photography. She spent her later years living at Bexhill-on-Sea in southeast England, where she died in 1986. Michel Remy, in his study of British surrealism, describes her as 'an outstandingly powerful visionary provocateur whose images, once seen, can hardly be forgotten'.

# PIERRE ROY

## The surrealist pioneer, whose temperament saw him abandon the movement in its early days

**BORN**: 10 August 1880, Nantes
**PARENTS**: Father a solicitor
**LIVED**: Nantes, 1880; Paris, 1899; Nantes, 1915; Paris, 1918
**PARTNER**: Adrienne Ridou, m. 1913–19
**DIED**: 26 September 1950, Milan

Pierre Roy is one of those artists whose work fitted perfectly with surrealist principles, but whose personality did not. Influenced by the early paintings of de Chirico, he produced dreamlike scenes in which familiar objects, meticulously portrayed, were assembled in irrational combinations. Birds' eggs, wine glasses, seashells, shoes, feathers, pebbles, anchors and flags were placed together as if they were performers on some unfamiliar stage, waiting to interact.

Little wonder that Roy, along with Jean Arp, Giorgio de Chirico, Max Ernst, Paul Klee, André Masson, Joan Miró and Man Ray, was included in the very first group exhibition of the surrealists in 1925. At this point, the critic André Salmon called him the 'true father of surrealism'. That may not have been music to the ears of André Breton, who rather pointedly omitted Roy from his seminal work *Le Surréalisme et la peinture* in 1928.

Roy was born in Nantes in 1880, the son of a solicitor. He grew up in a cultured, middle-class family where learning and scholarship were admired. His father influenced him to start making drawings at a very early age.

Roy also happened to be a relative of Jules Verne, whose work did much to define the genre of science fiction, and who was regarded by many surrealists as one of their greatest and most imaginative precursors. Verne's brother used to read Jules' fantastic tales to the young Pierre, igniting in the boy a longing to become a sailor and explore the world.

Instead, he had to make do with the less glamorous role of assistant in an architect's office in Nantes. Here, at least, he did develop his skills at precise draughtsmanship, but he soon became bored with the job and moved on to Paris to study art.

In 1913 he met and became friendly with de Chirico, but his career as an artist was interrupted when he was conscripted to serve in the military. After the First World War, in 1919, he started painting his first 'irrational juxtaposition' paintings, and in the early 1920s he became close with Breton, Ernst and their circle. He exhibited with them in several group shows and then, in 1928, had his own first solo exhibition. Two years later his first show in New York was a great success, and he was later included in the Museum of Modern Art's major surrealism exhibition of 1936.

The strength of Roy's work lay in its meticulous execution, but its weakness lay in the ornamental way he assembled the unrelated objects. His irrational juxtapositions were decorative rather than sinister or symbolic. It would not be going too far to describe his major visual preoccupation as 'the surreal still life'. In 1947 he said: 'As a painter, I have no philosophy whatsoever. When I paint anything at all, I do it out of the sheer pleasure of painting. I have no symbolic intention.'

Roy married Adrienne Ridou, who was the leading dressmaker to master couturier Paul Poiret and carried out Erté's designs. She died young in 1919, leaving Roy with a two-year-old child to care for. Roy was travelling abroad, on his way to attend an exhibition of his work in Italy, when he himself died suddenly in a hotel room in Milan in 1950.

# KAY SAGE



## The strong-minded American surrealist who was seen as a threat by André Breton

When Kay Sage arrived in Paris in 1937, she must have posed quite a problem for André Breton. She was thirty-nine years old, multilingual, strong-minded, well travelled and wealthy. She also had a powerful urge to succeed as an artist and was not going to take kindly to Breton's dictatorship. When she decided that surrealism was the perfect vehicle for her creativity, there was no stopping her.

Sage's moment of truth came when she attended the major surrealist exhibition of 1938 at the Galerie Beaux-Arts. She bought an early de Chirico and before the year was out was already exhibiting her own highly skilled works, featuring austere surrealist landscapes.

Kay Sage was born in 1898 in Albany, New York, into a family made rich as timber barons. She spent her childhood being dragged around Europe and North America by her highly strung mother and her travelling staff.

When her childhood came to an end, she settled in Italy, where she fell in love with a handsome young Italian prince. Marrying him, she became a princess – the Principessa di San Faustino – and lived in a palace, the Palazzo Rospigliosi. They led a high-society life for year after year until, eventually, Sage decided she had had enough. She moved alone to Paris and started to paint in earnest. Meeting the eccentric French surrealist Yves Tanguy changed her

**BORN**: 25 June 1898, Albany, New York, as Katherine Linn Sage

**PARENTS**: Father a wealthy politician; mother a bohemian

**LIVED**: Albany, 1898; Rapallo, Italy (childhood); Rome, 1925; Paris, 1937; New York, 1939; Woodbury, Connecticut, 1941

**PARTNERS**: Prince Ranieri di San Faustino, m. 1925–35; Yves Tanguy, m. 1940–55

**DIED**: 8 January 1963, Woodbury

life forever. Peggy Guggenheim recalled sending the impecunious Tanguy to ask the 'American Princess' if she would buy one of his paintings. Guggenheim later declared that Sage had bought not only the painting, but also Tanguy himself.

Sage became completely infatuated with Tanguy despite the fact that they were both married to other people at the time. The stronger their bond of attachment became, the more it riled Breton. Tanguy had been his protégé and now he was losing him to this American intruder. Sage must have known that Breton detested her, but she was not going let him to stand in her way. With the outbreak of the Second World War, she prepared to leave for New York and persuaded Tanguy to join her there. Tanguy was hers now, and in less than a year would become her legal husband – once she had dealt with the small matter of dumping her Italian prince.

Sage now played a masterstroke. Instead of leaving the penniless surrealists – who had despised her – to stew in wartime Paris, she began making arrangements to rescue them. She negotiated the fare for the Bretons to get them to New York, found them a suitable apartment and even paid their rent. André Breton's private thoughts about accepting this largesse are not known, but can easily be imagined.

Sage and Tanguy soon abandoned New York and moved out to Woodbury, Connecticut, where they bought an old farm whose outhouses they converted into studios. The walls of the house were hung with works by Miró, Calder, Delvaux, Magritte, de Chirico and Ernst.

When, in 1955, Tanguy died suddenly from a cerebral haemorrhage, Sage was totally distraught. She spent the following years working on a catalogue raisonné of his work. Once that was complete, she locked herself in her bedroom, aimed a gun at her chest, pulled the trigger and shot herself through the heart. Her ashes were mixed with those of Tanguy and buried on the coast of Brittany at Finistère, where Tanguy had enjoyed childhood vacations.

# KURT SCHWITTERS

## The German surrealist who was obsessed with turning rubbish into art

**BORN**: 20 June 1887, Hanover  **PARENTS**: Ran a ladies' clothing shop

**LIVED**: Hanover, 1887; Dresden, 1909; Hanover, 1915; Lysaker, near Oslo, 1937; Isle of Man (interned), 1940; London, 1941; Ambleside, 1945

**PARTNERS**: Helma Fischer, m. 1915–44; Edith Thomas, 1941

**DIED**: 8 January 1948, Kendal

Kurt Schwitters was a surrealist in everything except name. This was because he invented his own art movement, which he called *merzism*. A one-man movement, it ran parallel to surrealism and was similar in spirit if not in formal membership.

In 1918, Schwitters applied to join the Berlin dada group but was turned down because of his 'unpolitical attitude'. His response was to set up his own dada group in Hanover and, in 1919, to make his first *merz* pictures, using bits of rubbish he had picked up in the street. The fact that his raw material was despised by a despicable society made it admirable – the two negatives made a positive.

With this solid piece of logic under his belt, Schwitters set off on a crusade to make rubbish beautiful and devoted the whole of his life to this quest. The name *merz* was taken from the tail end of the German word *kommerz*, commerce. In other words, *merz* was concerned with the end-bits, the detritus, of the products of the commercial world.

Schwitters was born in 1887 in Hanover, where his parents were shopkeepers, and went to art school there. When he was twenty-one he became engaged to his cousin, Helma Fischer. In 1909 he moved to

Dresden to further his art studies and remained there until 1915, when he married Helma.

In the winter of 1918–19 he met Hans Arp for the first time, the start of a lifelong friendship. He said around this time, 'My ambition is the unity of art and non-art.... I don't see why one shouldn't use in a picture...things like old tram and train tickets, scraps of driftwood, cloakroom tickets, ends of strings – in a word, all the old rubbish which you find in dustbins or on a refuse dump.'

Soon he began to exhibit his *merz* pictures and made contact with various dadaists in Berlin, as well as with Max Ernst in Cologne. Throughout the 1920s he was actively exhibiting, and in 1929 his work was shown alongside the surrealists' in a mixed show in Zurich.

With the rise of Hitler, Schwitters came under attack, and some of his friends in Hanover were arrested and taken away by the Gestapo. When he heard that they were coming for him too, he fled to Norway. Helma stayed behind to care for their property in Hanover.

In 1940 the Germans invaded Norway and Schwitters had to flee again, this time taking passage to Scotland on an icebreaker. Because he was German, he was interned on arrival in the UK. Released in 1941, he moved to London, where he met Edith Thomas, a neighbour who would later become his companion. The following year they took a holiday in the Lake District, where he fell in love with the landscape.

The year 1944 was disastrous for Schwitters. Helma died of cancer in Germany, and he himself suffered a stroke that paralysed one side of his body for a time. When the war finally ended, Schwitters and Edith left London and moved to the Lake District, where he spent the last few years of his life. On 7 January 1948 he was, at long last, granted British citizenship, but he only enjoyed this new status for a matter of hours – the next day, at the age of sixty, he died in Kendal Hospital.

# KURT SELIGMANN

## The most scholarly of the surrealists, who was fascinated by the arcane and the magical



**BORN**: 20 July 1900, Basel
**PARENTS**: Father a department store owner
**LIVED**: Basel, 1900; Paris, 1927; New York, 1939; Sugar Loaf, New York, 1940
**PARTNER**: Arlette Paraf, m. 1935–62
**DIED**: 2 January 1962, Sugar Loaf, New York

Kurt Seligmann has been described as the seer of surrealism. He was the bibliophile of the group, accumulating a large library with a focus on magic and the occult; he even wrote a scholarly book on the subject, *The Mirror of Magic* (1948). What particularly excited him was the way in which arcane rituals could conjure up wonderfully strange and mysterious images. As he explained, 'The relics of ancient peoples indicate that religico-magical beliefs have given a great impulse to artistic activies.'

Kurt Seligmann was born in Basel at the start of the 20th century. His father, who owned a furniture store, wanted him to follow in the family business. Seligmann was reluctant to do this and managed to persuade his family to allow him to study art in Geneva instead. In 1927 he moved to Paris, met up with a friend from Geneva, the sculptor Alberto Giacometti, and was soon mixing with the surrealist circle around André Breton.

In 1935 he met and married Arlette Paraf, granddaughter of the fabulously wealthy art dealer Nathan Wildenstein, and the following year they travelled the world on a lavish year-long honeymoon. Back in Paris, Seligmann's involvement with the surrealists deepened to the point where in 1937, Breton formally accepted him as an official member of the group. In 1939, with war looming, he was the first of the European surrealists to cross the Atlantic and set up home in the United States. Once there, he and his wife did everything in their power to assist others in escaping to the New World.

In 1940 they moved to Sugar Loaf in Orange County, New York, where they bought a 55-acre farm estate and Seligmann built a large studio. Alexander Calder and Yves Tanguy were frequent guests. This was Seligmann's most productive period, when he created his best work and took part in important surrealist exhibitions in New York. After the war, in 1950, he and his wife both became American citizens.

Seligmann's death in 1962, at the age of sixty-one, is something of a mystery. On a freezing January morning, he picked up a gun and stepped out onto his property to shoot some rats that had been eating the food he had put out for wild birds. There was ice on the ground, and he slipped and fell. As he did so, the gun he was carrying went off accidentally and shot him in the head.

There are those who believe this was a suicide. Seligmann had recently suffered a severe heart attack and was known to be depressed; isolated in the country and anxious about his health, he might well have carefully contrived an 'accident' in order to avoid the stigma of suicide. We will never know. Arlette, his widow, bequeathed his entire estate to a private corporation dedicated to the preservation of Orange County.

# JINDŘICH ŠTYRSKÝ

**The co-founder of the Czech surrealist group, who was fascinated by the Marquis de Sade**

**BORN**: 11 August 1899, Čermná u Kyšperka, Bohemia
**LIVED**: Lower Čermná, 1899; Prague, 1922; Paris, 1925; Prague, 1929; Paris, 1935; Prague, 1935
**PARTNER**: Toyen (Marie Čermínová), 1922–42
**DIED**: 21 March 1942, Prague

Štyrský was the leading figure in the Czech surrealist group that formed in Prague in 1934. He is not well known in the West, in part because his life was cut short at forty-two by a fatal heart attack.

Greatly admired by Breton, he produced a series of powerfully erotic surrealist images, many of them collages. Surprisingly, he does not seem to have been censored or banned during the thirties – but once war broke out and Czechoslovakia was overrun by Nazis, all forms of surrealism, erotic or otherwise, were officially prohibited.

Štyrský was born in a small town in Bohemia at the end of the 19th century and studied at the Prague Academy of Fine Arts. By chance, while on holiday on the island of Korčula in Yugoslavia, he met another Czech artist – Marie Čermínová, later known as Toyen – who became his lifelong companion. In 1925 they went to Paris together to absorb the revolutionary mood that existed among the young artists there. Three years later, Štyrský was offered work as a theatrical director in Prague, and they returned to their home country.

Their friends in Prague were fascinated by the intensely close relationship that developed between

Štyrský and Toyen, referring to them jointly as a 'surrealist hermaphrodite'. There was a feminine side to Štyrský and a masculine side to Toyen, and it was felt that they had somehow managed to exchange their gender roles.

While he was with the surrealists in Paris, Štyrský had become fascinated by the writings of the Marquis de Sade. After his return to Prague, he decided to pay a visit to Sade's ruined castle in France, with the idea of taking photographs of what remained of the notorious Marquis's home. It was his intention to rebuild Sade's reputation.

In 1934, he and Toyen helped to establish the Prague surrealist group. André Breton was greatly impressed by what they were doing – especially the fact that they were busily translating many of his writings into their own language. When they invited him to pay them a visit he was keen to do so, taking along his wife, Jacqueline Lamba, and his surrealist friend Paul Éluard. He later claimed that they were given a hero's welcome, and Éluard wrote home to say, 'We live marvellously here...Delirious adoration and affection.' Later, Breton recalled his visit to Štyrský as 'one of the most beautiful memories of my life'.

With those reactions from the French visitors, it is no surprise that in 1935 Štyrský was warmly invited to return to Paris and take part in surrealist activities there. Sadly, when he arrived, his health began to deteriorate. His heart was so weak that at one point he was described as 'hovering between life and death'.

He returned to Prague, where, after the Germans invaded, surrealism became illegal and was driven underground. This did not eradicate the movement – quite the opposite, in fact. It seemed to attract more and more young people, to whom it represented free creative thought.

While this was happening, at the height of the war in 1942, Štyrský suffered his final heart attack. It was left to his partner, Toyen, to carry on the Czech surrealist tradition they had begun together.

# YVES TANGUY



## The surrealist who invented a unique dream-world of haunting landscapes

Yves Tanguy was a central figure of the surrealist group in Paris, celebrated by André Breton and faithful to the ideals of the movement for his entire life. Tanguy's dream-world landscapes were painted with the careful precision of an old master and proliferated with tiny details. When he put down his brushes, however, he became an eccentric, childlike extrovert, often causing havoc at social gatherings.

Part of Tanguy's problem was his susceptibility to alcohol. His friend Alexander Calder called him 'Three-Stage Tanguy'. There was the serious Tanguy who was dead sober. Then there was the charming Tanguy who was slightly drunk. And finally, there was the violent Tanguy who was completely drunk.

Tanguy was born in Paris, the son of a sea captain, on the fifth day of the 20th century. His childhood holidays were spent with his family on the Brittany coast, where he responded strongly to the dramatic rock formations and pebble-strewn beaches.

At the end of the First World War, Tanguy went to sea. He joined the Merchant Marine and over a period of two years would travel to both Africa and South America in cargo vessels. In 1920, he was called up for two years of military duty in the French army. He attempted to avoid service by swallowing spiders and eating his socks to suggest mental instability, but his efforts were in vain.

**BORN**: 5 January 1900, Paris, as Raymond Georges Yves Tanguy
**PARENTS**: Both of Breton origin; father a navy captain
**LIVED**: Paris, 1900; merchant navy, 1918; army, 1920; Paris, 1922; New York, 1939; Woodbury, Connecticut, 1941–55
**PARTNERS**: Jeanette Ducrocq, m. 1927–40; Peggy Guggenheim, 1938; Kay Sage, m. 1940–55
**DIED**: 15 January 1955, Woodbury

In 1925, he came into contact with the surrealists.
André Breton, recognizing the potential in this wild
young man, took him under his wing. Within a few
years Tanguy had begun to invent an exciting private
world of his own, in paintings that were sufficiently
successful to bring him his first solo exhibition in
1927. That same year he married for the first time, to
Jeanette Ducrocq. During the following decade he
worked hard to develop his landscapes of biomorphs
and geomorphs and exhibited with the surrealists –
but he sold little and was desperately poor.

Throughout the 1930s Tanguy had remained the
favoured disciple of André Breton. Then, with the
arrival in Paris of the American artist Kay Sage in 1937,
Breton had to witness his protégé being seduced by a
foreign intruder. How dare this interloper drive a wedge
between him and his faithful Tanguy? For his part,
Tanguy was basking in the financial glow of a seriously
rich American partner who had fallen deeply in love
with him. Sage was about to whisk him away to the
United States and, at last, a financially secure future.

In 1940, safely settled in America, Tanguy and
Sage set off on a jaunt to the West, where Tanguy
was overwhelmed by the wonderful rock formations.
They headed for Reno in Nevada, where they both
obtained divorces and then got married.

Tanguy and Sage bought a large farmhouse in
Woodbury, Connecticut in 1946, converting two
outbuildings into separate studios where they each
enjoyed a highly productive period of painting.
Tanguy, freed of financial worries, created some
of his greatest works there.

In 1955 Tanguy fell from a ladder at his home,
suffered a stroke and died. Sage, devoted to him until
the very end, threw herself into work on a catalogue
raisonné of his paintings – and then, once it was
completed, shot herself through the heart. Tanguy's
ashes had been carefully preserved; now they were
mixed with hers and taken by his old school friend,
Pierre Matisse, to be buried on the beach in Brittany
where he had walked as a child.

# DOROTHEA TANNING

## The American surrealist who loved Max Ernst and lived to be 101

**BORN:** 25 August 1910, Galesburg, Illinois
**PARENTS:** Swedish immigrants
**LIVED:** Galesburg, 1910; Chicago, 1930; New York, 1935; Sedona, Arizona, 1947; Paris and Sedona, 1949; France, 1957; New York, 1976
**PARTNERS:** Homer Shannon, m. 1941–2; Max Ernst, m. 1946–76
**DIED:** 31 January 2012, New York

Dorothea Tanning broke two records: she lived longer than any other surrealist, and of all the many relationships enjoyed by Max Ernst, hers lasted by far the longest. She lived for more than a century and was married to the libidinous Ernst for the last thirty years of his life.

Tanning's devout Lutheran parents emigrated from Sweden to the United States at the beginning of the 20th century, and she was born in Illinois in 1910. She grew up in what she called an atmosphere of eerie, bourgeois calm – an atmosphere that would later come to haunt many of her paintings.

By the age of seven she had already decided that she wanted to be an artist and, strangely, she began making surrealist images long before she had ever heard of the movement. At the age of fifteen, for example, she painted a naked woman with leaves for hair. In 1930, her parents allowed her to move to Chicago to attend art school.

After five years in Chicago, Tanning left for New York. It was a visit to the Museum of Modern Art in 1936 that changed her life, for it was there that she saw America's first major exhibition of surrealist art. Displayed on the gallery walls were the kind of painting she had been doing for some time, now presented as a serious new art form.

She was keen to meet the surrealists themselves and was able to do so during the Second World War, when many of them were living in New York. In 1942 she met Max Ernst at a party. Still unhappily married to Peggy Guggenheim, Ernst was attracted to the young American artist and soon paid a visit to her studio – and there began a love affair that would last until his death in 1976.

Tanning herself had been briefly married to the writer Homer Shannon, but they were divorced in 1942. Ernst and Guggenheim divorced in 1946, and soon afterwards he and Tanning were married in a dual ceremony with Man Ray and Juliet Browner, in Beverly Hills.

The couple decided to abandon New York and move to the wilds. They chose the Arizona desert, building a small house in a remote hamlet called Sedona, where they lived happily for a decade. Then, in 1957, they moved to France and settled in a new home in Provence, where they would remain until Ernst's death in 1976. Tanning subsequently returned to New York, setting up a studio, and stayed for the rest of her long life.

A remarkable feature of Tanning's years with Ernst is that her painting style was never influenced by that of her charismatic husband. From the start she had her own, haunted brand of oneiric surrealism. Painting with academic precision, she created a sinister world of bleak hotel rooms, corridors and landings where young girls interacted in odd ways with monsters, dogs or other strange beings.

Towards the end of her life, Tanning's compositions became more fragmented and less precise, eventually becoming almost abstract. In 2010, still mentally alert, she said, 'From the neck up I'm young and strong, but the rest of me is a hundred.' She never had children, preferring the company of Pekingese dogs.

# TOYEN

## The co-founder of the Czech surrealist group who dressed like a man

**BORN**: 21 September 1902, Prague, as Marie Čermínová
**LIVED**: Prague, 1902; Paris, 1925; Prague, 1929; Paris, 1947
**PARTNER**: Jindřich Štyrský, 1922–42; Jindřich Heisler, 1947
**DIED**: 9 November 1980, Paris

Toyen was born Marie Čermínová in Prague at the turn of the century, but later rejected that name out of a desire to be known simply as an artist – not specifically as a female artist. The name 'Toyen' is genderless, thought to be a contraction of the French word *citoyen*, a citizen. Toyen had a short, masculine haircut, often wore men's suits, and spoke Czech in the masculine form.

Determined from an early age not to play a traditionally feminine role, Toyen severed all family ties at the age of sixteen and lived an independent life with friends who had similar beliefs. After attending the School of Art in Prague and graduating in 1922, she visited the island of Korčula in Yugoslavia and met another young Czech artist, Jindřich Štyrský. They became partners, and the following year they both joined a group of avant-garde artists working in Prague.

Toyen and Štyrský left Prague again in 1925 and spent the next three years absorbing the stimulating atmosphere of the rebellious Parisian art world. The surrealist movement was at its peak during this period and it left its mark on both of them. When they returned to Prague, they became the joint founders of a surrealist group there.

Having discovered the Marquis de Sade through the surrealists, Štyrský undertook a pilgrimage to Sade's ruined castle, the Château de Lacoste. There he took a series of photographs of crumbling walls and overgrown stonework. Toyen was deeply moved by these sinister images and started to incorporate them into paintings.

In 1935 André Breton visited Prague, and a close relationship was established between him and the Czech surrealists. The Second World War put an end to this, with Breton fleeing to America. Forced to go underground to avoid persecution as a degenerate by the Nazis, Toyen kept working but exhibited nothing. During the war she and Štyrský took a major risk by providing shelter to a Jewish member of the Prague surrealist group, Jindřich Heisler, who lived in their bathroom for four years. Following Štyrský's death of a heart attack at the age of forty-two, Heisler became Toyen's second partner.

After the war Toyen was forced to flee from the Stalinist takeover of Czechoslovakia, and managed to escape to Paris along with Heisler. They arrived in 1947. Toyen would remain there for the rest of her life, becoming close to Breton and his circle.

Toyen's art revealed two main obsessions. The first was sex, reflected in the extensive collection of erotic objects that filled her studio. Even at the age of seventy, she reportedly still visited the cinema to watch adult films.

The second obsession was with animals. A quick search through her compositions reveals no fewer than thirty-four different species. Some are depicted realistically, but others are used as starting points for complex surrealist amalgams with other elements.

In 1953 Breton wrote of Toyen, who had become a close friend: 'Toyen, who catches my heart every time I think of her...the deep tremor within her co-existing with a rock-hard resistance to the fiercest attacks; her eyes which are cardinal points of light.'

# JULIAN TREVELYAN

## The British landscape artist who enjoyed an intense surrealist phase

**BORN**: 20 February 1910, Dorking, Surrey
**PARENTS**: Father a poet and scholar; mother a violinist
**LIVED**: Dorking, 1910; Cambridge, 1928; Paris, 1931; London, 1935
**PARTNERS**: Ursula Darwin, m. 1934–50; Mary Feddon, m. 1951
**DIED**: 12 July 1988, London

Julian Trevelyan was an imaginative landscape artist who went through an intense surrealist phase in the mid-1930s. His early life was spent in a country house near Dorking in Surrey, where his scholarly father entertained philosophers and art historians such as Bertrand Russell and Bernard Berenson. At the age of seven, young Julian was already filling sketchbooks with drawings; by eleven he had invented an imaginary town, designed entirely by himself, complete with detailed street maps.

From 1928 until 1931 Trevelyan read English Literature at Cambridge. In 1931, when he was twenty-one, he left England and spent four formative years in Paris. He took a studio in Montparnasse and, in his own words, 'Into this cauldron I flung myself avidly.' He soon found himself drinking in bars with Giacometti and other surrealists. His next-door neighbour was Alexander Calder, who was busy making the moving sculptures that would become known as 'mobiles'; Trevelyan bought one of the first of these.

During his first year in Paris, Trevelyan made his first surrealist drawings and paintings. The following year, he met the printmaker S. W. Hayter and attended his engraving school, working alongside Picasso, Miró, Masson and Ernst.

In 1934 Trevelyan married Ursula Darwin, a pottery student and great-granddaughter of Charles

Darwin. They left Paris for London the following year and bought a group of old riverside buildings on the Thames called Durham Wharf. There they set up their studios, and it would remain Trevelyan's home for the rest of his life.

Missing his Parisian friends, the gregarious Trevelyan set about creating a new network of contacts in London that included most of the British surrealists. His own work now took on a new flavour, influenced by Klee, Miró, Masson and Ernst, and by 1936 he had developed a highly recognizable, personal urban world that marked the peak of his surrealist involvement. He was invited to contribute to the International Surrealist Exhibition held that year at the New Burlington Galleries in London, where five of his works were shown.

It was also in 1936 that he and several other surrealists took part in an experimental trial of the hallucinatory drug mescaline at Maudsley Hospital. Trevelyan, who made drawings under the influence of the drug, found the experience exhilarating.

He was called up in 1939 and became a lieutenant in the Royal Corps of Engineers. In 1942 he was sent to the Middle East and North Africa. When German soldiers, carrying machine-guns and dressed as nuns, were descending from the clouds in parachutes, he commented that 'life had caught up with surrealism and surrealism with life'.

After the war, Trevelyan took a studio in Paris. His relationship with his wife, who still lived in London, became increasingly remote until, in 1950, the marriage came to an end. The following year he married the artist Mary Fedden and together they revived Durham Wharf as a centre for the London art world, with many social gatherings and parties.

In his later years he travelled a great deal, painting and sketching wherever he went. He was still painting vigorously in 1988, the year of his death at the age of seventy-eight. Fedden lived on for another quarter of a century, with one of his final paintings always hanging above her bed.

# CLOVIS TROUILLE



## The French surrealist who has been described as a salacious satirist

BORN: 24 October 1889, La Fère, France, as Camille Clovis Trouille
LIVED: La Fère, 1889; Amiens, 1905; Paris, 1920
DIED: 24 September 1975, Paris

The work of Clovis Trouille is slick, salacious and satirical, but with a strong surrealist flavour. Consider his subjects: a cardinal wearing female underclothing beneath his red cloak; two nuns in a passionate embrace; a naked girl in handcuffs studied by a man holding a whip; priests examining a girl's body with a magnifying glass. These paintings are not faintly suggestive – they are wildly erotic and anticlerical. They go to such outrageous extremes that they are amusing rather than offensive. Trouille has been described as an 'angel of bad taste' and André Breton called him 'the Grand Master of Anything Goes'.

Trouille was born in northern France in 1889, making him twenty-five when he was drafted into the French army at the start of the First World War. As with all the surrealists, the slaughter of that war so horrified him that it turned him into an anarchist. He spent the rest of his life ridiculing the establishment with his lurid, deliberately scandalous paintings.

After the war, despite being classically trained as an artist, he ended up earning his living as an employee in a factory making mannequins for shop windows. It was there, of course, that he found himself spending a great deal of time face to face with the female form in the shape of life-sized dummies of fashion models, and it is easy to see how this may have influenced the style and subject matter of his paintings.

His work was discovered by Dalí in 1930. Breton wanted to arrange a solo exhibition for him, but Trouille refused because he wanted to remain independent of any movement. Bizarrely, his first solo show did not take place until 1962, by which time he was seventy-three years old. Entry to his second show was forbidden to anyone under the age of eighteen or over the age of seventy. Excluding children was understandable, but the exclusion of the aged was less so; perhaps he felt that the older generation might be too prudish and would complain to the authorities.

Trouille's relationship with the surrealists was complex. Asked if he was a surrealist himself, he replied: 'Anarchist, surrealist – I don't know. I paint what I love, I paint feminine beauty. For me everything is erotic. It is the most wonderful feeling.' However, he was certainly attracted to the surrealists' rebellious ideas, and Breton and his friends were in turn attracted to the sacrilegious elements in Trouille's work. They found his blatantly anti-religious and anti-military images immediately appealing, but he was wary of their attempts to involve him more closely in their movement.

In 1969 the poster for the notorious Broadway sex comedy *Oh! Calcutta!* showed a large pair of naked female buttocks that had been painted by Trouille, who was quoted as saying 'The ass forms a perfect circle designed to suggest the conquest of the moon.'

Trouille died in Paris at the age of eighty-five. He even found the subject of his own death an amusing subject for his paintings. He completed three works on the topic, called *My Funeral*, *My Burial* and *My Grave*. In his funeral we see a magnificent procession through the streets of Paris, with his coffin being followed by a parade of bishops, soldiers and dogs. His grave is in a cemetery where naked girls wearing live bats on their crotches lie around nonchalantly, and on his gravestone it is just possible to read his last words: 'Here lies the artist who lost his life while earning it'.

# JOHN TUNNARD

## The eccentric British surrealist who invented a unique private world

**BORN**: 17 May 1900 in Sandy, Bedfordshire **PARENTS**: Wealthy landowners **LIVED**: Sandy, 1900; London, 1919; Manchester, 1921; Bridgnorth, Shropshire, 1926; London, 1928; Cadgwith, Cornwall, 1933; Lamorna, Cornwall, 1952; Penzance, 1970 **PARTNER**: Mary May Robertson, m. 1926–70 **DIED**: 12 December 1971, Penzance

Those who knew John Tunnard described him as a larger-than-life figure. Peggy Guggenheim, who gave him one of his first exhibitions at her gallery in London, commented on his bizarre behaviour at the private view. Overhearing a woman asking 'Who is John Tunnard?' he aimed himself at her from across the room and performed three somersaults, landing at her feet and declaring theatrically, 'I am John Tunnard.'

Tunnard was born in Victorian England at Sandy in Bedfordshire. His family were wealthy and enjoyed rural pursuits, so that as a child the young Tunnard saw a great deal of the English countryside. He was sent away to school at Charterhouse, where his skill at drawing was noted. When he left he moved to London, where, at the end of the First World War, he enrolled at the Royal College of Art.

After graduating, he became a teacher in design at a London art school in 1929. By now he was married to a fellow art student, Mary May Robertson, and relations with his family had soured. Moving to Cornwall in 1933, he and his wife set up a silk-printing business to raise money. In the years that followed Tunnard started painting scenes of the local landscape. Then, in 1935, a transformation took place. Suddenly his landscapes were populated by strange geometric elements mixed with natural forms – a private world of Tunnard's own creation. In 1937, he contributed work to two important surrealist exhibitions.

When he was taken up by Peggy Guggenheim, Tunnard's reputation in London art circles improved. Even so, although some of his work sold, he found himself in serious trouble financially; he and Mary had to take up crab-pot making to earn enough money to survive. During the Second World War, when he was a conscientious objector, Tunnard served as an auxiliary coast guard along the Cornish coast.

After the war he was once again desperately short of funds and earned a living teaching at the Penzance School of Art, which left little time for his own painting. But when his mother died he was at last freed from financial worries, and in 1952 he bought a house in which a local artist had once lived. It was a painter's paradise. He and Mary created a magnificent garden and he became involved with the protection of local wildlife. When he was at his easel, however, his obsession with natural history made few inroads into the subject matter of his work. Instead he disappeared into his own private visual world with its own rules and images, seldom straying from his characteristic biogeometric scenes.

Although never one of the best known modern artists, Tunnard had some high-profile admirers within the art world. When Mark Rothko visited Cornwall in 1958 he was delighted to find that Tunnard was still actively painting, as he had long been a respected figure among the American avant-garde. In the 1960s his painting continued unabated and he greatly enjoyed the fact that, at last, he was receiving critical acclaim. Mary died in 1970, and Tunnard was quick to follow her the next year.

# REMEDIOS VARO



## The feminist Spanish surrealist who moved to Mexico where she became famous

**BORN**: 16 December 1908, Anglès, Girona, Catalonia **PARENTS**: Father a hydraulic engineer; mother a devout Catholic Basque **LIVED**: Anglès, 1908; Madrid, 1924; Paris, 1930; Barcelona, 1931; Paris, 1937; Mexico City, 1941; Venezuela, 1947; Mexico City, 1949 **PARTNERS**: Gerardo Lizarraga, m. 1930; Esteban Francés, 1931; Benjamin Péret, 1936–47; Walter Gruen, m. 1952–63 **DIED**: 8 October 1963, Mexico City

Remedios Varo's early life was spent travelling all over Spain and North Africa, with her family kept constantly on the move by her father's work as a hydraulic engineer. He would often take Varo to museums, encouraging her interest in the fine arts from an early age. Finally, after a childhood of temporary homes, at the age of fifteen she was able to stay in one place for a while, when she attended the Academy of San Fernando in Madrid. One of her fellow students there was Salvador Dalí.

In 1930, as soon as Varo had finished her studies, she married another fellow student: the painter Gerardo Lizarraga. They had both been exposed to surrealist ideas during their time at the Academy, and the following year they moved to Paris to immerse themselves in the avant-garde. After a year they returned to Spain, settling in Barcelona. Their marriage was to be short-lived; Varo later had a brief affair with the Spanish surrealist Esteban Francés.

In 1936, when the Spanish Civil War broke out, she met the French poet Benjamin Péret, a close friend of André Breton's and a hardline surrealist. He was in Barcelona acting as a foreign volunteer, and he and Varo quickly fell in love. When he returned to Paris in 1937, she followed him there.

She was closely involved with Breton's surrealist circle from 1937 to 1939.

Péret refused to fight in the Second World War and was sent to prison in Rennes. Varo was also arrested and interned, simply on the grounds that she was Péret's companion. She was released just before the Nazis arrived in Paris and made her way to Marseille with some of the other surrealists. Later, Péret was able to join her after making the long journey south hidden in a wagonload of straw.

There followed an anxious period in the South of France, trying to arrange their escape from war-torn Europe. They finally reached Mexico in late 1941 thanks to the help of Peggy Guggenheim, who had agreed to pay for their passage. Once there, they found an almost derelict apartment in Mexico City and made it their new home.

They were hosts to Varo's ex-lover Esteban Francés and other displaced surrealists during this period. Leonora Carrington lived with them for a while, and their modest apartment became a focus for wartime refugees from Paris, despite being in a ramshackle tenement building. Their guests had to enter through a window, and were then warned to avoid the holes in the floor.

Six years later, with the war in Europe over, Péret returned to Paris – but Varo did not accompany him, and it was the end of their relationship. In 1952 she acquired a new partner in Walter Gruen, an Austrian exile who had undergone many hardships in Nazi concentration camps. He played an important role in her life, encouraging her to take her surrealist painting more seriously. Varo's career was just taking off when in 1963, at the age of fifty-four, she suffered a massive heart attack, dying in the arms of a grief-stricken Gruen.

Although not well known on an international scale, Remedios Varo enjoyed great fame in Mexico. In her short life, she created 384 remarkable paintings. A posthumous retrospective of her work held in Mexico City in 1971 had the largest museum audiences in Mexican history.

# EDWARD WADSWORTH

## The skilful, posh surrealist, who cared little for the activities of the official movement

**BORN**: 29 October 1889, Cleckheaton, Yorkshire **PARENTS**: Father ran a worsted spinning business, left a fortune **LIVED**: Cleckheaton, 1899; Edinburgh, 1903; Munich, 1906; Bradford, 1908; London, 1909; navy, 1916; Liverpool and Bristol, 1918; London, 1919; Maresfield, Sussex, 1927; Buxton, Derbyshire, 1940; Maresfield, Sussex, 1945 **PARTNERS**: Fanny Eveleigh, m. 1912; Kathleen Dillon, 1929–31 **DIED**: 21 June 1949, London

Edward Wadsworth denied being a surrealist, saying, 'Without hestitation...I am not. I am just interested in painting.' Even so, many of his immaculate compositions are full of surrealist elements. Some of the most celebrated surrealists, including Max Ernst and Alexander Calder, admired his work and recognized that although he would have nothing to do with the group, he was a natural surrealist – whether he liked it or not.

Wadsworth was born in a small mill town in Yorkshire in 1889, the son of a rich industrialist. He was sent away to boarding school in Edinburgh, where a strong work ethic was drummed into him. This may account, in part, for the meticulous finish that he gave to all his paintings.

There were plans for him to take over the family firm, but Wadsworth had other ideas, and he managed to persuade his father to let him attend the Slade School from 1909. He married in 1912, to a young violinist called Fanny Eveleigh, and in the same year paid a visit to Paris that enabled him to see the latest trends in art at first hand.

This phase was interrupted by military service. Wadsworth's first duty was to man an anti-aircraft gun at Paddington Station in London, with the aim of shooting down German zeppelins. Later, he worked on improving camouflage techniques. After the war he produced paintings influenced by the dazzle work that had been introduced on merchant vessels to confuse the U-boats.

In 1921 Wadsworth's father died and left his only son, aged thirty-two, a fortune equivalent in today's money to about £9,500,000. It was not in Wadsworth's character, however, to go wild and revel in the high life. Instead he began painting seriously in a demanding medium, egg tempera. He said, rather drily, that tempera suited his temperament.

A few years later the Wadsworths bought a house in the country, midway between London and the south coast. There were many house parties at their new home as friends in the art world flocked there to be entertained. Guests included Max Ernst, Pierre Roy, Henry Moore, Paul Nash and Roland Penrose.

In 1928 the couple took a house in Paris for four months. A major influence on Wadsworth's work at this point was the French artist Fernand Léger. His praise of the visual appeal of manufactured objects struck a chord with Wadsworth, giving him the courage to include such items as central elements in his own work. He lovingly displayed compasses, floats, sextants, lanterns, binoculars, barometers and set squares as though they were objects of great beauty, laid out for the viewer to examine and marvel at.

Whether or not Wadsworth cared to admit it, these strange assemblies of inanimate objects had an unquestionably surrealist flavour and a haunting quality reminiscent of early de Chirico. The surrealists themselves certainly thought so, and Wadsworth's work was reproduced in magazines alongside that of Ernst, Magritte, Klee and Miró.

When the Second World War broke out, Wadsworth and his family retreated to the north of England; some of his most memorable and most strongly surrealist works date from this period. After the war, however, his style became increasingly abstract, and would remain so until his death in 1954 at the relatively early age of fifty-nine.

# SCOTTIE WILSON

## The outsider artist who was a highly original, natural surrealist

**BORN**: 6 June 1888, Glasgow, as Louis Freeman

**PARENTS**: Lithuanian; father a furrier

**LIVED**: Glasgow, 1888; India and South Africa (army), 1906; Glasgow, 1911; France (army), 1914; Toronto, 1918; Glasgow and London, 1922; Toronto, 1932; Vancouver, 1938; London, 1945

**DIED**: 26 March 1972, London

Scottie Wilson was unique in being influenced by no other artist and, for that matter, influencing nobody. He stood alone, creating his own private dream world: a self-styled primitive and the only 'outsider artist' to be accepted by André Breton as a surrealist.

Wilson was born of Jewish Lithuanian parents in the Gorbals district of Glasgow in 1888. In those days the Gorbals was a dangerous slum, and young Scottie endured a tough childhood there. He left school at the age of nine and would never learn to read or write.

His first job was as a barefoot paper boy, after which he graduated to helping with his brother's market stall. His only pleasures were visits to the zoo and the circus, where he saw animals that would later play a major role in his compositions.

When war broke out in 1914, he joined the army and served on the Western front. After the war he eventually deserted, escaping to Canada. He settled in Toronto, where he opened a junk shop. Business was slow and Wilson passed the time doodling. He began to create more and more drawings and eventually took to hanging them up in the window of his little shop for people to see. Local collectors noticed them as they passed by and started buying them.

This was happening at the end of the 1920s. Wilson now had a new source of income, and by the early forties he was exhibiting his work in Toronto, Winnipeg and Vancouver. When the Second World War ended in 1945, he decided to return to Britain and settled in London. He then began a campaign to market his work using methods hitherto unknown in the world of art. A poster he designed informed you that at the Music Hall in Aberdeen, for one week only, you could see him at work. You were also promised an 'Exhibition of 300 of the most Amazing Dream Pictures ever shown to the public'. Admission was one shilling, children sixpence.

Wilson organized many such events and, quite by chance, Roland Penrose wandered into one of them. Stunned by what he saw, he bought the entire show. He then arranged a London exhibition for Wilson and his work was shown to André Breton, who immediately decided to include him in the big surrealist show he was organizing in Paris in 1947.

Wilson now found himself hailed as an honorary surrealist. He was making wonderfully complex coloured drawings, using an obsessional cross-hatching technique. Tiny parallel ink lines were drawn over each coloured shape, creating a unique style. The images he employed were limited in their range. A random selection of 100 of his works revealed a total of seventeen categories: bulbous faces (390); large birds (212); small birds (534); fish (615); butterflies (18); flowers (132); trees (22); houses (63); smoking chimneys (33); grasses (26); sun or moon (29); sea monsters (40); snakes or eels (11); goblins (13); insects (7); turtles (5); unidentified animals (10).

Towards the end of his life, in the 1960s, Wilson lived in a single rented room that served as his bedroom, living room and studio. He did his own very simple cooking. After his death, a suitcase stuffed full of banknotes was discovered underneath his humble bed.

# FURTHER READING

**MARION ADNAMS**
– Dalton, John. 1968. *Marion Adnams: Paintings, Watercolours, Collages.* Nottingham: Midland Group Gallery

**EILEEN AGAR**
– Agar, Eileen. 1988. *A Look at My Life.* London: Methuen
– Blaswick, Iwona et al. 2021. *Eileen Agar: Angel of Anarchy.* London: Whitechapel Gallery
– Byatt, A. S. 2005. *Eileen Agar, 1899–1991: An Imaginative Playfulness.* London: Redfern Gallery
– Lambirth, Andrew. 1987. *Eileen Agar: A Retrospective.* London: Birch & Conran
– Remy, Michel. 2017. *Eileen Agar: Dreaming Oneself Awake.* London: Reaktion Books
– Simpson, Ann. 1999. *Eileen Agar, 1899–1991.* Edinburgh: National Galleries of Scotland

**JOHN ARMSTRONG**
– Glazebrook, Mark. 1975. *John Armstrong, 1893–1973.* London: Royal Academy
– Lambirth, Andrew. 2009. *John Armstrong: The Paintings.* London: Philip Wilson

**JEAN (HANS) ARP**
– Arntz, Wilhelm F. 1980. *Das Graphische Werk, 1912–1966. L'oeuvre gravé. The Graphic Work.* Haag in Oberbayern: Verlag Gertrud Arntz-Winter
– Arp, Jean. 1948. *On My Way: Poetry and Essays, 1912–1947.* New York: Wittenborn, Schultz
– Bowness, Alan. 1962. *Jean Arp.* London: Arts Council
– Bozo, Dominique et al. 1983. *Jean Arp. Le temps des papiers déchirés.* Paris: Pompidou
– Cathelin, Jean. 1959. *Arp.* Paris: Georges Fall
– Giedion-Welcker, Carola. 1957. *Jean Arp.* London: Thames & Hudson

– Hancock, Jane et al. 1986. *Arp, 1886–1966.* Cambridge: Cambridge University Press
– Jean, Marcel. 1974. *Jean Arp: Collected French Writings.* London: Calder & Boyars
– Rau, Bernd, and Michel Seuphor. 1981. *Hans Arp. Die Reliefs Oeuvre-Katalog.* Stuttgart: Hatje
– Read, Herbert. 1968. *Arp.* London: Thames & Hudson
– Robertson, Eric, and Frances Guy. 2017. *Arp: The Poetry of Forms.* Otterlo: Kröller-Müller Museum
– Soby, James Thrall. 1958. *Arp.* New York: Museum of Modern Art
– Trier, Eduard. 1968. *Jean Arp.* London: Thames & Hudson

**FRANCIS BACON**
– Alley, Ronald. 1964. *Francis Bacon.* London: Thames & Hudson
– Birch, James. 2022. *Bacon in Moscow.* London: Cheerio Publishing
– Cappock, Margarita. 2005. *Francis Bacon's Studio.* London: Merrell
– Davies, Hugh, and Sally Yard. 1986. *Francis Bacon.* New York: Abbeville Press
– Edwards, John. 2001. *7 Reece Mews: Francis Bacon's Studio.* London: Thames & Hudson
– Farson, Daniel. 1994. *The Gilded Gutter Life of Francis Bacon.* London: Vintage
– Harrison, Martin. 2005. *In Camera: Francis Bacon.* London: Thames & Hudson
– Harrison, Martin. 2016. *Francis Bacon: Catalogue Raisonné.* 5 vols. London: Estate of Francis Bacon
– Peppiat, Michael. 1996. *Francis Bacon: Anatomy of an Enigma.* London: Weidenfeld & Nicolson
– Peppiatt, Michael et al. 2022. *Francis Bacon: Man and Beast.* London: Royal Academy of Arts
– Sinclair, Andrew. 1993. *Francis Bacon: His Life and Violent Times.* New York: Crown
– Stevens, Mark, and Annalyn Swan. 2021. *Francis Bacon: Revelations.* London: Collins

- Sylvester, David. 1975. *Interviews with Francis Bacon*. London: Thames & Hudson
- Sylvester, David. 2000. *Looking Back at Francis Bacon*. London: Thames & Hudson

## ENRICO BAJ
- Jaguer, Édouard. 1956. *Enrico Baj*. Milan: Schettini
- Petit, Jean. 1975. *Enrico Baj: Catalogue of the Graphic Work and Multiples*. 2 vols. Geneva: Rousseau
- Reynolds, Michael et al. 2017. *Enrico Baj: The Artist's Home*. New York: Skira Rizzoli
- Van de Velde, Ronny. 1998. *Enrico Baj: Modifications*. Antwerp: Van de Velde

## BALTHUS
- Clair, Jean. 2001. *Balthus*. London: Thames & Hudson
- Klossowski de Rola, Stanislas. 1996. *Balthus*. London: Thames & Hudson
- Leymarie, Jean. 1979. *Balthus*. Geneva: Skira
- Rewald, Sabine. 2013. *Balthus: Cats and Girls*. New York: Metropolitan Museum of Art
- Russell, John et al. 1968. *Balthus*. London: Tate
- Soby, James Thrall. 1956. *Balthus*. New York: Museum of Modern Art

## JOHN BANTING
- Banting, John. 1946. *A Blue Book of Conversation*. London: Nicholson and Watson
- Melly, George. 1971. *John Banting*. London: Hamet Gallery

## WILLIAM BAZIOTES
- Alloway, Lawrence. 1965. *William Baziotes: A Memorial Exhibition*. New York: Guggenheim Foundation
- Bross, Louise, and David Rubin. 1987. *William Baziotes: A Commemorative Exhibition*. Reading, PA: Albright College
- Preble, Michael. 1978. *William Baziotes: A Retrospective Exhibition*. Newport Beach, CA: Newport Harbor Art Museum
- Preble, Michael. 1984. *William Baziotes: Paintings and Works on Paper, 1952–1961*. New York: Blum Helman Gallery
- Preble, Michael. 2004. *William Baziotes: Paintings and Drawings, 1934–1962*. Milan: Skira

## HANS BELLMER
- Jouffroy, Alain. 1961. *Bellmer*. New York: Copley Foundation
- Pieyre de Mandiargues, André. 1979. *Le Trésor cruel de Hans Bellmer*. Paris: Le Sphinx
- Racine, Bruno et al. 2006. *Hans Bellmer. Anatomie du désir*. Paris: Centre Pompidou
- Taylor, Sue. 2000. *Hans Bellmer: The Anatomy of Anxiety*. Cambridge, MA: MIT Press
- Webb, Peter, and Robert Short. 1985. *Hans Bellmer*. London: Quartet Books

## JOHN BIGGE
- Neill, Roger. 2014. 'An Oxfordshire Artist and Two World Wars', *Oxfordshire Limited Edition*, May 2014

## PAUL-ÉMILE BORDUAS
- Gagnon, François-Marc. 1976. *Paul-Émile Borduas, 1905–1960*. Ottawa: National Gallery of Canada
- Gagnon, François-Marc. 1978. *Paul-Émile Borduas. Biographie critique et analyse de l'oeuvre*. Montreal: Fides
- Gagnon, François-Marc. 1978. *Paul-Émile Borduas. Écrits/Writings, 1942–1958*. Halifax: Press of the Nova Scotia College of Art and Design
- Gagnon, François-Marc. 2014. *Paul-Émile Borduas: Life & Work*. Toronto: Art Canada Institute

## CONSTANTIN BRANCUSI
- Geist, Sidney. 1983. *Brancusi: A Study of the Sculpture*. New York: Hacker Art Books
- Lemny, Doïna. 2023. *Brancusi et ses muses*. Paris: Gourcuff Gradenigo
- Miller, Sanda. 2010. *Constantin Brancusi*. London: Reaktion Books

- Neutres, Jerome. 2013. *Brancusi: New York 1913–2013*. New York: Assouline
- Pearson, James. 2019. *Constantin Brancusi: Sculpting the Essence of Things*. Maidstone, Kent: Crescent Moon

## VICTOR BRAUNER
- Alexandrian, Sarane. 1965. *Les Dessins magiques de Victor Brauner*. Paris: Éditions Denoël
- Bozo, Dominique. 1972. *Victor Brauner*. Paris: Musée National d'Art Moderne
- Brun, Jeanne et al. 2010. *Victor Brauner et les arts primitifs*. Paris: Schoffel-Valluet & Samy Kinge
- Ceysson, Bernard et al. 1988. *Cahiers Victor Brauner*. Saint-Etienne: Musée d'Art Moderne
- Davidson, Susan et al. 2002. *Victor Brauner: Surrealist Hieroglyphs*. Houston, TX: Menil
- Jouffroy, Alain. 1959. *Brauner*. Paris: Georges Fall
- Jouffroy, Alain. 1998. *Victor Brauner. Le Tropisme totémique*. Creil: Éditions Dumerchez
- Semin, Didier. 1990. *Victor Brauner*. Paris: Filipacchi
- Semin, Didier et al. 1996. *Victor Brauner*. Paris: Pompidou

## ANDRÉ BRETON
- Breton, André. 1936. *What Is Surrealism?* London: Faber & Faber
- Breton, André. 1946. *Les Manifestes du surréalisme*. Paris: Sagittaire
- Breton, André. 1947. *Arcane 17*. Paris: Sagittaire
- Breton, André. 1993. *Conversations: The Autobiography of Surrealism*. New York: Marlowe
- Breton, André. 1996. *Free Rein*. Lincoln: University of Nebraska Press
- Breton, André. 1999. *Nadja*. London: Penguin
- Breton, André. 2002. *Surrealism and Painting*. Boston: MFA Publishing
- Breton, André, and Marcel Duchamp. 1947. *Le Surréalisme en 1947*. Paris: Maeght éditeur
- Breton, André et al. 1957. *L'Art magique*. Paris: Formes et Reflets
- Breton, André et al. 1959. *L'Exposition internationale du surréalisme*. Paris: Galérie Daniel Cordier
- Goutier, Jean-Michel et al. 2003. *André Breton. 42 Rue Fontaine. Auction Catalogues*. 8 vols. Paris: Calmels Cohen
- Gracq, Julien et al. 1991. *André Breton. La Beauté convulsive*. Paris: Éditions du Centre Pompidou
- Pierre, José. 1986. *L'Aventure surréaliste autour d'André Breton*. Paris: Filipacchi
- Polizzotti, Mark. 1995. *Revolution of the Mind: The Life of André Breton*. London: Bloomsbury
- Rosemont, Franklin. 1978. *André Breton and the First Principles of Surrealism*. London: Pluto Press

## EMMY BRIDGWATER
- Millington, Ruth, Tor Scott and Lisa Rull. 2022. *Emmy Bridgwater: Edge of Beyond*. London: Mayor Gallery

## EDWARD BURRA
- Causey, Andrew. 1985. *Edward Burra: Complete Catalogue*. Oxford: Phaidon
- Chappel, William, ed. 1985. *Well, Dearie! The Letters of Edward Burra*. London: Gordon Fraser
- Drew, Joanna et al. 1985. *Edward Burra*. London: Hayward Gallery
- Martin, Simon et al. 2011. *Edward Burra*. Surrey: Lund Humphries
- Melly, George. 1985. *Edward Burra*. London: Arts Council
- Rothenstein, John. 1973. *Edward Burra*. London: The Tate Gallery
- Stevenson, Jane. 2007. *Edward Burra: Twentieth-Century Eye*. London: Jonathan Cape

## ALEXANDER CALDER
- Calder, Alexander. 1967. *Calder: An Autobiography with Pictures*. London: Allen Lane Press
- Grace, Ann et al. 2019. *Alexander Calder: Radical Inventor*. Milan: Five Continents Editions

- Manes, Cara. 2021. *Alexander Calder: Modern from the Start.* New York: Museum of Modern Art
- Perl, Jed. 2017. *Calder: The Conquest of Time.* New York: Knopf
- Perl, Jed. 2020. *Calder: The Conquest of Space.* New York: Knopf
- Prather, Marla. 1998. *Alexander Calder, 1898–1976.* New Haven, CT: Yale University Press
- Sweeney, James Johnson. 1943. *Alexander Calder.* New York: Museum of Modern Art
- Turner, Eliaabeth Hutton, and Oliver Wick. 2004. *Calder – Miró.* London: Philip Wilson

## LEONORA CARRINGTON

- Aberth, Susan. 2004. *Leonora Carrington: Surrealism, Alchemy, and Art.* Aldershot: Lund Humphries
- Carrington, Gabriel Weisz. 2021. *The Invisible Painting: My Memoir of Leonora Carrington.* Manchester: Manchester University Press
- Carrington, Leonora. 1976. *The Hearing Trumpet.* London: Penguin
- Chadwick, Whitney. 1994. *Leonora Carrington.* Mexico City: Consejo Nacional para la Cultura y las Artes
- Martin, Carlos et al. 2023. *Leonora Carrington: Revelation.* Barcelona: RM Editorial
- Moorhead, Joanna. 2017. *The Surreal Life of Leonora Carrington.* London: Virago Press
- Moorhead, Joanna. 2023. *Surreal Spaces: The Life and Art of Leonora Carrington.* London: Thames & Hudson

## MARC CHAGALL

- Chagall, Marc. 2018. *My Life.* London: Penguin Classics
- Compton, Susan. 1985. *Chagall.* London: Weidenfeld & Nicolson
- Haftmann, Werner. 1998. *Chagall.* New York: Abrams
- Metzger, Rainer, and Ingo F. Walther. 2016. *Chagall.* Cologne: Taschen
- Schlenker, Ines. 2021. *Chagall.* Munich: Prestel
- Sweeney, James Johnson. 1946. *Marc Chagall.* New York: Museum of Modern Art

## GIORGIO DE CHIRICO

- Baldacci, Paolo, and Gerd Roos. 2019–20. *Catalogue Raisonné of the Works of Giorgio de Chirico.* Turin: Allemandi
- Benzi, Fabio. 2023. *Giorgio De Chirico: Life and Paintings.* New York: Rizzoli Electa
- De Chirico, Giorgio. 1971. *The Memoirs of Giorgio De Chirico.* London: Peter Owen
- Faldi, Italo. 1949. *Il Primo De Chirico.* Milan: Alfieri
- Far, Isobella. 1968. *De Chirico.* New York: Abrams
- Joppolo, Giovanni et al. 1979. *De Chirico.* Milan: Mondodori
- Noel-Johnson, Victoria. 2019. *Giorgio de Chirico: The Changing Face of Metaphysical Art.* Milan: Skira
- Schmied, Wieland. 2002. *Giorgio de Chirico: The Endless Journey.* Munich: Prestel

## CECIL COLLINS

- Anderson, William. 1988. *Cecil Collins: The Quest for the Great Happiness.* London: Barrie & Jenkins
- Collins, Cecil, and Brian Keeble. 2002. *The Vision of the Fool.* Ashuelot, NH: Golgonooza Press
- Collins, Judith. 1989. *Cecil Collins: A Retrospective Exhibition.* London: Tate
- Comfort, Alex, and Conrad Senat. 1946. *Cecil Collins: Paintings and Drawings (1935–1945).* Oxford: Counterpoint
- Keeble, Brian. 2009. *Cecil Collins: The Artist as Writer and Image Maker.* Ashuelot, NH: Golgonooza Press
- Rowe, Nomi. 2009. *In Celebration of Cecil Collins.* London: Paul Holberton

## ITHELL COLQUHOUN

- Gale, Matthew, and Amy Hale. 2022. *Ithell Colquhoun: Bonsoir.* London: Tate

- Hale, Amy. 2011. *The Supersensual Life of Ithell Colquhoun*. London: Francis Boutle
- Hale, Amy. 2020. *Ithell Colquhoun: Genius of the Fern Loved Gully*. London: Strange Attractor Press
- Hale, Amy. 2024. *Sex Magic: Ithell Colquhoun's Diagrams of Love*. London: Tate
- Ratcliffe, Eric. 2007. *Ithell Colquhoun: Pioneer Surrealist*. Oxford: Mandrake
- Shillitoe, Richard. 2010. *Ithell Colquhoun: Magician Born of Nature*. London: Lulu

## JOSEPH CORNELL

- Ashton, Dore. 1974. *A Joseph Cornell Album*. New York: Viking Press
- Blair, Lindsay. 1998. *Joseph Cornell's Vision of Spiritual Order*. London: Reaktion Books
- Caws, Mary Ann. 1993. *Joseph Cornell's Theatre of the Mind*. London: Thames & Hudson
- Corman, Catherine. 2007. *Joseph Cornell's Dreams*. Cambridge, MA: Exact Change
- Edwards, Jason, and Stephanie L. Taylor. 2007. *Joseph Cornell: Opening the Box*. Bern: Peter Lang
- Hartigan, Lynda Roscoe et al. 2003. *Joseph Cornell: Shadowplay, Eterniday*. London: Thames & Hudson
- Lea, Sarah et al. 2015. *Joseph Cornell: Wanderlust*. London: Royal Academy of Arts
- Schafner, Ingrid. 2003. *The Essential Joseph Cornell*. New York: Abrams
- Solomon, Deborah. 1997. *Utopia Parkway: The Life and Work of Joseph Cornell*. London: Jonathan Cape
- Tashjian, Dickran. 1992. *Joseph Cornell: Gifts of Desire*. Miami: Grassfield Press
- Waldman, Diane. 2002. *Joseph Cornell: Master of Dreams*. New York: Abrams

## ARTUR DO CRUZEIRO SEIXAS

- Letria, José Jorge, 2014. *Cruzeiro Seixas: A Liberdade Livre*. Lisbon: Guerra e Paz

- Pinto de Almeida, Bernardo, Mario Cesariny et al. 2000. *Cruzeiro Seixas*. Famalicão: Centro de Estudos do Surrealismo, Fundação Cupertino de Miranda

## SALVADOR DALÍ

- Ades, Dawn. 2000. *Dalí's Optical Illusions*. New Haven, CT: Yale University Press
- Caws, Mary Ann. 2008. *Salvador Dalí*. London: Reaktion Books
- Cowles, Fleur. 1959. *The Case of Salvador Dalí*. London: Heinemann
- Dalí, Salvador. 1935. *Conquest of the Irrational*. New York: Julien Levy
- Dalí, Salvador. 1944. *Hidden Faces*. New York: Dial Press
- Dalí, Salvador. 1948. *The Secret Life of Salvador Dalí*. London: Vision Press
- Dalí, Salvador. 1994. *The Diary of a Genius*. London: Creation Books
- De Burca, Jackie. 2018. *Salvador Dalí at Home*. London: White Lion
- Descharnes, Robert. 1962. *The World of Salvador Dalí*. London: Macmillan
- Descharnes, Robert, and Gilles Neret. 1994. *Salvador Dalí 1904–1989*. 2 vols. Cologne: Taschen
- Etherington-Smith, Meredith. 1992. *Dalí: A Biography*. London: Sinclair-Stevenson
- Field, Albert. 1996. *The Official Catalog of the Graphic Works of Salvador Dalí*. New York: Salvador Dalí Archives
- Gérard, Max. 1968. *Dalí*. New York: Abrams
- Gibson, Ian. 1997. *The Shameful Life of Salvador Dalí*. London: Faber & Faber
- Gibson, Ian et al. 1994. *Salvador Dalí: The Early Years*. London: Thames & Hudson
- King, Elliot H. 2010. *Salvador Dalí: The Late Work*. New Haven, CT: Yale University Press
- Parinaud, André. 1977. *The Unspeakable Confessions of Salvador Dalí*. London: Quartet Books

- Romero, Luis. 1975. *Dalí*. Secaucus, NJ: Chartwell Books
- Schaffner, Ingrid. 2002. *Salvador Dalí's Dream of Venus*. New York: Princeton Architectural Press
- Secrest, Meryle. 1986. *Salvador Dalí: The Surrealist Jester*. London: Weidenfeld & Nicolson
- Shanes, Eric. 2010. *The Life and Masterworks of Salvador Dalí*. New York: Parkstone
- Whitaker, Robert. 2006. *In the Company of Dalí*. Sutton Valence, Kent: Touchstone Books

## JULIO DE DIEGO
- *Julio de Diego*. 1950. New York: Associated American Artists

## TONI DEL RENZIO
- Del Renzio, Toni. 2007. *Alter Ego Doppelganger (Surrealist Bulletin No. 1)*. Bradford: Northern Artists Gallery

## PAUL DELVAUX
- Brasseur, Camille. 2020. *Paul Delvaux: The Man Who Loved Trains*. Ghent: Snoeck
- Butor, Michel et al. 1975. *Delvaux. Catalogue de l'oeuvre peint*. Paris: La Bibliothèque des Arts
- Gaffé, René. 1945. *Paul Delvaux ou Les Rêves éveillés*. Brussels: La Boétie
- Langui, Emile. 1949. *Paul Delvaux*. Venice: Alfieri
- Rombaut, Marc. 1990. *Paul Delvaux*. Barcelona: Ediciones Polígrafa
- Scott, David. 1992. *Paul Delvaux: Surrealizing the Nude*. London: Reaktion Books
- Sojcher, Jacques. 1991. *Paul Delvaux*. Paris: Ars Mundi
- Spaak, Claude. 1954. *Paul Delvaux*. Antwerp: De Sikkel

## LEO DOHMEN
- Ceuleers, Jan. 1999. *Leo Dohmen. Photographs, assemblages and collages*. Leuven: Exhibitions International
- Ceuleers, Jan. 2000. *Leo Dohmen, 1929–1999: Look! Think! Win!* Antwerp: Ronny van der Velde
- Moffett, Cleveland et al. 1992. *Post-Columbian Art: Leo Dohmen*. Antwerp: Den Tijd
- Moore, S. Derrickson et al. 1998. *Leo Dohmen: Post-Columbian Art in Las Cruces*. Las Cruces, NM: Cutter Gallery

## ÓSCAR DOMÍNGUEZ
- Castro, Fernando. 1978. *Óscar Domínguez y el surrealismo*. Madrid: Catedra
- Guinon, Emmanuel et al. 1996. *Óscar Domínguez. Antologica 1926–1957*. Tenerife: Centro de Arte La Granja
- Serrano, Véronique. 2005. *Óscar Domínguez et le surréalisme 1906–1957*. Paris: Éditions Hazan
- Westerdahl, Eduardo. 1968. *Óscar Domínguez*. Barcelona: Ed. Gustavo Gili
- Westerdahl, Eduardo. 1971. *Óscar Domínguez*. Madrid: Direccion General de Bellas Artes
- Xuriguera, Gérard. 1973. *Óscar Domínguez*. Paris: Filipacchi

## ENRICO DONATI
- Selz, Peter H. 1965. *Enrico Donati*. Paris: Georges Fall
- Wolff, Theodore F. 1984. *Enrico Donati: The Most Recent Work*. Paris: Georges Fall
- Wolff, Theodore F. 1996. *Enrico Donati: Surrealism and Beyond*. New York: Hudson Hills Press

## MARCEL DUCHAMP
- Alexandrian. 1977. *Marcel Duchamp*. Switzerland: Bonfini Press
- Anderson, Wayne. 2011. *Marcel Duchamp: The Failed Messiah*. Geneva: Éditions Fabriart
- Baas, Jacquelynn. 2019. *Marcel Duchamp and the Art of Life*. Cambridge, MA: MIT Press
- Bailly, Jean-Christophe. 1986. *Duchamp*. London: Art Data

- Debray, Cecile. 2014. *Marcel Duchamp: La peinture meme: La peinture, meme.* Paris: Pompidou
- Hamilton, Richard. 1966. *The Almost Complete Works of Marcel Duchamp.* London: Arts Council
- Lebel, Robert et al. 2021. *Marcel Duchamp.* Zurich: Hauser & Wirth
- Marquis, Alice Goldfarb. 2002. *Marcel Duchamp: The Bachelor Stripped Bare.* Boston: MFA Publications
- Mink, Jnis. 2006. *Marcel Duchamp, 1887–1968: Art as Anti-Art.* Cologne: Taschen
- Schwarz, Arturo. 1969. *The Complete Works of Marcel Duchamp.* New York: Abrams
- Tomkins, Calvin. 1985. *The World of Marcel Duchamp, 1887–1968.* Amsterdam: Time-Life Books
- Tomkins, Calvin. 2014. *Duchamp: A Biography.* New York: Museum of Modern Art

## MAX ERNST
- Camfield, William A. 1993. *Max Ernst: Dada and the Dawn of Surrealism.* Munich: Prestel
- Derenthal, Ludger, and Jürgen Pech. 1992. *Max Ernst.* Paris: Nouvelles Éditions Françaises
- Ernst, Max. 1929. *La Femme 100 Têtes.* Paris: Éditions du Carrefour
- Ernst, Max. 1948. *Beyond Painting.* New York: Wittenborn, Schultz
- Ernst, Max. 1961. *Max Ernst.* London: Arts Council
- Ernst, Max. 1970. *Écritures.* Paris: Gallimard
- Ernst, Max et al. 1948. *Max Ernst: Beyond Painting.* New York: Schultz
- McNab, Robert. 2004. *Ghost Ships: A Surrealist Love Triangle.* New Haven, CT: Yale University Press
- Pretzell, Loni, Lothar Pretzell et al. 1971. *Hommage à Max Ernst.* Stuttgart: Verlag Kunstkreis
- Quinn, Edward. 1984. *Max Ernst.* Barcelona: Ediciones Polígrafa
- Russell, John. 1967. *Max Ernst: Life and Work.* New York: Abrams

- Spies, Werner. 1971. *Max Ernst, 1950–1970: The Return of La Belle Jardinière.* New York: Abrams
- Spies, Werner. 1975–2004. *Max Ernst. Oeuvre-Katalog.* 7 vols. Houston, TX: Menil Foundation
- Spies, Werner. 1991. *Max Ernst: A Retrospective.* Munich: Prestel
- Spies, Werner. 1998. *Max Ernst. Sculptures – Maisons – Paysages.* Cologne: DuMont Buchverlag
- Spies, Werner. 2006. *Max Ernst: Life and Work.* London: Thames & Hudson
- Spies, Werner. 2008. *Max Ernst. Une Semaine de bonté.* Paris: Gallimard
- Waldberg, Patrick. 1958. *Max Ernst.* Paris: Jean-Jacques Pauvert
- Warlick, M. E. 2001. *Max Ernst and Alchemy.* Austin: University of Texas Press

## MERLYN EVANS
- Gooding, Mel. 2010. *Merlyn Evans.* Moffat: Cameron & Hollis
- Jenkins, David Fraser et al. 1985. *The Political Paintings of Merlyn Evans: 1930–1950.* London: Tate
- Murray, Andrew et al. 1988. *Merlyn Evans 1910–1973: A Retrospective Exhibition.* London: Mayor & Redfern Galleries
- Pope-Hennessy, John et al. 1972. *The Graphic Works of Merlyn Evans.* London: Victoria and Albert Museum

## LEONOR FINI
- Brion, Marcel. 1955. *Leonor Fini et son oeuvre.* Paris: Jesan-Jacques Pauvert
- Fini, Leonor. 1994. *Leonor Fini: Peintures.* Paris: Éditions Michèle Trinckvel
- Jelenski, Constantin. 1968. *Leonor Fini.* Lausanne: Éditions Clairefontaine
- Overstreet, Richard, and Neil Zukerman. 2021. *Leonor Fini: Catalogue Raisonné of the Oil Paintings.* Zurich: Weinstein, Scheidegger & Spiess
- Selsdon, Esther. 1999. *Leonor Fini.* New York: Parkstone Press

- Villani, Tiziana. 1989. *Parcours dans l'oeuvre de Leonor Fini*. Paris: Éditions Michèle Trinckvel
- Webb, Peter. 2009. *Sphinx: The Life and Art of Leonor Fini*. New York: Vendome Press

## ESTEBAN FRANCÉS
- Francés, Esteban. 1997. *Esteban Francés 1913–1976*. Madrid: Dirección General del Patrimonio Cultural, Consejería de Educación y Cultura, Comunidad de Madrid
- Heathers, Anne, and Esteban Francés. 1961. *A Handful of Surprises*. New York: Harcourt, Brace & World

## WILHELM FREDDIE
- Freddie, Wilhelm. 2009. *Wilhelm Freddie: Stick the Fork in Your Eye*. Copenhagen: Statens Museum for Kunst
- Schmidt, Palle. 1976. *Wilhelm Freddie – den evige oprører*. Copenhagen: Chr. Erichsens Forlag
- Skov, Birger Raben. 1993. *Wilhelm Freddie: A Brief Encounter with His Work*. Copenhagen: Knudtzons Bogtrykkeri
- Thorsen, Jorgen. 1972. *Where Has Freddie Been? Freddie 1909–1972*. London: Acoris
- Villasden, Villads et al. 1989. *Freddie*. Copenhagen: Statens Museum for Kunst

## ALBERTO GIACOMETTI
- Bonnefoy, Yves. 2001. *Alberto Giacometti*. New York: Assouline
- Bouvard, Émilie. 2022. *Giacometti: Toward the Ultimate Figure*. New Haven, CT: Yale University Press
- Fontanella, Meghan, and Karole P. B. Vail. 2018. *Giacometti*. New York: Guggenheim Museum
- Giacometti, Alberto. 2022, *Why I Am a Sculptor*. Paris: Hermann
- Grenier, Catherine. 2018. *Alberto Giacometti: A Biography*. Paris: Flammarion
- Lord, James. 1986. *Giacometti: A Biography*. London: Faber & Faber
- Peppiat, Michael. 2023. *Giacometti in Paris: A Life*. London: Bloomsbury
- Sylvester, David. 1965. *Alberto Giacometti*. London: Arts Council

## HENRI GOETZ
- Bergstrom, Gunnar. 1973. *L'oeuvre gravé de Henri Goetz*. Stockholm: Sonet
- Geay, Jean-Pierre. 1989. *L'Univers nocturne de Henri Goetz*. Sauveterre: La Balance
- Trintignan, Helene et al. 2001. *Henri Goetz: Catalogue raisonné*. Paris: Éditions Garnier Nocera

## JULIO GONZÁLEZ
- Descargues, Pierre. 1971. *Julio González*. Paris: Le Musée de poche
- Gorvy, Brett, and Emmanuel Clavé. 1999. *Works by Julio González*. London: Christie's
- Hammacherm, A. M. 1999. *Julio González: face à face: dessins, sculptures*. Braine-l'Alleud: Centre d'art Nicolas de Staël
- Reid, Norman et al. 1970. *Julio González*. London: Tate Gallery
- Tabart, Marielle et al. 1999. *González Picasso Dialogue*. Paris: Pompidou

## ARSHILE GORKY
- De Chassey, Eric. 2007. *Arshile Gorky: Hommage*. Paris: Pompidou
- Gale, Matthew. 2010. *Arshile Gorky: Enigma and Nostalgia*. London: Tate Publishing
- Lader, Melvin P. 1985. *Arshile Gorky*. New York: Abbeville Press
- Rand, Harry. 1981. *Arshile Gorky: The Implications of Symbols*. London: Prior
- Spender, Matthew. 2001. *From a High Place: A Life of Arshile Gorky*. Los Angeles: UCLA Press
- Taylor, Michael R. 2009. *Arshile Gorky: A Retrospective*. Philadelphia: Philadelphia Museum of Art
- Theriault, Kim S. 2010. *Rethinking Arshile Gorky*. University Park: Pennsylvania State University Press

**EUGENIO GRANELL**
- Ballesté, Arbos, and Juan Manuel Bonet. 1989. *Eugenio Granell*. Seville: Caja San Fernando
- Bonet, Juan Manuel. 1993. *Eugenio Granell*. Santiago de Compostela: Consorcio da Cidade de Santiago
- Guigon, Emmanuel. 1995. *Eugenio Granell: Inventory of the Planet*. Santiago de Compostela: Fundación Eugenio Granell
- López Barxas, Francisco. 2000. *Eugenio Granell. O surrealismo felizmente vivo*. Vigo: Ir Indo Edicions

**JANE GRAVEROL**
- Scutenaire, Louis. 1962. *Peinture de Jane Graverol*. Brussels: Les Lèvres Nues

**SAM HAILE**
- Remy, Michel et al. 1987. *Sam Haile*. London: Birch & Conran
- Rice, Paul. 1993. *Sam Haile: Potter and Painter*. London: Bellew Publishing

**DAVID HARE**
- Goldwater, Robert. 1957. *Sculpture by David Hare and Sidney Gordin*. New York: The Gallery, Katonah Village Library, Katonah
- Goossen, E. C. et al. 1958. *Three American Sculptors: Herbert Ferber, David Hare, Ibram Lassaw*. New York: Grove Press

**S. W. HAYTER**
- Fröhlich, Fanchon, and Sylvie Le Seac'h. 2022. *S. W. Hayter's Research on Experimental Drawing*. Seoul: Bada Publishing
- Hacker, P. M. S. 1988. *The Renaissance of Gravure: Art of S. W. Hayter*. London: Clarendon Press
- Hayter, S. W. 1962. *About Prints*. Oxford: Oxford University Press
- Hayter, S. W. 1962. *New Ways of Gravure*. Oxford: Oxford University Press
- Hayter, S. W. et al. 1976. *S. W. Hayter. Peintures, 1940–1976*. Paris: Galérie de Seine

- Reynolds, Graham. 1967. *The Engravings of S. W. Hayter*. London: HMSO
- Robertson, Bryan. 1958. *S. W. Hayter Retrospective; 1929–1957*. London: Arts Council

**JACQUES HÉROLD**
- Alexandrian, Sarane. 1993. *Jacques Hérold: Étude historique et critique*. Paris: Georges Fall
- Poullain, Christine. 2010. *Jacques Hérold et le surréalisme*. Marseille: Musée Cantini
- Waldberg, Patrick. 1974. *Jacques Hérold. Aux frontières de l'extramonde*. Milan: Annunciata

**CHARLES HOWARD**
- Miller, Dorothy C. 1942. *Americans 1942*. New York: Museum of Modern Art

**GEORGES HUGNET**
- Baum, Timothy et al. 2003. *Georges Hugnet. Collages*. Paris: Éditions Léo Scheer
- Georgel, Pierre. 1978. *Peregrinations de Georges Hugnet*. Paris: Pompidou

**MARCEL JEAN**
- Jean, Marcel. 1960. *The History of Surrealist Painting*. London: Weidenfeld & Nicolson
- Jean, Marcel. 1971. *Marcel Jean: Paintings and Drawings, 1935–1948*. New York: Gimpel
- Jean, Marcel. 1980. *The Autobiography of Surrealism*. New York: Viking Press
- Jean, Marcel. 1991. *Au galop dans le vent*. Paris: Jean-Pierre de Monza

**HUMPHREY JENNINGS**
- Coombs, Neil George. 2014. *The Communicating Village: Humphrey Jennings and Surrealism*. Ph.D. thesis, Liverpool John Moores University
- Jackson, Kevin. 1993. *The Humphrey Jennings Film Reader*. Manchester: Carcanet

- Jackson, Kevin. 2004. *Humphrey Jennings*. London: Picador
- Jennings, Mary-Lou. 1982. *Humphrey Jennings: Film-Maker, Painter, Poet*. London: BFI Publishing

**FRIDA KAHLO**
- Beecroft, Julian. 2017. *Frida Kahlo Masterpieces of Art*. London: Flame Tree
- Burrus, Christina. 2008. *Frida Kahlo: 'I Paint my Reality'*. London: Thames & Hudson
- Herrera, Hayden. 2018. *Frida: The Biography of Frida Kahlo*. London: Bloomsbury
- Lozano, Luis-Martín. 2021. *Frida Kahlo: The Complete Paintings*. Cologne: Taschen
- Milner, Frank. 1995. *Frida Kahlo*. London: Chrysalis Books
- Serrano, Jessica et al. 2022. *Frida Kahlo: Her Universe*. Barcelona: RM Editorial
- Velasquez, Roxana. 2022. *Frida Kahlo: The Masterworks*. New York: Rizzoli
- Wilcox, Claire, and Circe Henestrosa. 2018. *Frida Kahlo: Making Herself Up*. London: Victoria and Albert Museum

**PAUL KLEE**
- Barr, Alfred H. Jr. et al. 1945. *Paul Klee*. New York: Museum of Modern Art
- Bourneuf, Annie. 2015. *Paul Klee: The Visible and the Legible*. Chicago: University of Chicago Press
- Eggelhöfer, Fabienne et al. 2020. *Paul Klee: Life and Work*. Berlin: Hatje Cantz
- Grohmann, Will. 1954. *Paul Klee*. Florence: Sansoni
- Grohmann, Will. 1987. *Klee*. London: Thames & Hudson
- Güse, Ernst-Gerhard, ed. 1991. *Paul Klee: Dialogue with Nature*. Munich: Prestel
- Hodge, Susie. 2014. *Paul Klee: Masterpieces of Art*. London: Flame Tree
- Jaffe, Hans L. 1972. *Klee*. London: Hamlyn
- Klee, Felix et al. 1987. *Paul Klee. Opere dal 1885 al 1933*. Mendrisio, Switzerland: Museo d'Arte Mendrisio

- Klee, Paul. 1973. *Pedagogical Sketchbook*. London: Faber & Faber
- Lanchner, Caroline. 1987. *Paul Klee*. New York: Museum of Modern Art
- Naubert-Riser, Constance. 1988. *Klee: The Masterworks*. London: Studio Editions
- Oliva, Achille Bonito. 1982. *Paul Klee. L'annunciazione del segno. Disegni e acquerelli*. Milan: Mazzotta
- Partsch, Susanna. 2023. *Klee*. Cologne: Taschen
- Rigo, Mario et al. 1986. *Paul Klee*. Milan: Mazzotta
- Rümelin, Christian et al. 1998–2004. *Paul Klee. Catalogue raisonné*. 9 vols. London: Thames & Hudson
- Sala, Aldo et al. 1992. *Paul Klee*. Milan: Mazzotta
- San Lazzaro, Gualtieri di. 1957. *Klee: A Study of His Life and Work*. London: Thames & Hudson

**FÉLIX LABISSE**
- Baligand, Françoise. 2005. *Félix Labisse 1905–1982: Exposition rétrospective du centenaire de sa naissance*. Douai: Musée de la Chartreuse
- Brachot, Isy, and Christine Brachot. 1982. *Félix Labisse*. Paris: Isy Brachot
- Cassou, Jean. 1979. *Labisse. Catalogue de l'Oeuvre Peint, 1927–1979*. Brussels: Isy Brachot
- Dotremont, Christian. 1946. *Labisse*. Brussels: Éditions La Boetie
- Martineau, Richard. 1972. *Félix Labisse*. Ghent: Snoeck
- Waldberg, Patrick. 1970. *Félix Labisse*. Brussels: André de Rache

**WIFREDO LAM**
- Alberro, Alexander et al. 2022. *Wifredo Lam: The Imagination at Work*. New York: Pace Publishing
- Amico, Giorgio. 2006. *Wifredo Lam: Il Grande Surrealista Cubano (1902–1982)*. Bolsena: Massari Editore
- Balderrama, Maria R. 1992. *Wifredo Lam and His Contemporaries, 1938–1952*. New York: Studio Museum, Harlem

- Benitez, Helena. 1999. *Wifredo and Helena: My Life with Wifredo Lam, 1939–1950*. Lausanne: Acatos
- Breton, André et al. 1979. *Wifredo Lam. XXe Siècle*, no. 52
- Cernuschi, Claude. 2019. *Race, Anthropology, and Politics in the Work of Wifredo Lam*. London: Routledge
- Fouchet, Max-Pol. 1976. *Wifredo Lam*. Barcelona: Ediciones Polígrafa
- Goizueta, Elizabeth T. 2014. *Wifredo Lam: Imagining New Worlds*. Boston: McMullen Museum of Art
- Laurin-Lam, Lou. 1996–2002. *Wifredo Lam: Catalogue Raisonné of the Painted Work*. 2 vols. Lausanne: Acatos
- Sims, Lowery Stokes. 2002. *Wifredo Lam and the International Avant-Garde*. Austin: University of Texas Press
- Tonneau-Ryckelynck, Dominique, and Pascaline Dron. 1993. *Wifredo Lam. Oeuvre gravé et lithographie. Catalogue raisonné*. Gravelines: Musée de Gravelines

## JACQUELINE LAMBA
- Lamba, Jacqueline. 2001. *In Spite of Everything, Spring*. East Hampton, NY: Pollock-Krasner House and Study Center

## LEN LYE
- Brobbel, Paul. 2018. *The Long Dream of Waking: New Perspectives on Len Lye*. Christchurch: Canterbury University Press
- Horrocks, Roger. 2001. *Len Lye: A Biography*. Auckland: Auckland University Press
- Lye, Len. 2015. *Zizz! The Art and Life of Len Lye*. Wellington: Awa Press
- Shiozaki, Erik. 1980. *Len Lye: Artist, Painter, Film Maker, Kinetic Sculptor*. MA thesis, California State University, Los Angeles

## CONROY MADDOX
- Levy, Silvano. 1995. *Conroy Maddox: Surreal Enigmas*. Keele: Keele University Press
- Levy, Silvano. 2003. *The Scandalous Eye: The Surrealism of Conroy Maddox*. Liverpool: Liverpool University Press
- Rosemont, Penelope, and Paul Garon. 2019. *Conroy Maddox: Letters to Surrealists in the USA*. Chicago: Black Swan Press
- Short, Robert. 1978. *Conroy Maddox: Surrealism Unlimited*. London: Camden Arts Centre

## RENÉ MAGRITTE
- Adams, Alexander. 2022. *Magritte: Masters of Art*. Munich: Prestel
- Allmer, Patricia. 2019. *Critical Lives: René Magritte*. London: Reaktion Books
- Benesch, Evelyn et al. 2005. *René Magritte: The Key to Dreams*. Ghent: Ludion
- Danchev, Alex. 2020. *Magritte: A Life*. London: Profile Books
- Gablik, Suzi. 1970. *Magritte*. London: Thames & Hudson
- Gohr, Siegfried et al. 2017. *Magritte: Attempting the Impossible*. Leuven: Davidsfonds/Infodok
- Hammacher, A. M. 1995. *René Magritte*. New York: Abrams
- Levy, Sivano. 2015. *Decoding Magritte*. Bristol: Sansom
- Meuris, Jacques. 2004. *Magritte*. Cologne: Taschen
- Oillinger-Zinque, Gisele, and Frederick Leen. 1998. *René Magritte, 1898–1967: Centenary Exhibition*. Brussels: Ludion
- Ottinger, Didier. 2017. *Magritte: The Treachery of Images*. Munich: Prestel
- Paquet, Marcel. 2015. *Magritte*. Cologne: Taschen
- Robbe-Grillet, Alain. 1975. *René Magritte. La Belle Captive*. Lausanne: La Bibliothèque des Arts
- Sylvester, David. 1992–1997. *René Magritte: Catalogue Raisonné*. 5 vols. London: Philip Wilson
- Waseige, Julie. 2021. *Magritte in 400 Images*. Brussels: Ludion

- Whitfield, Sarah. 2012. *Magritte: Newly Discovered Works. Catalogue Raisonné vol. 6*. Houston, TX: Menil Foundation

**GEORGES MALKINE**
- Malkine-Falvey, Fern et al. 1999. *Georges Malkine*. Paris: Paris Musées
- Vincent, Gille et al. *Georges Malkine. Le Vagabond du surréalisme*. Paris: Paris Musées
- Waldberg, Patrick. 1970. *Georges Malkine*. Brussels: André de Rache

**MARCEL MARIËN**
- Cannone, Xavier. 2014. *Marcel Mariën: The Stowaway*. Antwerp: Pandora
- Coadou, François. 2022. *Il créait des choses désagréables: Marcel Mariën et l'activité surréaliste*. Paris: Art Book Mag
- Mariën, Marcel et al. 1994. *Marcel Mariën. Monographie de l'arte moderne*. Brussels: Crédit Communal

**JOAN MASSANET**
- Malet, Rosa Maria et al. 1988. *Surrealismo en Catalunya, 1924–1936*. Barcelona: Ediciones Polígrafa
- Massenet, Joan et al. 2005. *Joan Massanet o el espectro de las cosas*. Madrid: Ediciones Aldeasa

**ANDRÉ MASSON**
- Ballard, Jean. 1968. *André Masson*. Marseille: Musée Cantini
- Gallissot, Nathalie, and Jean-Michel Bouhours. 2019. *André Masson: Une mythologie de l'être et de la nature*. Milan: Silvana Editoriale
- Lambert, Jean-Clarence. 1979. *André Masson*. Paris: Filipacchi
- Leiris, M., and G. Limbour. 1947. *André Masson and His Universe*. London: Horizon
- Masson, André. 1946. *Mythologies*. Paris: La Revue Fontaine
- Poling, Clark V. 2008. *André Masson and the Surrealist Self*. New Haven, CT: Yale University Press

- Rubin, William, and Carolyn Lanchner. 1976. *André Masson*. New York: Museum of Modern Art
- Sylvester, David et al. 1987. *André Masson: Line Unleashed*. London: South Bank Centre

**ROBERTO MATTA**
- Bozo, Dominique et al. 1985. *Matta*. Paris: Pompidou
- Ferrari, G. 1987. *Matta. Entretiens Morphologiques. Notebook No. 1, 1936–1944*. London: Sistan
- Ferrari, Germana Matta. 2012. *Casa Matta*. Mantova: Corraini Edizioni
- Micacchi, D. et al. 1980. *Matta: Index dell'Opera Grafica dal 1969 al 1980*. Viterbo: Edizione Viterbo
- Monahan, Thomas. 2015. *Matta: On the Edge of a Dream*. Milan: Skira
- Overy, Paul et al. 1984. *Matta: The Logic of Hallucination*. London: Arts Council of Great Britain
- Ozerkov, Dmitri, and Okansa Salamatina. 2020. *Matta and the Fourth Dimension*. Milan: Skira
- Rubin, William. 1957. *Matta*. New York: Museum of Modern Art
- Sabatier, Roland. 1975. *Matta. Catalogue raisonné de l'oeuvre gravé (1943–1974)*. Paris: Éditions Sonet

**F. E. MCWILLIAM**
- Ferran, Denise. 2008. *F. E. McWilliam at Banbridge*. Banbridge: F. E. McWilliam Gallery
- Ferran, Denise, and Valerie Holman. 2012. *The Sculpture of F. E. McWilliam*. Surrey: Lund Humphries
- Gooding, Mel. 1989. *F. E. McWilliam: Sculpture 1932–1989*. London: Tate Gallery
- Marle, Judy, and T. P. Flanagan. 1981. *F. E. McWilliam*. Belfast: Arts Council of Northern Ireland

**OSCAR MELLOR**
- Mellor, Phoebe. 2008. *The Paintings of Oscar Mellor*. Oxford: Taurus Gallery

- Morris, Desmond. 2023. *Oscar Mellor: Private Surrealist*. Rhos-on-Sea: Dark Windows Press

## JOHN MELVILLE
- Lucie-Smith, Edward. 1987. *John Melville 1902–1986: A Memorial Exhibition*. London: Gothick Dream Fine Art

## E. L. T. MESENS
- Melly, George. 2013. *Don't Tell Sybil*. London: Atlas Press
- Van den Bossche, Phillip et al. 2013. *E. L. T. Mesens: Dada and Surrealism in Brussels, Paris and London*. Ostend: Mu.ZEE

## JOAN MIRÓ
- Corredor-Matheos, J., and Gloria Picazo. 1980. *Miró's Posters*. Secaucus, NJ: Chartwell Books
- Cramer, Patrick, and Rosa Maria Malet. 1989. *Joan Miró: The Illustrated Books: Catalogue Raisonné*. Geneva: Patrick Cramer
- Dupin, Jacques. 1962. *Joan Miró. Life and Work*. New York: Abrams
- Dupin, Jacques. 1989–2001. *Joan Miró: Engraver. I–IV. 1928–1983*. New York: Rizzoli
- Dupin, Jacques. 1993. *Miró*. Paris: Flammarion
- Dupin, Jacques, and Ariane Lelong-Mainaud. 1999–2004. *Joan Miró: Catalogue raisonné. Paintings. I–VI. 1908–1981*. Paris: Daniel Lelong et Successió Miró
- Dupin, Jacques, and Ariane Lelong-Mainaud. 2008–2018. *Joan Miró: Catalogue raisonné: Drawings. I–VI. 1901–1981*. Paris: Daniel Lelong et Successió Miró
- Gimferrer, Pere. 1993. *The Roots of Miró*. Barcelona: Ediciones Polígrafa
- La Beaumelle, Agnes de. 2004. *Joan Miró. 1917–1934*. Paris: Pompidou
- Lanchner, Caroline. 1993. *Joan Miró*. New York: Abrams
- Leiris, Michel, and Fernand Mourliot. 1972–1992. *Joan Miró. Litografo. I–VI. 1930–1981*. Barcelona: Ediciones Polígrafa
- Lewenhaupt, Ann. 1993. *Joan Miró Posters*. Malmo Konsthall
- Malet, Rosa Maria et al. 1993. *Joan Miró. 1893–1993*. New York: Little, Brown
- Miró, Emelio Fernandaz, and Pilar Ortego Chapel. 2006. *Joan Miró: Sculptures: Catalogue raisonné: 1928–1982*. Paris: Daniel Lelong et Successió Miró
- Miró, Joan, and Josep Llorens Artigas. 2007. *Ceramics. Catalogue raisonné. 1941–1981*. Paris: Daniel Lelong et Successió Miró
- Rowell, Margit. 1987. *Joan Miró: Selected Writings and Interviews*. London: Thames & Hudson
- Serra, Pere A. 1986. *Miró and Mallorca*. New York: Rizzoli
- Wiese, Stephan Von et al. 2002. *Joan Miró: Snail Woman Flower Star*. Munich: Prestel

## PIERRE MOLINIER
- Fleischer, Alain. 2022. *Pierre Molinier, ou l'inceste extrême*. Paris: Louison Edition
- Mercié, Jean-Luc. 2010. *Pierre Molinier*. Paris: Les Presses du Réel
- Pierre, Petit. 2005. *Pierre Molinier et la tentation de l'Orient*. Paris: Pleine Page

## HENRY MOORE
- Berthoud, Roger. 1987. *The Life of Henry Moore*. London: Faber & Faber
- Compton, Susan. 1988. *Henry Moore*. London: Weidenfeld & Nicolson
- Garrould, Ann. 1996–2003. *Henry Moore: The Complete Drawings*. 7 vols. London: Lund Humphries
- Grigson, Geoffrey. 1943. *Henry Moore*. Harmondsworth: Penguin
- Hedgecoe, John. 1986. *Henry Moore: My Ideas, Inspiration, and Life as an Artist*. London: Ebury Press
- Strachan, W. J. 1983. *Henry Moore Animals*. London: Aurum Press

- Sweeney, James Johnson. 1946.
  *Henry Moore*. New York: Museum
  of Modern Art
- Sylvester, David. 1957. *Henry Moore:
  Sculpture and Drawings*. 6 vols.
  London: Lund Humphreys
- Wilkinson, Alan. 2002. *Henry Moore:
  Writings and Conversations*. London:
  Lund Humphries

## PAUL NASH

- Cardinal, Roger. 1989. *The Landscape
  Vision of Paul Nash*. London:
  Reaktion Books
- Causey, Andrew. 1980. *Paul Nash*.
  Oxford: Oxford University Press
- Causey, Andrew. 2000. *Paul Nash:
  Writings on Art*. Oxford: Oxford
  University Press
- Causey, Andrew. 2013. *Paul Nash:
  Landscape and the Life of Objects*.
  Surrey: Lund Humphries
- Eates, Margot. 1973. *Paul Nash:
  Master of the Image*. London:
  John Murray
- Fraser Jenkins, David. 2010. *Paul Nash:
  The Elements*. London: Dulwich
  Picture Gallery
- Kerrigan, Michael. 2018. *Paul Nash
  Masterpieces of Art*. London:
  Flame Tree
- Montagu, Jemima. 2003. *Paul Nash:
  Modern Artist, Ancient Landscape*.
  London: Tate Publishing
- Read, Herbert. 1944. *Paul Nash*.
  London: Penguin Books

## RICHARD OELZE

- Jaguer, Édouard. 1990. *Richard Oelze*.
  Paris: Filipacchi
- Kinkel, Hans. 2016. *Richard Oelze,
  1900–1980*. Cologne: Michael Werner
- Schick, Karin. 2000. *Richard Oelze*.
  Hamburg: Hamburger Kunsthalle

## GORDON ONSLOW FORD

- Bogzaran, Fariba et al. 2019.
  *Gordon Onslow Ford: Man on a
  Green Island*. Inverness, CA: Lucid
  Art Foundation
- Chipp Jones, Harvey L., and Herschel
  B. Chipp Jones. 1980. *Gordon Onslow
  Ford: Retrospective Exhibition*. Oakland,
  CA: Oakland Museum
- Hiekisch-Picard, Sepp. 2006. *Gordon
  Onslow Ford: The Formative Years:
  Paintings from the 1930s and 1940s*. San
  Francisco: Weinstein Gallery
- Miedzinski, Charles, and Fariba
  Bogzaran. 1993. *Gordon Onslow-Ford:
  Paintings of the Inner-Worlds*. San
  Francisco: Wittenborn Art Books
- Neufurt, Andreas. 1994. *Gordon
  Onslow Ford: Paintings*. Munich:
  Höcherl Verlag
- Sawin, Martica. 2010. *Gordon Onslow
  Ford: Paintings and Works on Paper
  1939–1951*. New York: Francis M.
  Naumann Fine Art
- Selz, Peter. 2003. *Gordon Onslow
  Ford: Exploring the Open Mind*. San
  Francisco: Weinstein Gallery
- Weinstein, Rowland. 2013. *Gordon
  Onslow Ford: Centennial Celebration*.
  San Francisco: Weinstein Gallery

## MERET OPPENHEIM

- Baur, Simon. 2022. *Meret Oppenheim:
  Enigmas*. Zurich: Scheidegger & Spiess
- Bhattacharya-Stettler, Therese,
  and Matthias Frehner. 2008. *Meret
  Oppenheim Retrospective*. Berlin:
  Hatje Cantz
- Burckhardt, Jacqueline et al. 1996. *Meret
  Oppenheim: Beyond the Teacup*.
  New York: D.A.P
- Curiger, Bice. 1990. *Meret Oppenheim:
  Defiance in the Face of Freedom*.
  Cambridge, MA: MIT Press
- Gardner, Belinda Grace et al. 2013.
  *Meret Oppenheim: Mirror of the Mind*.
  Berlin: Kerber
- Helfenstein, Josef. 1993. *Meret
  Oppenheim und der Surrealismus*.
  Stuttgart: Gerd Hatje
- Meyer-Thoss, Christiane. 1996. *Meret
  Oppenheim: Buch der Ideen*. Bern:
  Gachnang & Springer
- Pagé, Suzanne et al. 1984. *Meret
  Oppenheim*. Paris: Musée de l'art moderne

- Sinnreich, Ursula et al. 2001. *Meret Oppenheim: Kunst von Sinnen.* Zurich: TA-Media
- Wenger, Lisa, and Martina Corgnati. 2022. *Meret Oppenheim: My Album, from Childhood to 1943.* Zurich: Scheidegger & Spiess
- Zimmer, Nina et al. 2021. *Meret Oppenheim: My Exhibition.* New York: Museum of Modern Art

## WOLFGANG PAALEN
- Neufert, Andreas et al. 2019. *Wolfgang Paalen: Der Surrealist in Paris und Mexiko.* Berlin: Walther Koenig
- Pierre, José. 1980. *Wolfgang Paalen.* Paris: Filipacchi
- Winter, Amy. 2003. *Wolfgang Paalen.* Westport, CT: Praeger

## GRACE PAILTHORPE
- Remy, Michel et al. 1998. *Sluice-Gates of the Mind: The Collaborative Work of Pailthorpe and Mednikoff.* Leeds: Leeds Museum and Art Gallery
- Stefana, Alberto, and Lee Ann Montanaro. 2019. *Grace Pailthorpe's Writings on Psychoanalysis and Surrealism.* London: Routledge
- Wolf, Hope et al. 2019. *A Tale of Mother's Bones: Grace Pailthorpe, Reuben Mednikoff and the Birth of Psychorealism.* London: Camden Arts Centre

## MIMI PARENT
- Lord, Danielle. 2004. *Mimi Parent, Jean Benoit. Surréalistes.* Québec: Musée National des Beaux-Arts du Québec

## ROLAND PENROSE
- Penrose, Antony. 2001. *Roland Penrose: The Friendly Surrealist.* Munich: Prestel
- Penrose, Roland. 1939. *The Road is Wider than Long.* London: London Gallery
- Penrose, Roland. 1981. *Scrap Book: 1900–1981.* London: Thames & Hudson
- *Roland Penrose and Lee Miller: The Surrealist and the Photographer.* 2001. Edinburgh: Scottish National Gallery of Modern Art
- Slusher, Katherine. 2007. *Lee Miller – Roland Penrose. The Green Memories of Desire.* New York: Prestel

## FRANCIS PICABIA
- Borràs, Maria Lluïsa. 1985. *Picabia.* London: Thames & Hudson
- Camfield, William A. et al. 2014–2023. *Francis Picabia: Catalogue Raisonné.* 4 vols. New Haven, CT: Yale University Press
- Marcadé, Bernard. 2021. *Francis Picabia, rastaquouere.* Paris: Flammarion
- Mundy, Jennifer. 2008. *Duchamp, Man Ray, Picabia.* London: Tate
- Pagé, Suzanne et al. 2002. *Francis Picabia. Singulier idéal.* Paris: Paris Musées
- Pearlstein, Philip. 2023. *Picabia Inside Out.* London: Heni Publishing
- Umland, Anne, and Catherine, Hug. 2016. *Francis Picabia: Our Heads Are Round So Our Thoughts Can Change Direction.* New York: Museum of Modern Art

## PABLO PICASSO
- Baldassari, Anne. 2005. *The Surrealist Picasso.* Paris: Flammarion
- Baldassari, Anne. 2006. *Picasso; Life With Dora Maar.* Paris: Flammarion
- Cowling, Elizabeth. 2006. *Visiting Picasso.* London: Thames & Hudson
- Cowling, Elizabeth et al. 2002. *Matisse Picasso.* London: Tate
- Danchev, Alex. 2008. *Picasso Furioso.* Paris: Éditions Dilecta
- Duncan, David Douglas. 1961. *Picasso's Picassos.* London: Macmillan
- Elgar, Frank, and Robert Maillard. 1956. *Picasso.* London: Thames & Hudson
- Gilot, Francoise, and Carlton Lake. 1964. *Life With Picasso.* New York: Mcgraw-Hill

- Le Fur, Yves. 2017. *Picasso Primitivo*. Milan: Mondarori Electa
- Melville, Robert. 1939. *Picasso: Master of the Phantom*. Oxford: Oxford University Press
- Penrose, Roland. 1958. *Picasso, His Life and Work*. London: Gollancz
- Richardson, John. 1991–2022. *A Life of Picasso, vols 1–4*. London: Jonathan Cape
- Spies, Werner. 2000. *Picasso: The Sculptures*. Berlin: Hatje Cantz
- Staller, Natasha. 2001. *A Sum of Destructions*. New Haven, CT: Yale University Press
- Stepan, Peter. 2006. *Picasso's Collection of African and Oceanic Art*. Munich: Prestel
- Temple, Christine. 2016. *Picasso's Brain*. London: Robinson
- Utley, Gertje R. 2000. *Picasso: The Communist Years*. New Haven, CT: Yale University Press
- Warncke, Carsten-Peter, and Ingo F. Walther. 1992. *Pablo Picasso 1881–1973*. 2 vols. Cologne: Taschen

**ÀNGEL PLANELLS**
- García de Carpi, Lucía et al. 1995. *El Surrealismo en Espana*. Madrid: Museo Reina Sofía
- Malet, Rosa Maria et al. 1988. *Surrealismo en Catalunya, 1924–1936*. Barcelona: Ediciones Polígrafa
- Vives, Anna. 2019. *Angel Planell's Art and the Surrealist Canon*. London: Routledge

**PETER ROSE PULHAM**
- Pulham, Peter Rose. 1979. *Too Short a Summer*. York: Impressions Gallery

**MAN RAY**
- Braude, Mark. 2022. *Kiki Man Ray*. London: Two Roads
- De l'Ecotais, Emmanuelle, and Alain Sayag. 1998. *Man Ray: Photography and Its Double*. London: Laurence King

- Foresta, Merry et al. 1988. *Perpetual Motif: The Art of Man Ray*. New York: Abbeville Press
- Janus. 1990. *Man Ray: Oeuvres 1909–1972*. Paris: Celiv
- *Man Ray: Paintings, Objects, Photographs*. 1995. London: Sotheby's
- Mundy, Jennifer. 2016. *Man Ray: Writings on Art*. Los Angeles: Paul Getty Museum
- Mundy, Jennifer, ed. 2008. *Duchamp, Man Ray, Picabia*. London: Tate Publishing
- Naumann, Francis M. 2003. *Conversion to Modernism: The Early Work of Man Ray*. New Brunswick, NJ: Rutgers University Press
- Penrose, Roland. 1975. *Man Ray*. London: Thames & Hudson
- Ray, Man. 1988. *Self Portrait*. London: Bloomsbury
- Rocca, Robert et al. 2023. *Man Ray: 1890–1976: Genius of Light*. Milan: Silvana Editoriale
- Schaffner, Ingrid. 2003. *The Essential Man Ray*. New York: Abrams
- Ware, Katherine. 2023. *Man Ray*. Cologne: Taschen

**CERI RICHARDS**
- Bowness, Alan et al. 1981. *Ceri Richards*. London: Tate Publishing
- Gooding, Mel. 2002. *Ceri Richards*. Moffat: Cameron & Hollis
- Sanesi, Roberto. 1973. *The Graphic Works of Ceri Richards*. Milan: Cerastico Editore

**EDITH RIMMINGTON**
- Lesso, Rosie. 2021. *Edith Rimmington: Artworks and Famous Paintings*. New York: *The Art Story*

**PIERRE ROY**
- Bréhant, Cécile. 2001. *Pierre Roy et les marges du surréalisme*. Paris: Éditions L'Harmattan
- Cousseau, Henry-Claude et al. 1994. *Pierre Roy: Nantes 1880–Milan 1950*. Paris: Somogy

## KAY SAGE

- Miller, Stephen Robeson, and Jonathan Stuhlman. 2011. *The Surreal Worlds of Kay Sage and Yves Tanguy*. Katonah, NY: Mint Museum
- Noel-Johnson, Victoria, and Marzina Marzetti. 2023. *Kay Sage and Yves Tanguy: Ring of Iron, Ring of Wool*. Milan: Skira
- Sentival, Jessie et al. 2018. *Kay Sage: Catalogue Raisonné*. New York: Prestel
- Suther, Judith D. 1997. *A House of Her Own: Kay Sage, Solitary Surrealist*. Lincoln: University of Nebraska Press

## KURT SCHWITTERS

- Bader, Graham. 2021. *Poisoned Abstraction: Kurt Schwitters Between Revolution and Exile*. New Haven, CT: Yale University Press
- Boehm, Gottfried et al. 2004. *Schwitters – Arp*. Basel: Kunstmuseum Basel
- Bowness, Alan. 1958. *Kurt Schwitters*. London: Lord's Gallery
- Dietrich, Dorothea. 1995. *The Collages of Kurt Schwitters*. Cambridge: Cambridge University Press
- Gohr, Siegfried. 1985. *Kurt Schwitters: Die Spaten Werte*. Cologne: Stadt
- Luke, Meghan. 2014. *Kurt Schwitters: Space, Image, Exile*. Chicago: University of Chicago Press
- Martakies, Robin. 2006. *Kurt Schwitters, Free Spirit*. Bloomington, IN: Trafford Publishing
- Orchard, Karin et al. 2000–2006. *Kurt Schwitters. Catalogue Raisonné*. 3 vols. Berlin: Hatje Cantz
- Schultz, Isabel. 2020. *Kurt Schwitters: Merzkunst: Merz Art*. Munich: Hirmer

## KURT SELIGMANN

- Seligmann, Kurt. 1948. *The Mirror of Magic*. New York: Pantheon Books
- Seligmann, Kurt. 1973. *Kurt Seligmann: His Graphic Work*. Chicago: Allan Frumpkin Gallery
- Seligmann, Kurt. 2015. *First Message from the Spirit World of the Object*. San Francisco: Weinstein Gallery

## JINDŘICH ŠTYRSKÝ

- Srp, Karel. 2001. *Jindřich Štyrský*. Prague: Torst

## YVES TANGUY

- Ashbery, John. 1974. *Yves Tanguy*. New York: Acquavella Galleries
- Bozo, Dominique. 1982. *Yves Tanguy: Retrospective 1925–1955*. Paris: Pompidou
- Cariou, André et al. 2007. *Yves Tanguy. L'univers surréaliste*. Quimper: Musée des Beaux Arts de Quimper
- Marchesseau, Daniel. 1973. *Yves Tanguy*. Paris: Filipacchi
- Soby, James Thrall. 1955. *Yves Tanguy*. New York: Museum of Modern Art
- Tanguy, Kay Sage et al. 1963. *Yves Tanguy: A Summary of His Works*. New York: Pierre Matisse
- Von Maur, Karen. 2001. *Yves Tanguy and Surrealism*. Berlin: Hatje Cantz
- Waldberg, Patrick. 1977. *Yves Tanguy*. Brussels: André de Rache
- Waldberg, Patrick. 2002. *Tanguy: Peintures*. Washington, DC: Differences Press
- Wittrock, Wolfgang. 1976. *Yves Tanguy: The Graphic Work*. Düsseldorf: Kunsthandel

## DOROTHEA TANNING

- Bosquet, Alain. 1966. *La Peinture de Dorothea Tanning*. Paris: Jean-Jacques Pauvert
- Carruthers, Victoria. 2020. *Dorothea Tanning: Transformations*. London: Lund Humphries
- Mahon, Alyce et al. 2019. *Dorothea Tanning*. London: Tate
- Plazy, Gilles. 1976. *Dorothea Tanning*. Paris: Filipacchi
- Tanning, Dorothea. 2001. *Between Lives: An Artist and Her Work*. New York: Norton
- Waddell, Roberta et al. 1992. *Dorothea Tanning: Hail, Delirium! A Catalogue Raisonné of the Artist's Illustrated Books and Prints, 1942–1991*. New York: New York Public Library

**TOYEN**
- Bishof, Rita et al. 1987. *Toyen. Das malerische Werk.* Frankfurt: Verlag Neue Kritik KG
- Gorgen-Lammers, Annabelle et al. 2022. *Toyen 1902–1980.* Hamburg: Hamburger Kuntshalle
- Ivsic, Radovin. 1974. *Toyen.* Paris: Filipacchi

**JULIAN TREVELYAN**
- Manser, Jose. 2012. *Mary Fedden and Julian Trevelyan: Life and Art by the River Thames.* London: Unicorn
- Raine, Kathleen, and Julian Trevelyan. 1974. *A Place, A State.* London: Enitharmon Press
- Trevelyan, Julian. 1996. *Indigo Days: The Art and Memoir of Julian Trevelyan.* Aldershot: Scolar Press
- Trevelyan, Philip. 2013. *Julian Trevelyan: Picture Language.* Surrey: Lund Humphries
- Turner, Silvie. 2010. *Julian Trevelyan Catalogue Raisonné of Prints.* Surrey: Lund Humphries

**CLOVIS TROUILLE**
- Campagne, Jean Marc. 1965. *Clovis Trouille.* Paris: Jean-Jacques Pauvert

**JOHN TUNNARD**
- Martin, Simon et al. 2010. *John Tunnard: Inner Space to Outer Space.* Chichester: Pallant House Gallery
- Peat, Alan, and Brian Whitten. 1997. *John Tunnard: His Life and Work.* Aldershot: Scolar Press

**REMEDIOS VARO**
- Gruen, Walter. 2008. *Remedios Varo: Catalogo Razonado.* Mexico City: Ediciones Era
- Haskell, Caitlin et al. 2023. *Remedios Varo: Science Fictions.* Chicago: Art Institute of Chicago
- Kaplan, Janet A. 1988. *Unexpected Journeys: The Art and Life of Remedios Varo.* London: Virago Press
- Nonaka, Masayo. 2012. *Remedios Varo: The Mexican Years.* Barcelona: RM Editorial

**EDWARD WADSWORTH**
- Black, Jonathan. 2005. *Edward Wadsworth; Form, Feeling and Calculation.* London: Philip Wilson
- Cork, Richard, and Jeremy Greenwood. 2002. *The Graphic Work of Edward Wadsworth.* Suffolk: The Wood Lea Press
- *Edward Wadsworth: Paintings from the 1920s.* 1982. London: Mayor Gallery
- Glazebrook, Mark. 1974. *Edward Wadsworth: Paintings, Drawings and Prints.* London: Lund Humphries
- Lewison, Jeremy et al. 1990. *A Genius of Industrial England: Edward Wadsworth.* Bradford: Arkwright Arts Trust
- Wadsworth, Barbara. 1989. *Edward Wadsworth: A Painter's Life.* Salisbury: Michael Russell Publishing

**SCOTTIE WILSON**
- Melly, George. 1986. *It's All Writ Out for You: The Life and Work of Scottie Wilson.* London: Thames & Hudson
- Petullo, Anthony J., and Katherine M. Murrell. 2004. *Scottie Wilson: Peddler Turned Painter.* Milwaukee: Petullo Publishing

# ACKNOWLEDGEMENTS

I would like to acknowledge the help I have received with the subject of this book. I am especially grateful to Paul Conran, Silvano Levy, Andrew Murray, Michel Remy, Tor Scott and Abigail Susik, with whom I have had many valuable discussions over the years.

Sadly, all the artists that I have known, who were active in the surrealist movement between the 1920s and the 1950s, are now dead, but I would like to record my debt to them and my sincere thanks for all the stimulating ideas and amusing anecdotes they shared with me in earlier days.

I would also like to thank the team at Thames & Hudson for their encouragement, their meticulous attention to detail and their appropriately irrational colour scheme. In particular, Mohara Gill, Ginny Liggitt, Camilla Rockwood, Roger Thorp, Therese Vandling and Matthew Watson Young.

I should mention that, to celebrate the centenary of the surrealist movement in 2024, the book was originally going to be called *100 Surrealists*. It was felt that this was too logical and that *101 Surrealists* would be more in keeping with the perverse spirit of the movement.

# INDEX

First published in the United Kingdom in 2024 by
Thames & Hudson Ltd, 181A High Holborn, London
WC1V 7QX

First published in the United States of America
in 2024 by Thames & Hudson Inc., 500 Fifth Avenue,
New York, New York 10110

*101 Surrealists* © 2024 Thames & Hudson Ltd, London

Text © 2024 Desmond Morris

60% of the entries of this book are based on text
from *The Lives of the Surrealists* first published by
Thames & Hudson, 2018; and *The British Surrealists*,
first published 2022.

Designed by Therese Vandling




British Library Cataloguing-in-Publication Data
A catalogue record for this book is available from the
British Library

Library of Congress Control Number 2024934193

ISBN 978-0-500-02781-3

Printed and bound in China by Shenzen Reliance Printing Co. Ltd